EDUCATED IN WHITENESS

Educated
in Whiteness

GOOD INTENTIONS AND DIVERSITY IN SCHOOLS

Angelina E. Castagno

University of Minnesota Press
Minneapolis
London

MINNESOTA

KH

Portions of chapter 2 were previously published in "Making Sense of
Multicultural Education: A Synthesis of the Literature," *Multicultural
Perspectives* 11, no. 1 (2009): 43–48, and in "Multicultural Education and the
Protection of Whiteness," *American Journal of Education* 120, no. 1 (2013).
Portions of chapter 3 were previously published in "I Don't Want to Hear
That! Legitimating Whiteness through Silence in Schools," *Anthropology and
Education Quarterly* 39, no. 3 (2008): 314–33. Portions of chapter 4 were
previously published in "Common Sense Understandings of Equality and
Social Change: A Critical Race Theory Analysis of Liberalism at Spruce Middle
School," *International Journal of Qualitative Studies in Education* 22, no. 6
(2009): 755–68.

Published by the University of Minnesota Press
111 Third Avenue South, Suite 290
Minneapolis, MN 55401-2520
http://www.upress.umn.edu

Library of Congress Cataloging-in-Publication Data
Castagno, Angelina E.
  Educated in whiteness : good intentions and diversity in schools / Angelina E.
Castagno.
  Includes bibliographical references and index.
  ISBN 978-0-8166-8163-1 (hc : alk. paper) — ISBN 978-0-8166-8165-5 (pb :
alk. paper)
  1. Racism in education—Utah. I. Title.
  LC212.22.U83C37 2013
  370.8909792—dc23   2013028371

Printed in the United States of America on acid-free paper

The University of Minnesota is an equal-opportunity educator and employer.

21 20 19 18 17 16 15 14   10 9 8 7 6 5 4 3 2 1

10/17/15

Both engagement and commitment connote service. And genuine service requires humility. We must first recognize and acknowledge (at least to ourselves) that our actions are not likely to lead to transcendent change and may, indeed, despite our best efforts, be of more help to the system we despise than to the victims of that system whom we are trying to help. Then, and only then, can that realization, and the dedication based on it, lead to policy positions and campaigns that are less likely to worsen conditions for those we are trying to help and more likely to remind the powers that be that out there are persons like us who are not only not on their side but determined to stand in their way.

—DERRICK A. BELL JR., *FACES AT THE BOTTOM OF THE WELL*

CONTENTS

Whiteness, Diversity, and Educators' Good Intentions

Most educators are *nice* people with the best of intentions regarding the schooling they provide to students every day. Despite their good intentions and the general niceness among educators, most schools in the United States contribute to inequity every day. How does this happen? And what about the multitude of diversity-related efforts in schools that are supposed to help educators achieve the American ideals of "equality and justice for all" (Brayboy, Castagno, and Maughan 2007)? This book tells the story of educational policy and practice related to diversity in one urban school district in the western United States. Grounded in ethnographic data from a range of teachers and administrators, I build on current conversations about schooling in the United States by examining how well-intended policies and practices related to diversity actually maintain the status quo and entrench racial inequity. By going inside classrooms at two very different secondary schools, listening to teachers and administrators, and following policy as it gets implemented, we come to learn how popular educational discourses get employed in contradictory ways, how potentially transformative educational agendas get taken up in ways that run counter to the initial intent, and ultimately, how individuals with good intentions can produce structures that harm children. It is through knowledge of these patterns that we might come to the place of humility and genuine service that Derrick Bell (1992) suggests is necessary.

In one of my first interactions in Salt Lake City's Zion School District,[1] an administrator handed me a video that had been produced for the district earlier that year called "We Teach the World." As I listened to her describe the "diversity in our district" and the various ways the district addressed that diversity, I also observed the standard educator décor on the surrounding office walls—posters about "every child's ability to learn and succeed," knickknacks of apples and pencils, youth artwork, and quotes about "leaders who inspire." There was a clear undercurrent of what another district leader called a "culture of nice" in the stories she shared with me. When I watched the video at home later that evening, I was greeted with a similar storyline: differently raced youth smiling and laughing for the camera, White students counting to ten in Spanish, Mexican mariachi music, and Polynesian dancing and drumming. The feel-good video, the administrator's proud description of the diversity in the district, and the optimistic office décor were all mimicked over and over again during the following year—indeed, they are indicative of the nice ways diversity is taken up by educators across the nation. Educators' engagements with diversity, and especially with *race*, have become so inconspicuous, so normal, that they often elude critical examination. Through ethnography, this book problematizes dominant discourses of diversity and race in U.S. schools and illustrates how the well-intended, nice ways schools engage diversity-related policies and practices solidify inequity and reinscribe whiteness.

Some readers may wonder why this book is framed around the notion of "diversity"—especially since this word is usually taken up in nice ways and used as a nice cover for oppression and injustice. My response is that diversity offers an important entry point for an examination of equity in schools. Although the United States has always been a diverse nation, racial diversity has been a hot-button issue for at least the past thirty years. The No Child Left Behind Act (NCLB) spurred a frenzy of activity around the racialized achievement gap. Work like that of Jonathan Kozol has added fuel to the fire by making obvious the "savage inequalities" present in our school system. Policy makers, districts, schools, educational leaders, and teachers across the nation have been buzzing about with multiple and various answers to these problems. Lost in much of this work is a clear understanding of the way race, power, and whiteness form the foundation of our educational system and, indeed, our society.

Diversity is, of course, a buzzword that means different things to different people. For example, it can mean race, or culture, or all forms of diversity. Diversity also has various political attachments; it can mean diversity in a nice colorblind way or in an antagonistic way. This ambiguity is part of what I am drawing on in framing the book around "diversity." Diversity is taken up, addressed, and sometimes discarded in very particular ways in schools. Like many other sites across the United States, in the Zion School District, diversity is engaged in nice ways that fail to work toward equity and that ultimately reify whiteness.

Niceness and Whiteness in Action

The Zion School District sits in a relatively large urban area in the Rocky Mountain region of the United States. Serving about 25,000 students, more than half of whom are students of color, the district has long subscribed to common discourses about equal educational opportunity, providing a high-quality education to all students, and closing the proverbial achievement gap. Alongside this "normalcy" is a peculiar reputation that the larger community holds among outsiders as a very White, conservative, and unusual place. I was familiar with the district since I grew up in the area, knew a handful of educators in the district, and consistently read the local newspaper. When I had an opportunity to design a school-based ethnography around diversity and equity, the Zion School District seemed like an interesting locale.

Like most school systems around the nation, the Zion School District had a policy statement on multiculturalism that was intended to guide educators' efforts around diversity and equity. The policy statement offered a definition of multicultural education as "a philosophy stating that all students regardless of the groups to which they belong, such as those related to gender, ethnicity, race, culture, social class, religion, or exceptionality, should experience educational equity in the schools." The policy outlined categories of knowledge that "educational staff" should know and understand, such as the "similarities and differences among culturally diverse groups"; the culture, history, and contributions of various cultural groups; how "cultural factors" influence the development of students and their various "learning styles"; and the "background and rationale for current government regulations regarding desegregation, civil rights, equality of educational opportunities, and equity issues." The policy statement also outlined a number of action items that were supposed to be carried out by particular groups of people within the district, including that teachers would "adapt" curriculum and pedagogy to "include culturally diverse groups" and "use various teaching strategies to address differences in learning styles," and that schools would "develop strategic plans to address diversity."

The entire two-page policy offered a particular framework and guidance for the Zion School District's diversity initiatives. Specifically, the policy relies on neutral concepts (e.g., similarities and differences, cultural factors, learning styles) and open directives (e.g., adapt curriculum, various teaching strategies, strategic plans) to purportedly address an issue (inequity) that is specific, concrete, and pervasive. This nice approach to diversity is consistent with, and also reifies, whiteness. As such, it cannot possibly tackle the inequity it is meant to address. This policy is a poignant example of educators' good intentions, and as such, we might applaud its very existence. Indeed, leveling a critique at the policy—or any other attempt to address diversity, for that matter—risks appearing antiequity or, at a minimum, hostile to diversity-related efforts. But not leveling a critique is just as damaging, since nice approaches like this not only fail to address inequity but actually make the inequity harder to see and, thus, change.

Whiteness compels us to embrace diversity-related policy and practice uncritically and to praise any effort tagged with words like *multicultural*, *diversity*, and *equality*. But these are often tropes for policies and practices that do very little to advance equity or stop injustice. For example, although the crux of the Zion School District policy is that all students "experience educational equity," nowhere in the policy is "equity" defined. Reading through the rest of the policy and seeing how the policy gets translated into practice, it seems clear that equality (i.e., sameness) is truly what is meant. Furthermore, what is meant by the terms "culture" and "cultural group" used in this and other district communications? By framing these issues in terms of "culture," what is the actual way that these policy directives get taken up and implemented? And finally, how does the policy highlight differences among various groups of students, families, and communities, and what meaning and significance does the focus on difference hold for educators?

As later chapters illustrate, these concepts of culture, equality, and difference echo throughout the district. Tracing these themes and others from the central office to professional development and school leadership and into classrooms and teacher discourse illuminates their appeal and potency but also their toxicity. Within schools, niceness often defines appropriate—and even good—behaviors, interactions, norms, and policies. The power of niceness to shape daily phenomena is far reaching. Diversity and niceness are so intertwined that any engagement with diversity is necessarily, almost by definition, nice. This is not the case with engaging inequity and whiteness. But diversity in schools has been framed in such a way as to require a stance of inclusion, optimism, and assimilation. These concepts are, in turn, constitutive of the niceness we see in schools.

Educated in Whiteness

I grew up learning how to be a nice person, and I am generally quite good at it. The few times that I did not act in ways that were consistent with the niceness that was expected of me, I was quickly brought back into the fold. I can remember questioning an administrator in high school about what I perceived to be inequitable treatment based on the families to which students belonged. I can also remember being told that I was not simply wrong but also disrespectful and inappropriate in my accusations. For me, school was not the place where I learned about equity, oppression, or injustice. It was not until my early adult years that I started noticing these things. And it was only through explicit exposure to potentially uncomfortable concepts, relationships with people who were willing to challenge my worldview, and compelling evidence that injustice and unfairness were rampant in my community that I was able to see what was previously invisible to me. Once I started paying attention, I quickly became angry that my schooling was so inadequate. I was academically prepared to be very successful in college and beyond, and I had the critical thinking and writing skills that served as a helpful foundation, but I was never asked to think critically or write about things like racism, institutional oppression, homophobia, or social-class injustice. To have engaged in these kinds of issues would have been inconsistent with the nice White girl who I was and who I was expected to be.

When I spend time in schools now, I see the same patterns. When I spend time with my current students who are aspiring and practicing teachers and administrators, I see the same patterns. When I interact with my colleagues, who are seasoned educators charged with preparing future educators, I see the same patterns. And why wouldn't I? These norms of niceness are powerful motivators for educators in particular. Whiteness provides a fruitful context for these patterns, and whiteness is further reinforced by the recurrence of these same patterns.

Whiteness refers to structural arrangements and ideologies of race dominance. Racial power and inequities are at the core of whiteness, but all forms of power and inequity create and perpetuate whiteness. The function of whiteness is to maintain the status quo, and although White people most often benefit from whiteness, some people of color have tapped into the ideological components of whiteness for their own financial and educational benefits. Whiteness maintains power and privilege by perpetuating and legitimating the status quo while simultaneously maintaining a veneer of neutrality, equality, and compassion. Understanding the links between whiteness and diversity-related educational policy and practice is, therefore, an important, and yet relatively unexplored, task for educators.

To understand whiteness, it is helpful to step back and consider the meaning of race and racism. Race is primarily a socially constructed phenomenon, which means that people create race and give it significance.

Race comes to matter through our language, our relationships, the places we visit, the things we do, the institutions we inhabit, the policies we enact, and the knowledge we share. But the fact that we make race does not negate its reality, its importance, or its implications. Race, in fact, produces real, patterned, and lasting material effects.

In this book, race is analytically, materially, and ideologically salient. I do not mean to suggest that race is the sole form of dominance in schools, but the project of this book is to center race and racism as *analytic tools*, as *institutional structures* with material effects on both individuals and groups, and as *ideological constructs* that shape how we understand diversity-related policy and practice in the Zion School District. Critical race theory treats race as central to law, policy, history, and culture in the United States. Centering whiteness as an analytic tool facilitates analyses of racial power working with, through, and against other axes of dominance. The varying mechanisms of power that maintain inequity cannot easily be teased apart, but this book centers race and racism while simultaneously locating spaces where other "isms" operate. So while race is the primary axis of dominance within the context of this book, that is not to say that other forms of dominance are less important or damaging.

Racism is not simply, or even primarily, individualized prejudices, stereotypes, or negative thoughts about particular groups of people. Racism produces structural hierarchies of domination; it is pervasive and it is patterned (Bell 1992; Delgado and Stefancic 2001; Omi and Winant 1994). Prior research has meticulously explained the multiple ways in which institutional racism influences schooling (Abu El-Haj 2006; Frutcher 2007; Gillborn 2008; Gittell 2005; Ladson-Billings and Tate 2006; Lee 2005; Leonardo 2009; Vaught 2011). Racism works with and through other forms of dominance and injustice to make up whiteness. Whiteness is a foundational component missing from most studies of difference and power in schools. This book centers the notion of whiteness, illustrating how it works and what it means for youth, teachers, educational leaders, and efforts to achieve equity.

This book shifts the focus from the "underachievement" of individuals to the inequitable nature of institutions and the ways systems and structures of power may be contributing to the educational outcomes that have become so naturalized in the United States (Fine 1997). Rather than achievement gaps, we should be concerned with the educational debt (Ladson-Billings 2006). A focus on the "education debt" rather than the "achievement gap" highlights the *structural* and *cumulative* impact of centuries of educational inequities related to funding, curricula, resources, teachers, and segregation. "The education debt is the foregone schooling resources that we could have (should have) been investing in (primarily) low-income kids, which deficit leads to a variety of social programs (e.g. crime, low productivity, low wages, low labor-force participation) that require ongoing public investment. This required investment sucks away resources that could go to reducing the achievement gap. Without the education debt, we could narrow the achievement gap" (Ladson-Billings 2006). This education debt is composed of historical, economic, sociopolitical, and moral components and, therefore, requires a more holistic, historic, and comprehensive analysis of schooling than that implied by the focus on achievement gaps. Seeing how whiteness functions similarly encourages a comprehensive understanding of diversity and inequity in schools.

Although most people agree that whiteness is intimately connected with power, there is less consensus regarding what whiteness is exactly (Kincheloe and Steinberg 1998). Multiple scholars have written about whiteness as a set of unearned privileges enjoyed by White people, a normalization of what is right, and a norm against which everything else gets measured (Fine, Powell, Weis, and Mun Wong 1997; Frankenberg 1993, 2001; McIntosh 1988; Roediger 2000; A. Thompson 1999, 2003). Other scholars have provided illuminating historical analyses of whiteness—particularly how whiteness has been conflated with property and individual rights through the law (Harris 1993), how whiteness has been possessively invested in by groups throughout history to secure their own interests and guard those interests against the encroachment of others (Lipsitz 1998), and how whiteness has evolved and taken on new forms depending on time and context (Duster 2001). Clearly, history and the law have conspired to veil the fact that whiteness grants privilege and allows supremacy. They have also allowed White people to claim, and genuinely believe, that equality exists (Blanchett 2006; O'Connor and DeLuca Fernandez 2006; Reid and Knight 2006).

One helpful explanation of whiteness is provided by Michael Dyson, who argues that whiteness is an identity, an ideology, and an institution (Chennault 1998; Dyson 1996). As an identity, whiteness refers to the racial characteristic of being White. Although some good work has been done on whiteness as an identity in various contexts (Helms 1995; Perry 2002), this book focuses on whiteness as an ideology and an institution because of the ways this informs schooling and issues of educational equity. White people certainly have a central role in the maintenance of ideological and institutional whiteness, but whiteness is not just about White people. All of us engage dominant ideologies; sometimes it is in our interests to do so, and at other times it is not—but that is the nature of dominance. Whiteness serves as a "pervasive ideology justifying dominance of one group over others" (Maher and Tetreault 1998, 139). The ideology of whiteness also serves as "a form of social amnesia" that allows White people to forget or ignore how we are implicated in the maintenance of systems of privilege and oppression (McLaren 1998). The function of whiteness as an ideology is illustrated throughout this book.

As a system of ideologies and material effects (privilege and oppression), whiteness is also a well-entrenched structure that is manifested in and gives shape to institutions. It has thus become a norm against which others are judged and also a powerful, if sometimes unconscious, justification for the status quo. As a location of structural advantage, whiteness serves as "a discursive regime that enables real effects to take place" (McLaren 1998, 67). Michelle Fine highlights an important aspect of whiteness as an institution: "Whiteness was produced through the exclusion and denial of opportunity to people of color. . . . Institutional leadership and seemingly race-neutral policies/practices work to insure white privilege" (Fine 1997, 60). Thus, in examining and illustrating the structural and systemic nature of whiteness, it is important to highlight the exclusion and oppression it produces, reproduces, and maintains.

Most discussions of diversity, race, and equity tend to focus on individuals, interactions between individuals, and the identities of individuals, but this book asks readers to shift the focus to institutions and ideologies. Whiteness is not just attached to White individuals; whiteness is an umbrella system that organizes and coordinates multiple and various sites of power and dominance. What is essential to this system of whiteness is that dominance becomes normal, expected, and rationalized. Racial dominance is central to the mechanisms of whiteness, but whiteness is bigger than racism. So while the majority of data in this book center on race and racism, the inclusion of data that are not always centrally about race is essential for a more complete rendering of the system and mechanisms of whiteness.

Niceness as a Mechanism of Whiteness in Schools

A strategic element of whiteness that has yet to be explored in the literature is the notion of niceness—that is, being nice is intimately tied to engaging whiteness, and whiteness itself is aligned with niceness. School systems and the state of Utah provide two key intersecting contexts for exploring the role of niceness in the perpetuation of inequity. A central claim of this book is that *whiteness works through nice people*. The dictionary definition for *nice* is consistent with conventional understandings of the word: To be nice is to be pleasing and agreeable, pleasant and kind. What counts as nice is determined by people individually or in communities. Thus there is nothing factual about niceness. We construct the notion of niceness, and we connect it to particular behaviors, interactions, and discourses. A nice person is not someone who creates a lot of disturbance, conflict, controversy, or discomfort. Nice people avoid potentially uncomfortable or upsetting experiences, knowledge, and interactions. We do not point out failures or shortcomings in others but rather emphasize the good, the promise, and the improvement we see. Niceness compels us to reframe potentially disruptive or uncomfortable things in ways that are more soothing, pleasant, and comfortable. This avoidance and reframing are done with the best intentions, and having good intentions is a critical component of niceness. In fact, as long as one means well, the actual impact of one's behavior, discourse, or action is often meaningless.

Assets-based approaches to education, to working with youth, and to interventions are typical of the niceness so prevalent in education. Focusing on one's assets is supposed to facilitate greater resilience, optimism, and confidence in the person. It is also an individualistic approach to understanding people; it focuses on an individual's good qualities—not necessarily in a broader context or in relation to others or a larger community. A common phrase associated with assets-based approaches is to "change the way you see things"—in other words, wear a "new" pair of glasses that compels you to see the positive, the promise, and the good. These new glasses often obscure inequity, whiteness, and any aspect of the larger context that may hint at a disturbance in the status quo. Being nice provokes a sort of unspoken pact, or a tacit agreement, between people: If I am nice to you, I come to expect that you will also be nice to me in return. You will give me the benefit of the doubt if you notice something potentially problematic, because I have been nice in our previous encounters.

Although there are certainly different ideas about what counts as nice in different communities, there is also a sort of popularly understood, dominantly ascribed to understanding of what is *universally nice*. And what is universally nice is also conceptually and practically linked to whiteness. Being nice encourages us to gloss over ugly, tense, or otherwise hurtful things—and to do so carefully and precisely.

Niceness is illustrated throughout the stories in this book. But what is also illustrated through these same stories is the inequity that is produced and reproduced, and the whiteness that is engaged and protected, in these nice engagements with diversity in the Zion School District. Thus this book turns niceness on its head to highlight the ways in which niceness is not actually nice, good, or healthy for individuals and communities. The niceness running through diversity-related policy and practice in schools is only good for whiteness. As such, it may be "nice" for those who benefit from whiteness, but even those who benefit from whiteness do so only partially. Niceness is incredibly attractive and, at the same time, difficult to critique. But it is precisely this critique that this book engages. Nice people are educated in whiteness daily, and we, in turn, continue to educate in and for whiteness daily.

Being nice is not the same thing as being ignorant or having a lack of awareness. And whiteness is not the result of mere coincidence (Gillborn 2008). Within a frame of niceness, oppressive actions are not actually oppressive; they are just hurtful. They are assumed to be the result of individuals who have made bad choices or who just do not know any better. This framing diverts attention away from patterned inequity, structural oppression, and institutional dominance. But a structural phenomenon cannot be addressed with individual explanations (Vaught and Castagno 2008). Whiteness thrives when we limit our understanding of inequity and dominance to individual intentions, knowledge, instances, and interactions.

Central to making whiteness work is the way niceness connects to neutrality, equality, and compassion. Like niceness itself, neutrality, equality, and compassion are key qualities of whiteness. They are also qualities most of us would ascribe to good teachers. Indeed, the ties between education, niceness, and whiteness are so interwoven that they can be difficult to identify, locate, and pull apart. These ties are even more seductive because they appeal to our sense of fairness. While appearing fair because it centers equality and neutrality, whiteness also maintains a face of compassion. Importantly, "these frames form an impregnable yet elastic wall that barricades Whites from the United States' racial [and power] reality. The trick is in the way the frames bundle with each other—that is, in the wall they form" (Bonilla-Silva 2009, 47). These elements of neutrality, equality, and compassion are woven throughout the stories in this book, and they give whiteness its power in schools and among educators.

Seeing Whiteness through Ethnography

Talking and writing about whiteness is inherently difficult. Whiteness is systemic and systematic, which means that individual people engage whiteness and have some responsibility for acting against whiteness. But saying that we have a responsibility for whiteness is not meant to be a critique of particular people. There is a tendency for White people who encounter whiteness to feel threatened and to then occupy a defensive position against what we hear as accusations against us and our person-hood. When I described my work on this book to a family member, his response was to ask if I could use a word other than "whiteness" to describe what I was talking about, since "whiteness just seems to say that White people are all bad" and "makes you feel like you've done something wrong." Part of my response to this is that we have, in fact, done a number of things wrong if we genuinely value equity and justice for everyone in our communities.

But there is a complicated set of factors that contributes to these wrongs. They are not the result of independently acting people with horrible intentions. But they are also not the result of passive or ignorant individuals being duped by the system. In addition, there is a tendency for people of color either to distance themselves entirely from discussions of whiteness because they assume the conversation is about White people, or to personally reflect on how they engage whiteness but to keep those reflections safe from other's scrutiny. Whiteness works on all of us, and we all engage whiteness. Ethnography is a useful tool for making this phenomenon more accessible.

The stories—that is, the voices, observations, interactions, and texts—that I rely on to illuminate whiteness come primarily from an educational ethnography I conducted in 2005 and 2006 in an urban district in the state of Utah. My ethnography included immersing myself in the classrooms of twenty-four teachers in two different schools; attending as many board meetings, professional development offerings, assemblies, and other district events as possible; examining documents related to diversity as well as the everyday texts that teachers encounter (e.g., handouts, notes to parents, exams); and interviewing more than forty teachers and administrators. More recently, from 2010 to 2012, I conducted an additional thirty-seven interviews with teachers in one of the two schools while serving as an external evaluator for a federally funded turnaround grant the school received. Although I have not lived in the local community since 2006, I grew up there and return multiple times each year for both family visits and professional obligations.

Given my interest in examining diversity, and especially race, I purposefully designed this research to include two schools in the same district but with very different student demographics. I assumed that I would find significant differences between the ways the teachers at each school understood and addressed diversity. I did, in fact, uncover some important differences, but more important, I ended up finding remarkably similar patterns across the two schools. This similarity tells us much about the ways whiteness works and its consistent yet flexible nature.

We all have an incredible bank of racial knowledge. This book is centrally concerned with examining the ways educators engage racial knowledge, how they talk about and around diversity, how they make sense of the racial patterns they witness daily, and how their work with youth reflects what they think and know about diversity. Although the data are primarily about White teachers and administrators, this book should not be read as an indictment of individual White teachers or even of teachers in general. I am sympathetic to the challenges teachers face, the difficult work they engage, and the increasingly scripted context of schools. I am also deeply concerned about inequity and the impacts of whiteness on all communities. Each of us, individually and collectively, needs to be held accountable for the role we play in maintaining and reinforcing injustice. Listening to teachers, observing what happens in schools, and following policies as they hit the ground will help us better understand how whiteness is institutionalized and creates lasting patterns in our communities. Sabina Vaught (2011, 209) articulates the issue, and also the urgency, well: "The issue at the heart of racist schooling is not whether or not there exist individuals who are dedicated, talented, and successful. The issue is that our educational institutions, policies, and practices are structured by White supremacy, and as such they deny Black and Brown youth the myriad resources necessary for equitable schooling. It should not be an accident or a stroke of good fortune that a Black or Brown child receives a good education. It should be a systemic, structural guarantee." This call for a systemic, structural guarantee is made very difficult because we are educated in, and thus often educate for, whiteness. As a result, educators reify the very structures we are being charged with dismantling. Through this book, educators will come to see where, why, and how this occurs, so that we can begin to undo these patterns.

This Is the Place

As a young person, I attended predominantly White, though economically diverse, Catholic schools in the Salt Lake Valley. Being nice was commonly understood in my community as caring for others and being likeable, a team player, mild-mannered, and respectful. Being nice was never linked to justice or the pursuit of equity. This norm of niceness was powerful, pervasive, and so obvious that it hardly needed explanation or articulation. But there is something ironic about being in an overtly Christian space (i.e., a Catholic school) where niceness is expected and yet disconnected from justice. This irony similarly characterizes the research setting for this book.

Having been trained as an educational ethnographer, I am inclined to highlight the unique local context within which my research occurred. Indeed, Utah and the Zion School District are particular places with cultural elements that are not generalizable to other states and districts. Utah is in many ways a unique setting because of the dominance of the Mormon religion and the influence it exerts over politics, the economy, and social norms. At the same time, however, there is an increasing trend nationwide of conservative religious communities having an impact on national politics and norms; in this way, Utah is not that unusual. Having lived and studied in various other places around the country and having paid particular attention to the ways whiteness operates in these different contexts, I am also inclined, therefore, to articulate the common threads that my research setting shares with plenty of other settings across the United States. It is important to understand the local and culturally specific ways that educators in the Zion School District are engaging policy and practice related to diversity, and it is also important to think about how these patterns may be relevant in other contexts. Schools, like other social institutions, are situated within particular places, and those places significantly impact what occurs within the school walls.

The two most common associations with the state of Utah in the public imagination are most likely the words *Mormon* and *conservative*. And indeed, for the state as a whole, these are largely accurate characteristics, although they are beginning to wane slightly as Utah's population becomes more diverse. Still, in 2005, 62 percent of Utah residents were members of the Church of Jesus Christ of Latter-Day Saints (LDS or Mormon). Further, one national study found that Mormon teens are "the most intensely religious teens in the nation" (Hollingshead 2005, C9).

The Mormon Church has a somewhat paradoxical reputation among non-Mormons. On the one hand, it is viewed as a weird religion that allows polygamy, tries to "fix" gay and lesbian people, and ascribes to a number of outlandish beliefs. But on the other hand, it is viewed as being family oriented, generous, and helpful to both individuals and larger communities in times of need. This paradox was evident in Mitt Romney's 2012 run for president of the United States and the multiple ways in which he was portrayed by the media and perceived by the general public. Like the broader Utah context, Mormons are a particular kind of community, and yet they are not an entirely unique one within the United States. They have a specific history and worldview based on their shared identity as

LDS members, and yet we can find similar patterns and trends among other conservative religious groups across the county.

Although the Mormon Church boasts twelve million members worldwide, only about one-third of them are considered "active members" (Fletcher Stack 2005). But within Utah, the dominant culture is overwhelmingly shaped by and tied to the Mormon Church. As one local newspaper reported, "For as long as that church is vibrant, Utah culture will always be tied to it" (Canham 2005, A1). Illustrative of this connection is the fact that as I was writing this book in 2012, the local NBC affiliate in Salt Lake City, KSL, which is owned by the Mormon Church, refused to air a new "family comedy" called *The New Normal*. The sitcom was about a gay couple attempting to have a child via a surrogate mother, and the station offered the following comment: "As a communications company, we make decisions every day regarding our programming, and we made a decision to not broadcast this program because we feel it had a number of issues including sexually explicit content, demeaning dialogue, and inciting stereotypes. . . . We care about and value all members of our community, including LGBT people and their families, and are grateful when there can be . . . cordial and respectful dialogue" (Stanhope 2012). According to KSL, the broadcasting ban had nothing to do with the station's own potential disregard for queer families and issues pertinent to their daily lives; instead, it was about maintaining the compassionate, neutral, and generally nice position that it claimed as a local media outlet. The rationale offered here flips accusations about the station being antigay by claiming to actually be "protecting" the community from stereotypes, disrespectful dialogue, and sexually explicit content. Appealing to "cordial and respectful dialogue" is another way to leverage niceness and, thus, to reify whiteness. KSL's position—as operating from a place of concern that is simultaneously void of any relationship to power, oppression, or marginalization—is indicative of patterns seen across White, Christian religious communities in the United States.

These appeals to neutrality, equality, compassion, and niceness run deep in the state of Utah as well as in its schools and school districts. In 1999, the local community was outraged when the Gay Straight Alliance at a Salt Lake City high school sponsored a six-minute slide show that defined terms such as *gay*, *lesbian*, and *bisexual* and identified symbols and events of importance to the queer community. The slide show was part of the annual multicultural assembly, but community pressure caused school officials to publicly announce that future multicultural assemblies would "only include groups representing particular geographic areas and cultures and, thus, the gay club would not be allowed to participate" (McCormick 2000, 273). Administrators in the Zion School District remembered this incident vividly, and one explained to me that she believed the framing of the ban was "indicative of a culture of nice we have here."

Rather than the "new normal" potentially represented in this particular television show and the presence of student groups allied with the queer community, the "normalcy" of Utah and its close ties to the Mormon Church is captured in the state slogan that claims, "This is the place!" This phrase can be seen on license plates, on large billboards along the highway, and in countless other marketing efforts across the state of Utah. The phrase has its roots in history; the story goes that Mormon pioneers arrived in the Salt Lake Valley and exclaimed that "this is the place!" after a difficult journey. The phrase now frames Utah's official state song:

> Utah! People working together.
> Utah! What a great place to be.
> Blessed from Heaven above,
> It's the land that we love.
> This is the place! . . .
>
> Utah! With its focus on family,
> Utah! Helps each child to succeed.
> People care how they live.
> Each has so much to give.
> This is the place!

Throughout every verse, the state song evokes a number of images central to American identity. These verses highlight the cooperative, hardworking, and family-oriented aspects of both American and Utah cultures. These are nice cultural elements that evoke feelings of pride, belonging, and optimism. The song also appeals to ideologies of patriotism ("the land we love"), Christianity ("blessed from heaven"), determination in the face of adversity ("they kept on going"; "the trials they had to face"), success ("they reached the Great Salt Lake"), hard work ("farms and orchards"; "pioneer spirit"), manifest destiny ("across the plains"), and the American dream ("the place where dreams come true"). This song, the images it evokes, and the social imaginary to which it appeals are constitutive of whiteness. There is an overarching message about what is good and right conveyed here, but it is conveyed without explicitly naming it as such. *You just know.* And so it is with the goodness and rightness implied in most educational policies and practices related to diversity. And so, too, it is with the niceness, compassion, equality, and neutrality implied by whiteness.

According to the 2010 census, Salt Lake City proper (as opposed to the entire Salt Lake Valley, which includes Salt Lake City suburbs) is home to approximately 188,000 people, 75 percent of whom identified as White, 22.3 percent "Hispanic" (primarily Mexican or Mexican American), 4.4 percent Asian, 3.7 percent multiracial, 2.7 percent Black, 2.0 percent Native Hawaiian and Pacific Islander, and 1.2 percent American Indian or Alaska Native.

As I will elaborate, the Zion School District is even more racially and ethnically diverse in terms of its student population. Furthermore, within Salt Lake County, 16 percent of residents speak a language other than English at home; within Salt Lake City, that number jumps to 25 percent. Although close to one hundred languages have been identified in area census reports, Spanish is by far the most widespread non-English language spoken. Approximately 60 percent of those who speak an alternative language speak Spanish (Sanchez 2005). This language diversity is particularly prevalent on the west side of Salt Lake City, where in two zip code sectionals more than half the residents speak a language other than English at home. Racial and ethnic diversity among young people in the Salt Lake area is even higher than it is among the elderly population, so ten years from now, this diversity will be even more apparent.

The divide between the "west side" of the city versus the "east side" is particularly salient and part of the shared discourse among local residents. The social geography of the Salt Lake Valley mirrors patterns seen in other urban spaces. The valley is surrounded by mountains in every direction, but the highest and most picturesque mountains are the Wasatch Range on the east side. These granite peaks and tree-covered slopes house the area's popular ski resorts. Although some high-end neighborhoods are tucked into the mountains, the most populated high-income areas sit in the foothills of these mountains. These are highly sought-out areas for those who can afford them: Homes range from hundreds of thousands of dollars to multimillions, and they feature exquisitely landscaped yards with green grass. Parks are also plentiful. Moving down the foothills, one eventually enters the downtown area, with older homes that have been remodeled; newly developed urban condominiums; and artsy, hip neighborhoods that are more modestly priced and interspersed with cafes and locally owned shops. Continuing west, one abruptly runs into the primary interstate that cuts through the valley and a maze of railroad tracks that mark a clear divide between east and west. Here, too, are many industrial buildings, a few homeless shelters, and the beginning of neighborhoods with homes that are less expensive and mixed with apartment buildings, convenience stores, and payday-loan shops.

At least two superfund sites sit along the Jordan River that runs through the west side of the Salt Lake Valley. These spaces have been covered with clay to contain the hazardous waste and then nicely "beautified" with landscaping and park benches. Because of their appearance, it is easy to miss the fact that the sites contain toxic materials. Moreover, they are only blocks away from west-side schools; no such sites encroach on the east-side communities of Salt Lake City. These geographic divides also mark clear distinctions along racial and social-class lines. Like its urban sisters across the nation, the Salt Lake area houses patterned gentrification and segregation—both of which are evident in the local public schools.

Schools in Salt Lake City fall within two of Salt Lake Valley's many districts, all of which are nestled between two large mountain ranges. Just as Salt Lake City is far more demographically diverse than the rest of the state, the Zion School District is also the most demographically diverse school district in the state. During the fall of 2010, the district served more than 24,000 students—40 percent of whom were designated as English-language learners (ELL), 56 percent of whom were students of color, and 60 percent of whom qualified for free or reduced-price school lunches. This diversity is a fairly recent phenomenon that has occurred over the past three decades. As in most diverse school districts, however, teachers, administrators, and those with decision-making power are still largely White, middle class or upper class, and English speaking. In the Zion School District, they are also frequently Mormon.

The Zion School District's history and context are more fully described and analyzed in the following chapter, but here I want to introduce readers to the two schools that are the focus of this book. Mirroring the gentrification across the city, schools in the Zion School District were largely divided by race.

Birch Secondary School

Walking through the parking lot and into the front doors of Birch Secondary School in 2006, visitors were greeted by a large sign at eye level that read, "Welcome to [Birch Secondary] School—where failure is not an option, and success is the only option. Together We Can." This theme of "together we can" was also displayed in other parts of the school, including on flags in the auditorium and on banners over some of the stairwells. Immediately next to this large colorful sign were two smaller wooden signs that announced Birch's "countdown to excellence." In the middle of the wooden signs there was a mirror at eye level with the inscribed statement "I can do it!" and on either side of the mirror, there was a countdown sign for language arts and math that indicated the number of days until students took the district's standardized tests in these subjects. Students were reminded of the "countdown to excellence" almost daily during the morning announcements as well. Before every late bell at Birch, the theme music from the television game show *Jeopardy* played over the loudspeaker, which indicated that students had only a few more seconds to make it to their next class on time. From the main entrance, visitors could proceed down a maze of hallways or up the stairs to the second floor. Each of the halls was lined with student lockers and classrooms. The walls displayed signs in English, Spanish, and Tongan as well as numerous poster-size photographs of multiracial youth engaged in various activities.

The students at Birch were the most concentrated group of students of color and students from low-income backgrounds in all the district's ten secondary schools. In 2005, students of color represented approximately 86 percent of the student body at Birch; 77 percent of the students were designated English-language learners (ELL), and 96 percent qualified for free or reduced-price school lunches. Most ELL students were native Spanish speakers, but there were also growing numbers of students from Somalia and Sudan who spoke native tribal languages. Of the students of color at Birch, 62 percent were Latino (primarily of Mexican descent), 13 percent were Pacific Islander (primarily Samoan and Tongan), 4 percent were African American, 4 percent were Asian American, and 3 percent were American Indian or Alaska Native. Just 14 percent of students were White.

Standardized test scores at Birch were consistently low compared to east-side schools in the district, and achievement gaps were evident between White students and students of color. On the language arts exam, for example, the highest percentage of students scoring in the lowest percentile bracket were Black students, and only half of the school's Latino students, who constituted the majority of the school's population, earned proficient scores. Thus, while Birch test scores were slowly rising, they did not differ substantially from patterns seen in other urban schools across the nation in terms of achievement gaps according to race and language.

Fourteen Birch teachers and administrators participated in my research. The total group included five men and three people of color, which represented about one-third of the classified staff at Birch. The teachers I worked with taught every grade level of mainstream, special education, and English-as-a-second-language (ESL) classes, and they taught a range of subject areas, including math, language arts, physical education, fine arts, science, and social studies. Some of the teachers had been at Birch for more than ten years, and others were just beginning their careers the year I collected data. Although most of this book focuses on teachers, I also interviewed the administrative team and spent time observing them at faculty meetings and assemblies.

Birch's principal, Mr. More, was a White man who had been a teacher, assistant principal, and principal throughout the district at the elementary, middle, and high school levels before coming to Birch as principal in 2003. He was extremely hopeful about the direction Birch was going and emphasized the goal of becoming a "90/90/90" school. Mr. More talked about the 90/90/90 research every chance he had. He noted that 90 percent of the Birch population already consisted of students of color and low-income students and that the school was working hard to achieve 90 percent in high academic achievement. In collaboration with other staff, Mr. More guided the faculty toward emphasizing reading and math during the year I was collecting data, and he planned to incorporate a "writing across the curriculum" element the following year. He was also instrumental in hiring an additional full-time administrator to focus exclusively on student behavior.

Overall, Mr. More believed that "our primary focus at [Birch] is closing that achievement gap. That has to happen." His focus on academics was evident during morning announcements, faculty meetings, assemblies, and reports to the district as well as in the décor around the school. Being new to Birch but a veteran of the district, Mr. More recognized and willingly admitted that Birch "has a tremendous amount of baggage associated with it" in terms of its poor reputation and image as a "toxic environment." He was, however, quick to note that "that is changing in major ways." Mr. More waged a focused "PR campaign" of changing Birch's image within the district—an agenda that centered around improved academic performance (the 90/90/90 goal and emphases on reading, writing, and math) but also on discipline (hiring a new administrator and "setting clear boundaries"), a clean school ("this place might be falling down around us but it's going to be clean"), and a welcoming environment when someone called or visited the school (the school phone greeting was always "It's a wonderful day at [Birch]!").

Spruce Secondary School

At Spruce Secondary School, a large colorful banner hung outside the school's front door that announced Spruce's exemplary status as a "community of caring." The front doors opened into a foyer with the library, auditorium, and main office all within view. Spruce had long been considered a "good" school within the Zion School District, and its annual performance on the state standardized tests had been consistently high. In any given year, approximately 80 percent of Spruce students post proficient scores on the state standardized exams. When Spruce's test score data are disaggregated by race/ethnicity and language status, achievement gaps are evident, but they are not as disparate as those among Birch's students.

Spruce sits in the east-side foothills, just below the mountains, and in an older but highly desirable neighborhood. The school's immediate community was largely White and middle to upper-middle class, but the enrollment boundaries included areas farther west that served working-class and lower-income families. The student body at Spruce was still more than 70 percent White, but almost 50 percent of students qualified for free or reduced-price school lunches, and 25 percent of students were classified as English-language learners. These students, who were almost entirely Spanish dominant and newly immigrated to the United States, spent more than half their day in segregated classes with a small group of ESL teachers who were White and monolingual English speakers.

Of the fourteen educators at Spruce who participated in my research, five were men, two were people of color, and two were administrators. The twelve teachers with whom I spent the most time taught all grade levels and both ESL and mainstream classes; like the research participants at Birch, they composed about one-third of the teaching staff at Spruce. The subjects they taught included math, science, social studies, fine arts, language arts, world languages, and health. Because Spruce had very low teacher turnover each year, none of the teachers with whom I worked were new to the school. The amount of time they had been teaching at Spruce ranged from five to twenty-five years. Some had taught for a number of years before coming to Spruce—in other words, they could all be considered veteran teachers.

The classrooms of the teachers I worked with at Spruce had a similar feel to them. Every room had classroom rules and consequences, the five Community of Caring values (respect, trust, family, caring, and responsibility), and the school's mission ("empower every student") and vision ("every student achieves") posted prominently around the room. The shared spaces around the school had a similar emphasis on school rules and values.

Spruce's principal, Ms. Smith, was a White woman who had occupied her position for more than seven years. She lived in the community surrounding Spruce and clearly perceived Spruce as an east-side school that commanded high expectations from students. In our formal interview, she talked at length about how Spruce used to be the district's ESL magnet school and how "the bar was lowered" during that time because "teachers accepted poor-quality work." She explained: "At one time, they [teachers] did lower the grading scale, and we need to readjust that, which is why our goal is high-quality work." When the district moved away from the magnet model and reverted back to being a neighborhood school, the enrollment boundaries changed and Spruce began to enroll fewer students of color because ELL students went to their neighborhood schools on the west side. The new boundaries, however, did bring a sizable population of lower-income White students to Spruce. Whereas Birch's principal was focused on "closing the achievement gap," Ms. Smith did not feel that a focus on the achievement gap was what her school needed. She believed that focusing on closing the achievement gap resulted in the "high-end kids" being ignored and "losing percentage points":

> Generally, when you bring your lower-end students and your higher-end students [together], your lower-end students progress and your higher-end students come down several percentages. That happened. That happened here. I started watching the neighborhood Caucasian scores drop—1, maybe 2, percent. So what's happening is, and this was a conversation in the school, we are spending so much time on closing the achievement gap, are we still working on those on the cusp and the high-end kids? And we did, we spent hours and hours looking at data and the lowest percentile. Well, I can tell you who my lowest percentile kids are. I can tell you by their name, and I can tell you maybe eight or ten of their reading scores. And they do not change. They do not. You have a certain percentage of kids, and it is so sad, but no matter what you do, we can't make a difference. And we've tried everything. We've tried calling parents and saying, "We've got a special class to get them caught up. We have a special reading class. We need them to do this." The parents refuse: "No, they are not giving up an elective to take another class." There will always be a percentage in society [who] are going to bottom out. And so, we look at those kids, who are the rough kids, who are the kids [who] are suspended. Caucasian—White, I mean, African American . . . um, you know, it's not particularly one or another. Race has nothing to do with it, but a lot of it is lack of family support.

Ms. Smith expressed a firm commitment to serving the "high-end" students at Spruce, and this commitment was evident in the numerous advanced and honors classes the school offered and the recent decline in

ESL and remedial offerings. She also made it clear that, in her mind, "race has nothing to do" with success and failure.

The themes of neutrality, equality, and compassion already come to life in these short introductions to Birch and Spruce. We can also begin to see the various ways niceness is engaged by the two principals. Despite very different school contexts and the different philosophical emphases of the school leaders, whiteness—that is, a system of material and ideological race dominance—is employed and reified. I hope that by looking closely at diversity-related policy and practice at both Spruce and Birch secondary schools, we can learn something about how schools and educators across the nation are engaged in these issues. Indeed, it is important to see how a particular school district is educated in whiteness, so that we can begin to examine our own schools and consider how we might educate against whiteness.

Overview of the Chapters in This Book

With critical race theory and whiteness studies as a foundation, this book employs concepts like interest convergence, liberalism, meritocracy, and colorblindness to better understand diversity-related educational policy and practice. This sort of theoretical framework and the resulting analyses are not nice. Gloria Ladson-Billings highlighted this tension in 1998 when she asked, "What is Critical Race Theory doing in a nice field like education?" (Ladson-Billings 1998). But niceness is a White construct and, as such, works to reify whiteness.

Although this book is grounded in ethnographic data, it is organized around concepts and theory rather than data. As a conceptually driven ethnography, I am trying to do two seemingly different things here: First, I hope to provide rich and detailed data that describe one district's diversity-related work and the impact of that work. Second, by examining two schools in the state of Utah, I hope to offer a nuanced theoretical discussion of whiteness as it relates to schooling in the United States. I use stories and narratives to see how theory is enacted every day, *and* I use theory to unpack and make sense of the stories and narratives. In an effort to capture both the rich stories and the power of theory, the chapters are organized thematically. Each chapter introduces two key concepts that are illuminated through data; each of these concepts is central to the operation of whiteness in U.S. schools.

Chapter 1 discusses interest convergence and responsibility. Chapter 2 discusses colorblindness and powerblindness. Chapter 3 examines silence and politeness. Chapter 4 examines equality and meritocracy, and chapter 5 highlights individualism and a critique of liberalism. These concepts are clearly interconnected, so it is impossible to completely separate one from another. But by focusing each chapter on two distinct elements of whiteness, I am better able to both fully explain the ideas and paint a picture of them on the ground.

The chapter organization also allows a close examination of the various contexts that make up the stories in this book. Chapter 1 examines the Zion School District from the district, or central office, level. Within the district, central office leaders claimed equity as a priority but simultaneously claimed that the responsibility for failed attempts at equity resided in individual schools. When there existed a convergence of interests, some progress was made around diversity, but this progress was always narrowly defined and limited by the possessive investment in whiteness. When no such interests converged, responsibility for equity was consistently displaced elsewhere. It becomes difficult to hold anyone accountable when no one is really "at fault." Having set up the district context, the remaining chapters go inside Birch and Spruce and offer close encounters with a range of teachers.

Chapters 2 and 3 discuss and analyze patterns that were similar in both schools. Chapter 2 examines the ways teachers at Birch and Spruce understood and engaged multicultural education as either "powerblind sameness" or "colorblind difference." Although these framing concepts appear to be logically inconsistent with one another, educators subscribed to both simultaneously. These two frameworks of sameness and difference serve as a dual system of support for whiteness.

Chapter 3 discusses some of the meaningful silences around— and silencing of—race and sexuality in schools. Even though done with the best of intentions, efforts at maintaining politeness end up maintaining the status quo rather than facilitating social change. This chapter also highlights three teachers who served as exceptions to these norms of silence and, therefore, provide some insight into what classrooms might look like where issues of race and sexuality are not silenced.

Although the ways teachers engage multicultural education and enforce polite silences were patterns shared across Spruce and Birch, there were certainly differences between the two schools. These differences are the focus of chapters 4 and 5. Chapter 4 highlights how schools differently engage diversity and, specifically, the notion of equality. At Spruce, a powerblind, colorblind understanding of equality shaped the ways educators understood excellence and the efforts they made to provide a high-quality education to Spruce students. At Birch, however, educators engaged a more race- and power-conscious form of equality, but they were so constrained by the pressures of standardized accountability that their diversity-related efforts were also limited and ultimately failed to approximate what was needed to advance equity.

Chapter 5 examines current federal efforts to "turn around the nation's worst schools" through targeted School Improvement Grants. Birch received one of these grants in 2010, and this chapter considers how the immediate and short-term influx of resources impacted the school, what it meant for teachers and students, and how it is yet another iteration of whiteness in schools. With a foundation in individualism and classical liberalism, this school-reform model results in the loss of students, teachers, and actual schools. The resulting neoliberal transformation exacerbates inequity and reifies whiteness.

The concluding chapter suggests that while whiteness shapes what diversity-related policy and practice look like, the resulting policy and practice, in turn, further strengthen whiteness. Thus whiteness operates as an almost perfect system. It is effective and efficient at what it does. But there are spaces of possibility within this system. There have to be. The challenge, then, is to locate those spaces of possibility, pry them open, and use them to dismantle the system. This is where educating against whiteness comes in. Teachers have an opportunity to facilitate the kind of education that would highlight inequity and dominance and then encourage action that brings about equity, chips away at whiteness, and ultimately creates more space for even more action. This sort of work is not consistent with the niceness found in typical diversity-related policy and practice in schools. This niceness, in fact, stands as a seductive obstacle for educators. As a key element of whiteness in schools, niceness makes educating against whiteness very difficult, so we must be awake, vigilant, and strategic. Being educated in whiteness increases the challenge before us; it also increases the stakes.

CHAPTER ONE

"Equity Has to Be a Priority"

Converging Interests and
Displacing Responsibility

I have stressed the importance of looking beyond the superficial
rhetoric of policies and practices, in order to focus on the material
and ideological work that is done to legitimate and extend race
inequity. When judging education policy, therefore, it is pertinent
to ask some deceptively simple questions. . . . These are by no
means the only relevant "tests" of equity and policy, but they are
among the most revealing and fundamental because they go beyond
the expressed intent of policy-makers and practitioners to examine
how policy works in the real world. First, the question of priorities:
Who or what is driving education policy? Second, the question
of beneficiaries: Who wins and who loses as a result of education
policy priorities? And, finally, the question of outcomes: What are
the effects of policy?

—DAVID GILLBORN, "EDUCATION POLICY
AS AN ACT OF WHITE SUPREMACY"

I entered the Zion School District with the intention of studying "multicultural education" on the ground—in schools and among teachers in different school contexts. In 2005, this was the language used in schools and colleges of education to reference work around diversity and sometimes equity. Consistent with this national trend, I knew the Zion School District had a policy on the books titled "Policy on Multicultural Education" as well as a district administrator charged with implementing the policy. As the chapters in this book highlight, I learned something about how the district and particular teachers engaged this thing called multicultural education, but I also learned much about how educators engaged whiteness in their various approaches to diversity.

Before going inside schools and hearing about how teachers engage diversity-related policy and practice, it is useful to consider how the Zion School District's central office understood, engaged, and shaped efforts around diversity. One obvious starting point for this analysis is to look directly at the multicultural education policy. Indeed, the policy itself and work surrounding the policy composed a significant portion of the central office's leadership around diversity. But widening the lens to examine other diversity-related work is also important for understanding how issues of equity and whiteness get taken up, used, and discarded in particular contexts. This chapter focuses on the narratives of central office leaders and the work done at the central office in order to provide a more complete rendering of the context surrounding what happens at Birch Secondary School and Spruce Secondary School. Starting with the central office's policy and practice begins to answer David Gillborn's call for better understanding the "material and ideological work that is done to legitimate and extend race inequity" in schools (2005, 492).

I return, first, to the district policy initially introduced in the previous chapter. The policy's origin and implementation are indicative of larger trends in the central office's work around diversity. By examining the policy, we begin to see how interest convergence and the displacement of responsibility for equity play out on the ground. Then I shift focus to other diversity-related work engaged by central office leaders and the ways they described the work being done in the district. Here I suggest that the central office leverages its responsibility for equity when it is so compelled because of external pressure from the No Child Left Behind Act (NCLB) and the Office of Civil Rights (OCR). In these cases, we see a convergence of interests among federal mandates, district priorities, and communities of color. When there are no such interests converging, however, the central office displaces responsibility for equity back to the schools. When equity is solely a policy imperative driven by mandates or funding, diversity-related efforts end up being limited and temporary. In these instances, whiteness and the interests of those with power are always maintained, because—whether shaped by federal mandates, site-based decisions, or accountability pressures—diversity-related policy and practice in the Zion School District are consistent with niceness and thus rarely disrupt the status quo or challenge inequity.

Policy on the Books, Policy in Practice

As I mentioned in the introductory chapter, the Zion School District developed a diversity and multiculturalism policy in 1997. The development and adoption of this policy followed a series of events that brought attention to diversity-related concerns in the district. In 1994, the Office of Civil Rights (OCR) found that at least seven Utah school districts were not meeting the federal guidelines for educating English-language learners (ELL), and in 1995, a member of the Zion School Board resigned from his position due to frustrations regarding the board's "inability to face issues of diversity, religious conflict, site-based management, and inequitable building programs." The board member who resigned was quoted in a newspaper article saying, "The school board [members are] really sharp, but they are insensitive to people who are different from them," and "the board's greatest challenge is to get in touch with the district's increasing minority presence."[1] Within the next couple of years, members of the Latino community filed suit against the district with the OCR, citing the district's failure to properly educate ELL and special education students.

When I was in the Zion School District in 2005 and 2006, one central office leader told me that the district had had an "ethnic affairs person" in the mid-1990s, and when he resigned, a committee was formed to "look at what we needed to move things forward. It was a matter of what do we need." She noted that the committee was not formed "out of any particular problem," but that the group was charged with examining "how to work better with our students of color and our families." The committee ultimately determined that "we needed a policy to bring importance to the whole idea [of diversity and multicultural education]." So when district leaders perceived a need to respond, the multicultural education policy was created.

The development of this policy was clearly a reaction to community pressure, changing demographics, and tensions among district constituents. Not insignificantly, central office leaders described the policy's initial development in nice ways. They were quick to point out that there was not "a problem" that needed to be addressed. There was some sort of "need" and a desire to "work with" communities of color. This framing gets repeated in other diversity efforts, and while there is nothing inherently wrong with it, it simultaneously absolves the central office from any wrongdoing and positions the staff as proactively engaging diversity-related work. It does not position the central office as protecting its investments in whiteness, and it fails to highlight the way action emanates from the convergence of interests.

The theory of interest convergence suggests that people believe what benefits them, and the majority group tolerates and/or pursues advances for racial justice only when it suits its own interests to do so (Bell 1979, 1980, 1987; Castagno and Lee 2007; Tate 1997; Taylor 1999). Thus the interests of people of color to achieve racial equity will only be accommodated when they converge with the interests of White people. When the price of such racial remedies becomes too high or costly for Whites, progress is halted and the status quo is maintained. The price of racial remedies is more than just financial costs. It also refers to ideological, psychological, and relational costs incurred as a result of undoing whiteness. Similarly, George Lipsitz (1998) suggests that the status quo of whiteness is maintained through the ways in which White people invest in our/their own interests and maintain sole possession over those interests. Incremental change is made when those interests are perceived to converge with the interests of communities of color, but only to the extent to which such changes do not significantly disrupt the dominant cultures, ideologies, or institutions.

In the development of the multicultural education policy in the Zion School District, we see the convergence of interests between the district and minoritized communities. Students of color were not being well served in district schools, so the community pressed the district through various means (e.g., lodging a formal complaint, resigning from certain roles in protest). The district had an interest in appearing responsive to community needs and in appearing to ensure the success of all district students. The convergence of these interests resulted in the development of a policy explicitly framed around multiculturalism and equity. But as we will see, the way the policy got subsequently taken up and implemented was determined by leaders' possessive investment in whiteness and the extent to which diversity-related efforts encroached on whiteness.

When the Zion School Board approved the policy in 1997, it also approved money for a full-time administrator to ensure the policy was carried out. The district conducted a national search to fill this newly created position, and it ultimately hired Ms. Garrison, a woman of color who had many years of experience working with schools and educators around issues of diversity. Ms. Garrison was still in the position ten years later, but she had been responsible for a number of other programs during her tenure, so multicultural education never represented more than 40 percent of her job responsibilities. One district administrator explained that when the policy was created, the Board of Education "really didn't have a clear idea about what multicultural education was" and that the policy "hasn't moved since" it was created. Many others agreed that very little progress had been made in the decade following the development of the policy. Perhaps the price of real progress toward equity was too high and the investment in whiteness too great for the Zion School District.

Because the possessive investment in whiteness is rarely explicitly acknowledged or named, there must be other, presumably legitimate, ways to explain what happened with this policy's failed implementation. Ms. Garrison attributed the lack of movement to the absence of support needed to do her job well. She described herself as staunchly committed to diversity and equity, but she also admitted that she had not been able to successfully implement the policy during her time in the Zion School District. She did not, however, fault herself for this failure; rather, she cited a number of other factors, including the fact that her budget had not grown since her first year of employment, that she was "never brought to the table" for discussions about strategic planning and academic achievement, and that "multicultural education was simply not a priority in the district." Ms. Garrison noted that "the district is here [while she made a fist with one hand] and I'm here [while she made a far-away fist with the other hand], and the gap or distance is getter further and further apart. We've been working for months on strategic planning, and I'm not a part of it. If I'm not there, nobody raises [the issue of diversity]." She also said, "I've never believed that I had the support of the administration." She added that the exception was her first year in her position, when "there was a lot of buzz around multicultural education because the policy had just been created." In the years since, however, Ms. Garrison lamented that other priorities had been identified that "took precedence over everything else in this district." Here we see Ms. Garrison displacing responsibility for the policy's lack of implementation around equity "up"—that is, to the larger entity of the central office. She cites other district priorities, her not being part of key district initiatives, and a lack of financial support for work around multicultural education.

Some central office leaders agreed that the conditions within the district had not been right for the diversity policy to be effectively implemented and added that "[Ms. Garrison] is just one person." In contrast to Ms. Garrison, who placed responsibility for the policy's ineffective implementation on her central office colleagues and supervisors, the central office leaders pointed to the schools as failing to initiate work around diversity and equity. They were able to do this because of the district's site-based leadership context—an issue that I return to later in this chapter.

Here we see other central office leaders displacing responsibility for action around equity "down" and relinquishing their own accountability. One central office leader explained that when Ms. Garrison approached schools during her first year about developing strategic plans around multicultural education, the "schools said, 'Back off, and we'll let you know when we need you.'" Highlighting the local authority of schools speaks directly to the district's norms around site-based leadership and the lack of power and influence this particular policy had over individual schools.

It also speaks to the way in which whiteness protects and encourages a business-as-usual approach to schooling.

Although most central office leaders of color and some White leaders believed that factors outside Ms. Garrison's control were largely to blame for the slow progress of diversity-related efforts in the district, some of the White central office leaders were more critical of Ms. Garrison, did not believe that she had a clearly outlined agenda, and held her largely responsible for the lack of progress around multicultural education and equity. Placing responsibility for the failure to achieve system-wide equity on one individual is absurd, but it is illustrative of a common approach seen in school districts across the country. Hiring one person to serve as *the* leader for diversity and equity efforts often results in the isolation of both the person and the efforts, as well as scapegoating the hired person so that she is held responsible for any program problems or failures. Furthermore, these diversity-related positions are often the only higher-ranking leadership positions held by people of color, which serves to exacerbate their marginalization and increase the likelihood of their "failure."

At every turn, we see how the possessive investment in whiteness and the price of racial remedies shaped the way the multicultural education policy was taken up, dismissed, and rationalized. One central office leader told me that the policy was never implemented because it "required things the schools weren't ready to do." In addition, the central office was also not ready to do what was needed to pursue equity. The price of this work is high for school systems whose foundations rest on racial hierarchies. It is also high for educators whose understanding of school success rests on assumptions of colorblindness, equality, and meritocracy. Uprooting these foundations is difficult and potentially scary; it is far easier, not to mention nicer, to continue operating as if the foundation is stable. Indeed, if we widen the lens from this specific policy to the central office as a whole, we can see how these trends operate on a larger scale. This widening of the lens also brings whiteness into relief.

Displacing Responsibility for Equity to Individual Schools

Central office leaders in the Zion School District largely talked about diversity-related efforts by using the language of "equity." And equity was primarily understood as "providing equal educational opportunity" and "closing the achievement gap." Not insignificantly, equity and equality were collapsed into the same idea, making them synonymous, so that fairness and justice (equity) is equated with sameness (equality). Central office leaders further described their goals as "all students having access to high-quality programs" and "all our kids are learn-ing and succeeding." More than half the central office leaders I spoke with characterized diversity-related efforts—and especially "equity"—as a "high priority" in the district. Equity was variously explained as "one of our top priorities," "[something] we talk about all the time," and "a central office goal." This diversity discourse is a familiar one among educators. Indeed, to not talk about equity—or, at least, equality—as a priority would run the risk of being critiqued.

But this default diversity stance is too often paired with real, material inequity in schools. Although Zion School District leaders said equity was a priority, they were simultaneously faced with data that indicated the prevalence of achievement gaps and the academic failure of many students within district schools. The patterns were similar to those seen in districts across the United States: Almost 90 percent of White students scored within the proficient range on the state's standardized test in language arts, while less than two-thirds of Latino students and just over half of African American students received a proficient score. Simi-larly, 80 percent of White students—compared to barely half of Latino students and less than half of African American students—received a proficient score on the state math exam. In addition, students of color were 2.2 times more likely to receive out-of-school suspensions than White students. Clearly, these are not acceptable outcomes. How did central office leaders make sense of these data, and where did they place responsibility and calls for accountability? Tellingly, they often pointed to the schools.

Overall, most central office leaders believed that although there was a strong sense of the importance of diversity-related efforts and pursu-ing equity at the district level, this urgency tended to break down at the school level. Many central office leaders named one or two schools that they believed were "doing a good job" addressing diversity and equity issues, but they agreed that most schools in the district were not addressing these issues. Central office leaders offered three main reasons for this break-down at the school level: site-based leadership, deficit discourses, and no sense of need for diversity-related efforts. Displacing responsibility to the schools is a key mechanism for abrogating accountability for equity within the district. It also highlights the degree to which educational lead-ers invest in whiteness and minimize the cost of upsetting the status quo. The resulting pattern is one where central office leaders reify whiteness in the name of honoring each school's authority to manage their own affairs. This is a nice approach to leadership that not only permits but virtually ensures continued inequity.

Site-Based Leadership

The Zion School District has a history of patterned decentralization. Beginning in the 1950s, superintendents began the process of decentralization so that individual schools had more immediate control over their affairs. During the 1970s, the notion of "shared governance" really took hold as a philosophy that valued the voices and perspectives of multiple constituencies. During my time in the district thirty years later, I heard less about shared governance and more about site-based leadership. Although the district's website had a manual titled "Shared Governance Guide: Active Cooperation for More Effective Education," the extent of shared governance appeared to be that schools maintained "school improvement councils" (which were primarily composed of a small number of staff from a particular school) and "school community councils" (which included local community members and were supposed to be representative of the school's student demographics). Both central office leaders and teachers made frequent reference to site-based leadership, particularly in the context of our conversations about equity and diversity-related work in the district.

Because the Zion School District has a long history of site-based leadership and local control over schools, there is a well-established tradition of the central office being fairly hands-off when it comes to decisions affecting individual schools. Most central office leaders who believed equity was a priority for central office leadership explained that the implementation of this priority was variable within schools because of individual school leadership. Ms. Benson's explanation was representative of what many of her colleagues told me:

> [Central office] leadership people see it [equity] as a priority, but site-based management makes it a more complicated issue because each school is its own little kingdom within a larger kingdom. And so the priorities that the district, board, and superintendent set, everyone is aware of, but they only give lip service to it. . . . I think districts that are more top-down probably have an easier time with something like this because there are fewer options. So I would say there is a lot of variation on understanding and implementation and willingness to march along. But I think our district leaders are very sensitive and very aware. I am really impressed with their ability to see the needs.

Ms. Benson clearly attributed the absence of equity efforts in schools to site-based leadership. Her reference to a "kingdom within a kingdom" is a nice way to recognize the presumed authority and autonomy of both individual schools and the central office. In a similar vein, Ms. Venidos, the Director of English Language Services, talked about how the support she provided schools and individual teachers to meet the needs of English-language learners was "voluntary because we are a site-based management district." She went on to explain that this often resulted in a lack of communication between the central office and schools and among various schools, so that, in the end, "everyone goes at everything differently" and "there is little collaboration."

Thus, from the perspective of the central office leaders, district-level policies, services, and support opened up a number of doors for diversity-related efforts, but site-based leadership seemed to close many of them at the school level. This notion of site-based leadership was the most frequently cited reason among central office leaders for the lack of effective diversity and equity efforts in the schools. In other words, site-based leadership allowed, and even encouraged, the central office to displace responsibility for equity to the schools. Absolving themselves of this responsibility also meant that central office leaders could not be held accountable for equity. When displacement of responsibility occurs, even well-intended and vocal appeals for equity are meaningless.

One central office leader of color articulated this well when she said that although there were "pockets of really exemplary work" around equity, "there is no overarching vision" within the district. Instead, there was "poor communication" about what the commitment to equity actually was. In contrast to many of her colleagues, she located these "exemplary pockets" and "missing vision" across both the central office and the schools. She did not abrogate the responsibility of central office leaders but rather identified equity as an institutional, systemic issue. Indeed, maintaining that continued inequity is simply the result of site-based leadership within the district seems to miss the complexity of the issue. As I illustrate later in this chapter, site-based leadership *does not* stop the central office from mandating particular diversity-related policies and practices within the schools.

Deficit Beliefs about Youth of Color

The second most frequently cited reason among central office leaders for the lack of diversity-related work in the schools was the prevalence of a "deficit discourse" throughout the district. Every central office leader of color and one White central office leader I spoke with referenced how teachers, school-level administrators, and some central office personnel were "still working from deficit models" about particular groups of students. They said that these deficit ideologies resulted in strongly held beliefs about students and families being to blame for low academic achievement. The deficit discourse, according to a number of central office leaders, allowed teachers to continue doing what they had always done in the classroom and to avoid any responsibility for the consistently low academic performance of particular groups of students. Ms. Harding, for example, noted that "people have to start changing their attitudes" and begin to question their assumptions of deficit. For her, this was why multicultural education was so important—because she believed it forced teachers and administrators to be aware of and reflect on their assumptions and how those assumptions might be affecting educational practice. As we will see, however, the way multicultural education was engaged in the Zion School District actually did little to disrupt patterned inequity.

Recognizing deficit ideologies in individuals is important, but any effective approach to equity must be systemic and systematic (Vaught and Castagno 2008). Part of the difficulty in advancing this sort of structural approach stems from the value we place on niceness and individual goodwill. Ms. Luna highlighted the pervasiveness of niceness among educators when she noted, "People are now less likely to talk negatively about certain people, but they still don't challenge each other's assumptions." Ms. Venidos agreed and explained that the resistance to diversity-related efforts and the persistence of deficit assumptions stemmed from two different positions: "For some, it's truly a matter of not knowing, while others are more purposeful," but "either way, it's harmful to our students." Ms. Venidos was clear that the outcome of "harm" is what is most important. But when harm is understood as perpetuated by individuals who primarily "don't know any better," and this understanding is situated in a context where leaders displace the responsibility for change to other individuals, action toward equity is unlikely. Being educated in, and for, whiteness creates a powerful set of conditions and operating mechanisms that sustain inequity.

The data I collected at the Birch and Spruce secondary schools were consistent with these central office leaders' analyses regarding the presence of deficit ideologies. As I illustrate in later chapters, a deficit ideology was clearly subscribed to by many teachers and was a significant barrier for working toward greater equity and educating against whiteness. My point here is that a number of central office leaders were well aware of the prevalence of a deficit ideology within the district, and yet they seemed to do little work to confront it. Pairing this explanation with the previous one of site-based leadership highlights how nicely framed diversity rhetoric and good intentions for equity are meaningless if responsibility is displaced and accountability disappears. Site-based leadership encourages a passing of the buck. In this context, the price of leveraging its responsibility for equity is too high for the Zion School District.

Subscribing to deficit beliefs about particular groups of students—and their families and communities—is not necessarily nice if *nice* is understood to mean thinking and behaving in ways that are kind and positive in relation to others. In other words, we might say that educators who maintain deficit assumptions are not nice toward the people they believe are deficient. But deficit ideologies are often revealed in seemingly neutral and compassionate ways—a point that becomes more obvious in later chapters. Furthermore, educators and leaders who simultaneously critique deficit ideologies in private (i.e., in an interview with a researcher or among a small group of close colleagues) and ignore or fail to confront them in public (i.e., at a staff meeting or when deficit discourses are actually observed) are engaging niceness in powerful ways. Central office leaders who balance this private/public tension maintain the "culture of nice" within the Zion School District.

Perceiving "Need"

The final reason referenced by central office leaders for the lack of diversity efforts in the schools related to the demographic context of particular schools and areas of the city. A number of people mentioned one or two schools they felt were doing "really exemplary work" and "were more aware" of issues related to diversity. All the "exemplary" schools they mentioned were on the west side of the district and served largely students of color. Ms. Benson summed up this theme well when she said that on the east side, "there is not a sense of urgency, and I don't think there is a real feeling of need. . . . I really think it has to do with need. If there is a pressing need, then you make the effort and you try to adjust your behaviors or your thought patterns. If you don't, then I think it's just too comfortable to stay where you are." Ms. Benson followed up this remark by explaining that more schools on the west side that serve diverse student populations seemed to recognize that there was "a need" to do something different in order to better serve their students, whereas most east-side schools with larger percentages of White and middle-class and upper-class students were content with a business-as-usual approach, since the schools' test scores were generally high at the aggregate level.

The No Child Left Behind Act makes "need" at the school level obvious because of the way it requires data to be collected, disaggregated, and publicly available. Schools that have not been successful at meeting Adequate Yearly Progress (AYP) and demonstrating improved academic achievement on standardized tests are, therefore, more likely to feel a sense of need and urgency to do something different to meet the expectations being placed on them by federal and state governments and their local school districts. When success is defined by tests, there is no perceived diversity problem or need at schools with high aggregate test scores. Lost in this dynamic are the students of color who are not being well served in east-side schools and who essentially become invisible through the prioritizing of need as defined by test scores.

The notion that only schools whose leaders perceive a need will pursue diversity-related work points to the reactive nature of many diversity efforts. When equity is pursued as a reaction to a perceived need, the strategies employed are often limited and temporary. But this path is presumably the only nice one to take, because proactively working for equity requires naming whiteness and changing the institutional and ideological foundation of schools. Sitting back, waiting, avoiding potentially difficult work, and then responding appropriately when so compelled are constitutive components of niceness; these behaviors also allow whiteness to grow unhindered. The limited and temporary nature of reactive diversity efforts is highlighted by turning to instances where the central office did engage in diversity-related work.

When Interests Converge and Equity Is a Policy Imperative

If the Zion School District followed a pure system of site-based leadership, then the story of diversity-related policy and practice would be solely about schools, and the central office would be absent from the discussion. This, however, was not the case. Alongside central office leaders' discourse about the absence of diversity efforts in most schools were narratives of relatively successful efforts coming out of the central office. In the following sections, I examine these efforts in order to shed light on when, how, and why the central office leaders acted inconsistently with the philosophy of site-based leadership and with their typical pattern of displacing responsibility for equity to schools.

As we will see, the central office leverages its responsibility for equity when there is a convergence of interests stemming largely from policy or funding pressures. In these cases, the interests of minoritized communities, the Zion School District, and the federal government intersect and prompt action. Significantly, action occurs primarily because of the presence of federal pressure. Most central office leaders referenced either the Office of Civil Rights or NCLB regulations and explained that equity "has to be a priority" given these two imperatives from the federal government. A number of central office leaders cited both the desire to be released from OCR review and the mandate to comply with federal NCLB regulations in order to maintain access to federal funding *as reasons for* equity being a high district priority. In other words, equity was articulated as a policy imperative—that is, something that derived from external pressure, sanctions, or funding. The central office's efforts around assessment services, language services, and refugee services highlight the spaces where interests converged in the Zion School District. Even in these spaces, however, action was limited and investments in whiteness were protected.

Assessment Services

Within the Zion School District, the central office led multiple efforts throughout the year to gather data and disseminate it to students, families, and teachers. These assessment services came out of a department in the central office with at least five staff members who were skilled in statistics, testing, and evaluation. The central office allocated significant resources toward the development and use of "practice" standardized tests and toward the collection and dissemination of multiple forms of achievement data. Math teachers at Birch, for example, were required to administer tests that resembled the end-of-the-year proficiency test, and they were expected to use the data obtained from these weekly assessments to shape their curriculum and instruction.

Central office leaders talked about these efforts as "accountability measures," and they pointed directly to NCLB regulations as the primary driver behind these efforts. Although the Zion School District examined disaggregated data prior to the No Child Left Behind Act, state and federal accountability models forced central office leaders to analyze disaggregated achievement data more deeply and make such data publicly available. Interest convergence is operating here because minoritized communities have an interest in publically available achievement data if it helps advocate improved schooling for their children, and the Zion School District has an interest in such data if it ensures their compliance with federal mandates and, in turn, ensures access to federal funds. In addition to the financial gain for the district, there is a less tangible, but no less real, reputational gain in being responsive to community and constituent concerns.

Examining and publicly sharing disaggregated achievement data pushes the norms of niceness because it brings achievement gaps into clear view.

A nicer approach would be to ignore such data, but even disaggregated data can be understood in nice ways. Although data are needed to see where problems exist, the real test of whiteness occurs in how problems are understood and subsequently addressed. Disaggregated achievement data can easily be used to reinforce deficit beliefs about particular groups of students. When faced with clear achievement gaps based on race, socioeconomic status, language, or disability, educators can look either internally or externally for an explanation and subsequent remedy. Looking internally to the system of schooling and working for institutional change would be a step toward ensuring equity. But looking externally and locating the cause with students, families, and communities reproduces deficit ideologies. Although deficit frameworks are not exactly nice toward those groups, they are nice in that they shelter oneself, one's colleagues, and the institution of schooling. This choice functions to protect whiteness, even when niceness may be slightly compromised.

Linda Skrla and James Scheurich (2001) have suggested that the assessment efforts and accountability mandated by NCLB regulations make educational inequity visible and therefore serve an important role in changing educators' deficit views. The collection and dissemination of data are a necessary step in achieving equity, but it is not sufficient. Some of the staff in the Zion School District's assessment department were keenly aware of the multiple ways data could be used and understood, and they struggled against the tendency of various audiences to read data in simplistic and deficit-oriented ways. As the next two sections illustrate, since central office leaders primarily engaged diversity-related work through efforts related to language services and refugee services, it is not unreasonable to believe that achievement data served to legitimate this deficit-oriented work.

Language Services

Diversity efforts related to language services were particularly prevalent in the work of central office leaders and in central office professional development programs and student services. Approximately five years prior to my research in the Zion School District, a Latino community member filed a complaint with the Office of Civil Rights against the Zion School District. The complaint alleged that the district discriminated against ELL students by not providing services necessary for them to participate meaningfully in the district's educational programs. The Zion School District entered into a "Commitment to Resolve" agreement in which it voluntarily agreed to resolve the allegations and compliance issues but did not

admit guilt or a finding of violation. The interests of the Latino community to ensure a high-quality education for their youth converged with the
district's interest in avoiding sanctions from the federal government. So
the district's hand was forced, but whiteness shaped how the hand ultimately moved. Through the Commitment to Resolve, the district was able
to avoid acknowledging the legitimacy of the claims being made—here,
whiteness was operating in the district's ability to determine the meaning
of the issue (Harris 1993). The district positioned itself as being responsive to the needs of ELL youth and families, which served to protect it
from accusations of wrongdoing, racism, and inequity. This protection is
an important gain for institutions.

One of the major changes in the district stemming from the OCR case
was that all teachers would be trained in second-language-acquisition
knowledge and models. As a result, the district sponsored a multiday
professional development series in the "Specially Designed Academic
Instruction in English" model for all teachers hired prior to 2001, and all
teachers hired after 2001 had to obtain an "English as a secondary language" (ESL) endorsement by the third anniversary of their employment.
By spring 2005, almost five hundred educators in the district possessed
their ESL endorsement, and another 150 were in the process of obtaining
this endorsement. Reactions to this mandate were mixed; some teachers
and administrators thought it made sense, while many others thought it
was either "overboard" because not all teachers worked with ELL students or "pointless" because the endorsement programs did not teach
them anything new. District administrators felt strongly that they had
long since complied with the agreements outlined in the Commitment to
Resolve and were hoping that the Office of Civil Rights would soon close
the case against the Zion School District.

One teacher spoke at length about the district's focus on ELL students and the primary role language services played in the central office's
diversity-related efforts: "Yeah, usually in our career-ladder days or in-
services, especially before school, we gather in different places, and after
school too, and have these big in-services [for the entire district], and
the last few years they have been pretty much about, you know, ESL
students." This district-level focus on language services was especially
evident in the marketing and popularity of a professional development
program called SIOP, an acronym for Sheltered Instruction Observation
Protocol. The SIOP program came up in many conversations I had with
teachers and administrators about multicultural education and diversity.
SIOP is a national model that was developed specifically for use with
ELL students—as is evidenced in the program handbook's title, *Making*

Content Comprehensible for English Learners: The SIOP Model. The SIOP offerings by the central office were in addition to the ESL endorsement required of all teachers.

This emphasis on language services was prevalent throughout the district, and it is a theme that reemerges in later chapters. The point here is that it was a key way in which the central office engaged diversity-related work, and it was a reactive response stemming from a convergence of interests and significant federal pressure. Interests converged because the district had a high stake in both avoiding federal sanctions and advancing its reputation as a responsive and "equity-oriented" institution, and the Latino community had a high stake in the quality of schooling young people received. But the actual policies and practices emanating from these interests converging represent a low-cost approach because educators' investments in whiteness are hardly touched by efforts aimed at assimilating students into the dominant culture. The focus on language is also a decidedly nice approach to engaging diversity since it emphasizes inclusion into the mainstream, dominant linguistic fold.

Refugee Services

In addition to language services, refugee students and their families were also on the forefront of a number of district initiatives and funding decisions. The Salt Lake Valley has long been a United Nations refugee relocation site, so there has been a large population of refugees in Utah since at least the 1970s. During the late 1970s and 1980s, the majority of refugee students came from Southeast Asian and Eastern European countries. By 2005, the vast majority of refugee students were from African countries, primarily the Congo, Sudan, and Somalia. These students had often spent their entire lives in refugee camps and had little or no access to schooling or the English language. This presented a unique challenge for the Zion School District since it was the first time it saw so many students who were nonliterate in their own language, came from families who spoke no English, and had no history of formal schooling.

According to every central office leader with whom I spoke, the Zion School District's recent focus on refugee students and services was the direct result of the arrival of Somali Bantu youth.[2] One district leader explained that "previous refugee groups from Eastern European countries seemed to integrate fairly quickly," but that with the current group of refugees, "we are training them almost as infants because they come with little or no formal schooling and have lived their entire lives in refugee camps." The district hired a private consultant to work exclusively on this issue by building collaborative relationships with social service agencies that serve refugee families and by developing workshops for teachers, administrators, and even the refugee families themselves. The workshops I attended all emphasized skills that the district believed refugee families and students lacked, including, for example, how to wash their hands, shampoo their hair, eat a "well-rounded" meal, and exercise.

For the Zion School District, refugee students were a significant concern because they were highly unlikely to earn proficient scores on the standardized NCLB measures of achievement. Because so much of the district's reputation, funding, and autonomy rested on how well students performed on these tests, the central office had a substantial interest in "stepping in"—and thus side-stepping site-based leadership norms. Interests converged around the need to better serve refugee students, but the direction of the efforts was shaped by whiteness. There was a shared sense of sympathy and compassion among educators, which drove the deficit-oriented approach to the refugee services offered by the Zion School District. Sympathy and compassion are part of niceness, so here again, the focus on refugee services engages niceness in ways that are expected and accepted among educators.

Converging Interests and Cost Controls

How diversity-related policies were implemented and subsequent diversity-related efforts were enacted in the Zion School District seem to fall under two general frameworks. There are those policies that were mandated by the central office and those that were readily left up to the schools to implement. When it came to diversity-related efforts, those mandated by the central office were only and always the policies that had, in turn, been mandated or funded by the federal government. Everything else was left up to the schools, which meant that school leadership had a significant amount of discretion in determining when equity was pursued and when it was not. What this meant in the Zion School District was that those schools that primarily served students of color *and* that had not been meeting accountability standards were more likely to take up diversity efforts as a means to achieving this end. But schools that were secure in their aggregate performance on standardized assessments generally did not see diversity initiatives as useful or necessary. Interest convergence and the possessive investment in whiteness provide a way to understand this phenomenon because schools are acting in ways that protect their own interests; sometimes these interests converge with the interests of minoritized communities, and at other times they do not.

Interest convergence brings both good news and bad news. The good news is that if and when interests converge, some good work can be engaged and progress can be made toward equity. The bad news is that when those interests go away (or if they never converged to begin with), progress is halted, priorities shift, and whiteness once again reigns supreme. In the Zion School District, interests converged to push particular diversity efforts—most notably work related to assessment, language, and refugees. At the same time, in schools and spaces where those interests did not converge, very little got done and responsibility for not engaging diversity efforts was displaced back to schools.

Interest convergence is an important concept for understanding diversity-related work. But it is also important to realize that the convergence of interests is not usually equally weighted. In the Zion School District, the key element in the convergence was actually the presence of federal pressure. All three areas of service were reactions to federal imperatives. Diversity-related efforts at the central office generally grew out of the perceived need to do something, but that need arose out of a policy imperative or mandate and the subsequent convergence of interests. The resulting action was reactive and therefore limited and temporary.

Furthermore, taken independently, interest convergence leaves an incomplete rendering of how and why diversity-related efforts get advanced in schools. Pairing interest convergence with the price of racial remedies and the possessive investment in whiteness provides a more robust explanation. *How* diversity-related efforts are enacted is shaped by the possessive investment in whiteness and the price of racial remedies, which means that the resulting action is unlikely to truly produce greater equity or dislodge whiteness. Indeed, the extent to which diversity-related efforts advance equity is determined by the investments we make in whiteness and the loss we are willing to incur on those investments.

In fact, the ways the three areas of service were carried out by the Zion School District reify whiteness. Providing language services through an ESL model and providing refugee services grounded in deficit assumptions fail to draw on the strengths and funds of knowledge of students and communities (Gonzalez, Moll, and Amanti 2005; Moll, Amanti, Neff, and Gonzalez 1992). The implied goal here is assimilation into the dominant cultural norms. Assessment measures may draw attention to perpetual achievement gaps, but unless they are paired with structural explanations and trainings to address institutional inequity, they fail to close such gaps. In the end, then, the power relations and structural inequities in society are merely reproduced, maintained, and legitimated in schools. In other words, although NCLB regulations and the Office of Civil Rights empower key leaders to force equity efforts in spite of a system of site-based leadership, the scope of these efforts is limited. They are limited by educators' possessive investment in whiteness. Undoing structural inequity would require structural and systemic approaches; it would also require work that might call into question the value we typically place on colorblindness, meritocracy, and equality. This is not the sort of work associated with niceness or consistent with being educated in whiteness.

Investing in Whiteness at the Expense of Equity

In the Zion School District, central office administrators overwhelmingly said that "equity is a priority" within the central office and that federal pressure meant "equity has to be a priority." These leaders were critical of schools because they did not think schools placed the same kind of priority on equity as did the central office. Central office leaders said their hands were tied not only because of strong norms around site-based leadership in the district but also because schools did not feel the same kind of urgency to bring about equity. When the central office did lead diversity-related efforts, these efforts almost always stemmed from externally imposed mandates, which primarily came from the federal government and were tied to funding. Because the efforts of central office leaders around assessment, language, and refugees all stemmed from federal pressure, the federal government became both the common enemy and the buffer for the central office to act in spite of, and in contradiction to, site-based leadership norms. In this way, blame got displaced in at least two directions: first to the schools for not acting in particular ways and second to the federal government for forcing action. Leaders in the Zion School District typically had good intentions around diversity and equity, but when responsibility is displaced, accountability for equity is difficult to locate.

Whiteness thrives on well-intended people, policies, and efforts. Part of being nice entails having good intentions toward other people. How often do we hear "But I didn't mean to do that," or "I wasn't trying to be hurtful," or "My heart was in the right place" after some sort of harm has been experienced by an individual or group? The fact is that the harm still occurred regardless of whether one meant it to occur or not. Whether the outcome was intended or not is a distraction. When we focus on the intent, we generally lose sight of the real, material outcome. If racial equity and justice are what we seek, we need to move away from an emphasis on whether somebody or something "meant well." Good intentions mean very little if we do not take responsibility and cannot be held accountable.

Within school districts, it is quite likely that a number of policies are either "on the books" or assumed among central office leaders to be priorities, and yet these policies are not known to teachers. Even when actors know about a policy, there is no guarantee that they will interpret it in the way policy makers intended or in the same ways as other actors within the community. Individuals necessarily understand, adapt, ignore, and adopt policies in various ways depending, in part, on their previous experiences, beliefs, worldviews, and resources (see, for example, Burch 2002; Lipsky 1980; Spillane 2002). In the process of making sense of policies, actors often encounter competing and ambiguous policy priorities and therefore must also make decisions about which priorities to privilege. Districts have an important role in conveying to educators what policies are and what sense they should make of them.

In my interviews with teachers at Birch and Spruce secondary schools, I always asked if they were aware of any policies in the district related to diversity, and I consistently heard responses such as, "I'm not aware of any," "I don't think we have any actual policies," and "There is nothing coming from this school or from the school district." In fact, none of the twenty-four teachers in my research knew about the policy on multicultural education. When I told teachers about the policy, some of their responses were, "Oh, do they let teachers in on this?" and "Is it just for appearances?"

Many teachers also told me that the district did not convey a sense of pressure or expectation that equity and diversity *ought* to be priorities for teachers. In my interviews with teachers, I always asked if they felt any sort of encouragement or pressure to be doing diversity-related work, and not one person indicated that he or she felt either encouragement or pressure. One Birch teacher said, "I think there is an appreciation if it's being done, but there is not an expectation of it being done," and a Spruce teacher noted, "Personally, I don't feel any pressure." Harking back to the idea that west-side schools may be more inclined to engage diversity, teachers at Birch were more likely to feel "appreciated" if they did engage diversity-related efforts than were teachers at Spruce.

One central office leader agreed, saying, "I think teachers, a lot of them, know how to talk about multicultural education and ESL issues, but they don't do anything differently in their classrooms. And there really is little support for them to do something different. And there's really honestly, I think, very little accountability for them to do something different." While she was critical of schools and teachers for not making equity a priority, she also recognized that they were provided very little support for this work and were not held accountable for it. Indeed, providing real support and holding educators accountable for addressing inequity would not be a nice role for the central office to play. It is nice to *talk* about diversity and equity; it is not so nice to force action around it. This is especially true in districts with strong norms around site-based leadership.

What, then, is to be done? And how do we make sense of inequitable outcomes alongside the presence of educational leaders who maintain that equity is a top priority and that students' best interests are what drive their work? In his examination of educational policy, Gillborn (2005, 498–99) offers the following observation: "Scholarship on race inequity . . . has long argued that a deliberate intention to discriminate is by no means a necessary requirement in order to recognize that an activity or policy may be racist in its consequences. . . . That racist measures are not only retained, but actually extended, suggests that policy-makers have decided (tacitly, if not explicitly) to place race equity at the margins—thereby retaining race injustice at the center." My data suggest that although whiteness is at the center, central office leaders articulate this in other ways—ways that are void of race altogether. They articulate it by talking about their own good intentions and the simultaneous responsibility (and, hence, accountability) of others. Indeed, focusing on the intentions of educators may not be the best course of action if educating against whiteness is what we seek. We must, instead, look to the outcomes of educational policies and practices and ask what those outcomes tell us about patterned, structured inequity. We must also consider what it might mean and how it might look to invest in equity rather than whiteness.

Throughout this chapter, I have suggested that some progress is made toward equity when interests converge and external pressure forces something to be done. I have also suggested that the resulting reactive measures are limited because of educators' investments in whiteness and the high cost of losing those investments. Later chapters will examine some of the specific ways educators are invested in notions of powerblindness and colorblindness, politeness, equality, individualism, and liberalism. These are the workhorses of whiteness. The allegiance to these ideologies is indicative of the ways we invest in whiteness, diversify our portfolio to ensure the overall investment is strong, and cash in on those investments at strategic times. But what I hope also becomes clear through this book is that there are significant costs involved with maintaining these allegiances and continuing to invest in whiteness. The cost is perpetual, pervasive, and widening inequity; unhealthy communities; and an absent sense of relationality and reciprocity (Brayboy and Maughan 2009) with those around us. This toxicity harms us all and is a high price to pay for whiteness.

CHAPTER TWO

Engaging Multicultural Education

Safety in Sameness or Drawing Out Difference?

I see the problem of racism as a problem of power. Therefore, the intentions of individual actors are largely irrelevant to the explanation of social outcomes. Second, based on my structural definition of racism, it should also be clear that I conceive racial analysis as "beyond good and evil." The analysis of people's racial accounts is not akin to an analysis of people's character or morality. Lastly, ideologies, like grammar, are learned socially, and, therefore, the rules of how to speak properly come "naturally" to people socialized in particular societies.

—EDUARDO BONILLA-SILVA, *RACISM WITHOUT RACISTS*

Over the past forty years, educators have advocated multicultural educa-tion as an educational approach with the explicit purpose of improving the school experiences of students, increasing learning and achievement in diverse school contexts, and ultimately bringing about greater equity. Unfortunately, these goals have not been achieved, despite the growing body of scholarship and the rising numbers of educators who claim to engage in this thing we call multicultural education. Instead, when multicultural education is examined in schools, what we find are nebu-lous explanations of what multicultural education actually is alongside business-as-usual practices (Sleeter and Grant 2003) that reproduce the very conditions multicultural education is supposed to change. *Mul-ticultural education* has become a weasel word to denote something that has to do with diversity in educational contexts but that fails to address inequity. As such, multicultural education is a nice way to engage diversity.

This chapter examines how teachers in the Zion School District engaged this particular educational approach and suggests that the way teachers understand multicultural education shifts between ideologies of sameness and difference. The specific forms of sameness and difference change depending on the context and particular demographics of the students being taught, but multicultural education is almost always equated with either what I call *powerblind sameness* (i.e., denying difference) or *colorblind difference* (i.e., denying racial difference while recognizing other forms of difference).

Teachers' allegiance to both sameness and difference was highlighted in an interaction I had with a White, male social studies teacher at Birch Secondary School. After a class discussion about the recently aired Super Bowl and the various commercials that objectified and demeaned women, Mr. James looked toward the table where I was sitting with some students and said that he was thinking about a conversation he and I had had earlier in the day and was wondering if multicultural education "includes the gender piece." I asked if he was asking me or his students, and he said he was asking me and added, "Does multicultural education target girls?" One of the young women of color in the class called out "Yes!" and another said, "I'm multicultural." I explained how some people would claim that multicultural education is only about race, but that many others believe it is about race, gender, sexuality, language, religion, and disability.

I then asked Mr. James how he would have answered that same question if I would have asked him it. He said, "I don't know; it should because there is also a gender issue." I asked whether he also thought multicultural education was about other categories besides just race and gender, and he said he was unsure. He asked, "If you include everyone, then is it really multicultural education?" because "then we're just treating everyone the same" and "you aren't differentiating." He was quiet for a moment and then he added, "I guess then we'd be better off." He trailed off this sentence with a thoughtful or possibly confused look on his face, and he started the day's "official" lesson about the American Revolution.

The curiosities articulated by Mr. James (e.g., "Does multiculturalism cover the gender piece?" or "Are we worried about more than race?") and conclusions he draws (e.g., "We'd be better off not differentiating") were echoed by many other teachers at both Birch and Spruce. The tentative nature of his musings about difference, gender, and treating everyone the same are familiar and acceptable ways for teachers to engage diversity. Most teachers have a genuine curiosity about diversity, but they engage the issues in nice ways that never actually threaten inequity. Dancing between valuing sameness on the one hand and difference on the other hand is a common manifestation of whiteness. By exploring how teachers take up multicultural education, this chapter also highlights how whiteness is reified through appeals to powerblind sameness and colorblind difference.

Numerous frameworks define what multicultural education is in theory, and most of these frameworks articulate a range of approaches that all fall under the broad umbrella of "multicultural education" (Banks 2001; Castagno 2009; Gay 2000; Nieto 2004; Sleeter and Grant 2003). The following six approaches capture the range that is represented in most theoretical discussions of multicultural education:[1]

1. *Educating for Assimilation.* In this approach, diversity is perceived as a threat and something to be ignored or downplayed. Power and neutrality are located in the dominant mainstream culture. Students are educated to assume their role in the current social order.

2. *Educating for Amalgamation.* This approach is neutral toward diversity. Commonalities across people and groups are emphasized in order to reduce prejudice and promote unity.

3. *Educating for Pluralism.* This is a cultural relativist position. Cultural differences are celebrated and respected.

4. *Educating for Cross-Cultural Competence.* In this approach, competence and acculturation in different and multiple cultural settings are encouraged.

5. *Educating for Critical Awareness.* This approach facilitates increased awareness—and questioning—of the status quo, relations of power, and social structures.

6. *Educating for Social Action.* In addition to being aware of the status quo and inequity, in this approach students must work to change structural inequities and promote social change.

Each of these approaches relies on different assumptions about the purpose of education in a multicultural and democratic society. Each also inspires very different curricula, pedagogy, and educational policies.

The kind of education I advocate is aligned with the sixth approach—that is, education that focuses on equity, culture, and power by requiring high academic expectations for all students; centering multiple perspectives, cultures, people, and worldviews in the curriculum; and equipping students with an understanding of issues of power, privilege, and oppression as well as ideas about how they might educate against whiteness. I recognize that I set a very high bar here and that the kind of education I advocate stands in stark contrast to the nice approaches to education typically seen in schools. But the purpose of this chapter is not to promote what multicultural education is, is not, or should be. Instead, the purpose is to examine how multicultural education is engaged by real teachers at Birch and Spruce as one avenue for understanding how whiteness gets reified through well-intended, and typically nice, diversity-related efforts in schools.

Multicultural Education as Powerblind Sameness

Teachers in the Zion School District held two general understandings of multicultural education that were both iterations of a concept I call powerblind sameness. *Sameness* refers to the belief that all students are the same and do not possess any differences that matter for the teaching and learning process. *Powerblindness* takes the notion of colorblindness and broadens the scope to include identity categories beyond race. In other words, powerblindness includes colorblindness but also includes other elements. Whereas *colorblindness* refers to our reluctance and avoidance of race and the role race plays in our everyday lives (Bonilla-Silva 2009; Delgado and Stefancic 2001; Frankenberg 1993; Gotanda 1995; Haney-Lopez 2006; Lewis 2003; Pollock 2004), *powerblindness* refers to our reluctance and avoidance of race, social class, language, gender, sexuality, and other aspects of identity that are linked to power (or lack thereof) and the distribution of resources in the United States. Some aspects of identity are minimally linked to one's access to public goods and power structures. The term *powerblindness* references those identity categories that are intimately linked to the access and distribution of power. Thus *powerblind sameness* refers to the denial of power-related difference.

At both Spruce and Birch, teachers' understanding of multicultural education as powerblind sameness was articulated in their belief that multicultural education is for "all students." After my second visit to a Spruce language arts classroom, the teacher came up to me and wondered what I had been writing notes about, because she thought what she had done that day "was a pretty universal lesson" that was applicable to and effective for all her students. She went on to tell me that she did not "distinguish between colors" and that "I just teach learners" because her "students are all learners no matter what their culture is." The investment teachers have in "universal lessons" aimed at "all learners" can be seen in the way they link multicultural education to learning styles and to human relations. But in its presumed inclusivity and neutrality, the appeal of education for "all children" actually reifies whiteness. "All children are somehow benignly the same. 'All' is not a word that carries heterogeneity. It suggests instead likeness and similarity. It implies children who are different slowly becoming more like all of us (whoever we are)" (Ball and Osborne 1998, 395). Teachers' investments in powerblind sameness operationalize these assimilationist assumptions about diversity and legitimate them within a presumably inclusive, and thus nice, framework.

Learning Styles

One of the most common ways that teachers associated multicultural education with powerblind sameness was in their reference to "learning styles." When I asked, "How would you characterize or describe multicultural education?" teachers from both Spruce and Birch answered with multiple references to learning styles. The teachers' explanations of multicultural education were peppered with phrases such as "different levels and styles of learning" and "my students don't all learn the same way." These explanations of multicultural education often reflected a tendency toward powerblind sameness through claims that "we are all just learners" who simply "learn differently." Ms. Howard summed up this sentiment well when she said, "Multicultural education to me means reaching a diverse audience as far as it comes to learning and teaching. There are so many different learning styles, so I just try to use a lot of visuals and check in with students and make sure they are getting it."

Teachers also, then, associated multicultural education with the necessity of using a variety of teaching strategies in order to best meet the needs of students with various learning styles. Much like Ms. Howard, Ms. Pela explained, "There [are] a lot of hands-on and visual-learning techniques where you can teach the same thing just in different ways, different strategies." Reflecting this same idea, other teachers talked about multicultural education in terms of "addressing kids on different levels" and using "different teaching strategies because of different skill levels."

> AUTHOR: So what does multicultural education mean? I mean, how would you explain multicultural education to someone who is unfamiliar with that concept?
>
> MR. PERRY: Well, I think it's just because I've been teaching so long, that I just think it [multicultural education] is just part of good education. Because I know there are certain kids that, I mean, that's why I use the videos and the visuals because they can see it written and they can hear it, but they don't know how to spell it. Because when I'm just doing things and dictating they have a horrible time,

but when they see it up there, they are much more keyed in. . . . So I
think you just try to hit everybody.

Mr. Perry believed that multicultural education was about how students
learn differently; so his responsibility as a teacher was to employ various
techniques to "hit everybody." Like Mr. Perry, Christine Sleeter and Carl
Grant (2003, 39) explain, "Many teachers see themselves as responsible for helping students fit into the mainstream of American society.
They believe that students who do not readily fit in because of cultural
background, language, learning style, or learning ability require teaching strategies that remediate deficiencies or build bridges between the
student and the school." Mr. Perry also noted that he was talking about
not just "kids who are multicultural" (by which he later explained that
he meant students from other countries whose first language is not English) but rather any student—regardless of background, language, or
race—who might struggle with particular styles of teaching.

Scholars of this learning-styles construct stress repeatedly that *everyone*
has a learning style; although we each have different learning styles, we all
at least have *some* learning style (Brandt 1990; Dunn, Beaudry, and Klavas 1989; Sims and Sims 1995). Much of the literature on learning styles
also makes some connection between learning styles and diversity: One
author notes that "the importance of having a thorough understanding
of learning styles becomes more critical when applied to diverse populations" (Anderson 1995, 76), and another claims that "learning styles
can help us in a practical way to value diversity" (Brandt 1990, 13). As
the teachers in the Zion School District illustrate, however, relying on
concepts such as learning styles and teaching strategies allows educators
to erase—or at least ignore—other meanings of diversity and focus on
the commonality that "everyone has a learning style." Furthermore, if all
students have a learning style, and if that is what is emphasized, the logical conclusion is that it is the primary role of teachers to diversify their
teaching techniques in an effort to reach those who learn differently. The
role is not, then, to focus on race, gender, or any other form of difference among students, which is consistent with most teachers' preferences
toward powerblind sameness (L. Johnson 2002; Marx 2006; McIntyre
1997; Sleeter 1996).

At both Spruce and Birch, the teachers' regular appeals to ideas about
learning styles provided a way for them to avoid talking about power-related
differences among their students and instead maximize the similarities
between them. In other words, an important function of the learning-
styles discourse was that it allowed teachers to talk about students in

nice ways—ways that avoided reference to power-related aspects of their identities. This avoidance protects whiteness because race and structural arrangements of power are obscured.

The strong appeal of the learning-styles and teaching-strategies discourse is fundamentally rooted in a desire to achieve and/or maintain a powerblind society. Believing that multicultural education is really about learning styles and teaching strategies allows educators to maintain the belief that schooling is apolitical and disconnected from the inequities outside the school walls. These beliefs, then, explain and justify the absence of educational practices that might begin to critique and change current social arrangements. The links to niceness are not hard to find.

The teachers' explicit associations between multicultural education, learning styles, and diverse teaching strategies led most teachers to the conclusion that multicultural education is no different from "good education." When I asked teachers, "How would you describe the relationship between good education and multicultural education?" I often heard something close to the following: "I think that they are exactly the same. I think that regardless of what culture or socioeconomic status or ethnicity they are, a teacher is always going to have to find ways to reach students that learn differently than others. I think regardless that is your goal . . . to find what works for certain students." Teachers at both schools described the relationship between multicultural education and good education by noting, "I actually think that all education is multicultural," "I think it's the same because education in general, multicultural or not, is based on life experiences," "Well, they should be the same thing actually," and "I think they are kind of the same. You can't have one without the other." As these quotes illustrate, the tendency of teachers to equate multicultural education with good education was overwhelming.

Gloria Ladson-Billings explains how when she spoke with teachers about her research on excellent teaching for African American students, the usual response was for teachers to claim that she was merely describing "good teaching" rather than "some 'magic bullet' or intricate formula and steps for instruction" (Ladson-Billings 1995a, 159). Her concept of "culturally relevant pedagogy" (Ladson-Billings 1995a, 1995b) is, in fact, what many educators would consider "good teaching," but it is not merely connected to "teaching strategies," as many teachers seem to believe. Ladson-Billings explains how the good teaching that she describes in culturally relevant pedagogy is much more related to "the philosophical and ideological underpinnings of their practice, i.e., how they thought about themselves as teachers and how they thought about others (their students, the students' parents, and other community members), how they structured social relations within and outside of the classroom, and how they conceived of knowledge" (Ladson-Billings 1995a, 162–63). This is not unlike Lilia Bartolome's (1994) argument that the persistent "methods fetish" among teachers solely concerned with finding the "right" teaching strategies misses the importance of the ways power and dominance are reproduced in schools, the deficit view held by many educators about students of color, and the institutional oppression that affects students' performance in school.

Some multicultural education scholars promote multicultural education as "good education" (see, for example, Banks 2001; Nieto 2004) in order to make it more legitimate and palatable to teachers in a range of school settings. While this makes sense in theory, teachers often take up the language of multicultural education to describe what they do even though they do not subscribe to the meaning of multicultural education that most leading scholars have articulated. In other words, teachers have co-opted[2] the name *multicultural education* to describe what they have always done. This, then, illustrates an important concern in packaging transformative educational strategies as "just good education." Whiteness encourages the co-opting of potentially disrupting philosophies and practices in order to maintain inequity. This reframing of potentially dangerous concepts is also consistent with niceness because of the way it obscures structural dominance behind individually focused issues.

Human Relations

The second way teachers in the Zion School District understood multicultural education as powerblind sameness was through a commitment to improving human relations skills. Most teachers believed that improved human relations were both the goal of multicultural education and the actual effect of engaging multicultural education. Teachers at both Spruce and Birch talked about how they believed multicultural education would expand their students' worldviews and therefore lead them to be more respectful and accepting of diversity.

Spruce teachers talked about the goals of multicultural education as exposing people to the "interesting" and "diverse and rich" cultures that are in Utah, expanding students' understandings of the world, and teaching students that everyone has a culture that is deserving of appreciation. These teachers also believed that multicultural education affects students by encouraging them to get along and treat each other better, creating more unity among people, and gaining a better perspective on life by recognizing that the world is bigger than they thought.

> AUTHOR: What do you think the goals or purposes of multicultural education are?
>
> MS. SEAN: I think students get along better. They treat each other better. I mean, they are happy; they just have a better perspective on life because they are not just thinking about themselves, and they have more unity. They just . . . um, yeah, [have] better well-being.

Birch teachers also referenced the goal of making students more well rounded by having them interact with those who are different from them and the effect of students becoming more understanding of differences. In discussing the goal of multicultural education, Ms. Ramirez, for example, explained, "So I think that is the main idea that students should get, that their way is not the only right way. That there are many ways, and they all could be right." She went on to talk about some of the effects of multicultural education: "I think it makes them more understanding of differences. It teaches them to be respectful of differences, to let them know that their way is not the only way." In a similar vein, Ms. Wendall noted that multicultural education is "very important, and it makes us all much more well-rounded to meet people from different ethnicities, from different cultures." Teachers consistently highlighted the importance of students being exposed to difference (i.e., different cultures and ideas), but in none of these instances was difference problematized, linked to power, or associated with inequity. Exposure to difference, then, served a larger purpose of advancing sameness, unity, and niceness.

Educational practices related to human relations were evident throughout the Zion School District in their adoption of the Community of Caring program. Although the Community of Caring program is not explicitly packaged as multicultural education, more than half the teachers I spoke with talked about it as an example of how they engaged multicultural education. Community of Caring is a national program that the Zion School District had selected to serve as a framework for its "character education" efforts. The district's website explained: "Community of Caring is a K–12, whole school, comprehensive, research-based, character-education program with a unique focus on students with disabilities. Community of Caring was founded in 1982 by Eunice Kennedy Shriver. The five core values of caring, respect, responsibility, trust, and family are integrated into every aspect of school life, including the existing curriculum. The program emphasizes the idea that the ability to reflect upon and act upon values is essential in shaping lives, illuminating goals, and guiding responsible decisions." Lessons relating to one or more of the Community of Caring values (i.e., caring, respect, responsibility, trust, and family) were most common during the homeroom/"advisory" period at both Birch and Spruce.

One teacher at Birch, for example, facilitated a thirty-minute discussion about lying with her advisory class. She initiated the discussion by asking the group, "What is a lie?" One student answered that it could be good or bad, and the teacher asked what kinds of lies might be good and then what might be good about a lie. She returned to her original question and asked again, "So what is a lie?" She also asked if it was "still lying when you know the truth but don't say it," and then, "If you lie and don't get caught, does it really go away in your heart or soul?" And finally, "Is there a difference between a big lie and a little lie?"

After students offered various responses to these questions, the teacher read a story about a girl whose mom lied to her about gang activity so she would not go out after the school dance; the girl went out after the dance anyway. Her friend lied to the original girl's mom about coming home right after the dance, and finally, the friend's mom failed to tell the original girl's mom what really happened. After reading this story, the teacher asked which was the "worst lie" in the story, and the students debated their different opinions for a few minutes. Then a student asked, "What if what you did was so bad that you can't tell them; then how do you get your conscience back?" The teacher said, "That's a good question, let's ask the group."

This was one of the more effective human-relations lessons I observed. This teacher was skilled at facilitating conversations and eliciting comments from most students through the use of provocative questions and examples to which students could relate. But this example also illustrates how human-relations lessons generally focus on individual ethics and personal decisions rather than on structural or institutional issues. Even at their best, human-relations educational practices generally do not facilitate equity because of the individually based morality they advance. In other words, they emphasize individual and interactional niceness, which in turn solidifies institutional and ideological whiteness.

Although some of these lessons were engaging for students, most lessons that were taken directly from the Community of Caring resource binder seemed overly packaged and disconnected from student interests. One activity required that each student write something "nice" about every other student in their class. Another asked students to write answers to a list of questions about "honest Abe" (i.e., Abraham Lincoln) and how he demonstrated the value of trust throughout his life. And still another directed students to draw a cartoon illustrating one of the five Community of Caring values. While these activities are not necessarily bad, they highlight the limited nature of human-relations approaches to multicultural education. They are illustrative of the nice ways educators engage diversity and how we typically school youth in niceness.

This notion of multicultural education as human relations is a common theme in the literature. Similar to the belief expressed by teachers in the Zion School District, "Advocates of human relations . . . believe the approach needs to be fostered in everyone, and in all schools, to make our democracy work and bring about world peace" (Sleeter and Grant 2003, 81). The goals of human-relations approaches to multicultural education are working toward greater harmony in social relations among all students, encouraging students to learn about cultural differences while respecting others' right to deviate from the norm, creating unity and tolerance among people, and reducing prejudice (see, for example, Gibson 1984; Kincheloe and Steinberg 1997; McLaren 1994; Nieto 2004; Sleeter 1996; Sleeter and Grant 2003).

While these goals certainly have some value, a number of critiques have been leveled against human-relations approaches to multicultural education, including that they fail to address the structural nature of inequity, can be assimilationist, implicitly accept the status quo, and are only concerned about diversity when it threatens the perception of harmony and unity (Sleeter and Grant 2003). Thus, while many teachers equate multicultural education with human relations, most scholars in the field argue that a narrow focus on human relations does not go far enough in working for greater educational equity and, ultimately, in challenging whiteness. I would add that a focus on human relations as a manifestation of multicultural education merely reinforces whiteness through its valuing of niceness. Part of being nice means not talking about potentially conflict-laden topics such as discrimination, privilege, and oppression (Boler 2004; Castagno 2008; Howard 1999). In order to "just get along," it becomes necessary to maintain this niceness in the face of often obvious and explicit marginalization and systemic inequity.

The curricular emphasis at Spruce and Birch on human relations was especially interesting because students at both schools seemed to get along fairly well, work cooperatively in groups when that was required, and treat their peers and adults with respect. This is not to say the students were "perfectly behaved," but it is to say that most of them already had a strong sense of the values human-relations education tried to instill. What the students lacked, however, was knowledge "about their own position in the social structure and what to do about it" (Grant and Sleeter 1996, 83). Lessons aimed solely at human relations rarely, if ever, address issues of the larger social structure, our place within it, what that means, and strategies for social change.

In fact, part of the appeal of human-relations approaches to multicultural education is precisely that they do not require teachers to broach these complex and potentially threatening subjects. By focusing on personal values and how to get along, educators can believe that this alone will solve society's social problems, and more important, they can locate the blame within individual people who are "immoral" rather than in everyone's role in maintaining structural inequalities and relations of power. There exists a clear tension between the individualized, nice interaction called for in human relations and the collective agitation required for social change,[3] and whiteness both supports and is supported by an emphasis on the former.

Safe Engagement with Diversity

The investment teachers have in powerblind sameness shapes how they engage students and issues of diversity that arise in their classrooms. Even when they did broach topics related to diversity, teachers at both Spruce and Birch engaged the issues in nice ways—that is, in ways that avoided conflict, inequity, and power. One example occurred in an art class when the teacher asked students to sketch six scenes depicting themselves preparing a meal. Almost all the students decided on meals that were representative of their ethnic background, and after hearing that a Mexican American girl drew herself preparing a rice dish, a Vietnamese American girl asked, "You cook rice? Me too." This small bit of dialogue illustrates how this particular lesson could have been used to initiate a discussion about food practices among diverse families, the types of foods that are readily available in particular communities, and even how that is related to larger political and economic structures on a global scale. In other words, rather than simply presenting a lesson that asked students to reflect on and illustrate their own food preparation, this art lesson could have been a jumping off point for a meaningful dialogue about equity, power, and whiteness.

Another instance occurred in a class that was developing posters to hang around the school hallways to encourage students to read. The teacher asked her students why reading was important, and someone replied that "it helps you get farther in life." Another student then asked, "Can I do a picture of someone picking up trash and then a lawyer and write 'who will get farther in life?'" The teacher replied, "Sure; that's a great idea." I observed many similar examples where students equated not succeeding in school with "working at McDonalds" and other presumably undesirable jobs, and in none of these instances did the teachers question the assumptions being made about meritocracy, equal opportunity, or capitalism. Instead, the teachers implicitly agreed with the students and perpetuated the myth of meritocracy that says if everyone succeeds in school, then they will all have pleasurable, high-paying, and rewarding employment upon graduation. "According to this framework, merit is the only difference between the haves and the have nots" (Lee 2005, 71).

By assuming that true meritocracy exists, educators fail to expose students to ideas about how structures limit the opportunities of particular groups of people and thus imply that if you work hard and still do not "get ahead," then it is entirely your fault. In other words, although meritocracy might be a worthy ideal, it is not a reality in the United States, and by believing that it is a reality, we are unable to see inequities and therefore will not work to eradicate those inequities. Thus, because of the ways it masks structural inequities, meritocracy is yet another iteration of powerblindness.

But it was not just students' assumptions and comments that encouraged nice responses from teachers; teachers' lessons and their own exhibited knowledge were also consistent with powerblind sameness and therefore engaged diversity in safe ways. One example occurred in an English-as-a-second-language (ESL) class in U.S. history when students were learning about "westward expansion." The teacher mentioned that the New Mexico Territory was once Mexican land but was "given up" to the United States. A Mexican American student said in a surprised and possibly disappointed tone of voice, "So Mexico just gave it up?" The teacher nodded her head and said, "Yes. . . . through treaties . . . and by force." The teacher then moved on to another topic, even though the class of predominantly Mexican immigrant youth was clearly interested in this topic and unsatisfied with the history as it was presented. Although teachers often believe that they are offering neutral, fact-based information in their classrooms, knowledge is always from a particular perspective, and in U.S. schools, it is almost always from the dominant perspective; thus it results in the marginalization of other knowledge (Apple 1993; Connell, Ashenden, Kessler, and Dowsett 1982; Lee 2005; Nieto 2004).

Another example occurred in a class that was learning about basic economics: The teacher introduced some vocabulary terms and distinguished between "needs" as "something you must have to survive" and "wants" as "things that make life better." He proceeded to talk about how "we have a choice in our economy because that's how capitalism works" and that that was different than if we were living in a third-world country because we would then be "immediately concerned with our needs." He concluded that in the United States, "We pretty much take our needs for granted and can just deal with our wants." This teacher failed to recognize—or at least acknowledge publicly—that he was talking from a very specific perspective and that there *are* people in the local, and certainly national, community that do have to be concerned with their needs rather than wants. He clearly assumed a middle-class perspective, even though the distinction between needs and wants could have been a starting point from which to do some critical work around social class, capitalism, and economic relations of power. Here again we see how teachers' presentations of issues of diversity and equity are consistent with niceness. By avoiding structural issues and framing issues in presumably neutral ways, teachers advance nice engagements with diversity that ultimately do very little to advance equity.

Powerblind Sameness and Whiteness

Teachers' investments in ideologies of powerblindness, meritocracy, and the value of sameness over difference lead them to take a business-as-usual or assimilationist approach to education. By maintaining their commitment to notions of sameness, educators are compelled to avoid teaching about ideas that may either disrupt the perceived unity of all people or question ideologies of sameness. These are nice ways for teachers to take up multicultural education. Significantly, educators' tendencies to link multicultural education with sameness generally served to perpetuate their belief in the possibility and value of powerblindness. Whether they were psychologizing students by focusing on learning styles and teaching methods, humanizing students by focusing on human-relations education, or engaging diversity in safe ways, teachers maintained a strong loyalty to a powerblind ideology—an ideology that protects and reifies whiteness.

Ultimately, teachers understood multicultural education in terms of both learning styles and human relations, and they believed multicultural education was simply "good education" for all students. Although *in theory* multicultural education is important for all students (Baker 1994; Nieto 2004; R. Powell 2001; Sleeter and Grant 2003), I am not convinced that *in practice* this discursive appeal to sameness and all students has the same meaning. Multicultural education is intended to highlight, and thus reduce, inequities, but the sameness discourse instead serves to hide such inequities. Powerblind sameness also protects whiteness by assuming a White norm, since the sameness implies that everyone is the same as "us." By associating multicultural education with sameness, educators are adopting a nice, powerblind perspective that erases any political or potentially threatening form of difference. In other words, good teachers respond to learners and help students get along, but they do not see or respond to things like race, social class, or gender. This stance privileges the individual and offers little impetus to pursue equity. In this way, it is a decidedly nice approach to diversity.

Powerblind sameness is also intimately connected to ideologies of meritocracy and equality. Believing that everyone has the same access to—and opportunities for—success and ignoring the ways in which structural arrangements maintain power hierarchies results in the reproduction and reinforcement of whiteness. By associating multicultural education with powerblind sameness, teachers fail to work toward the promise of multicultural education even though they have adopted its language.

Multicultural Education as Colorblind Difference

Whereas teachers' sameness discourse was powerblind and thus allowed them to avoid multiple important identity categories, their difference discourse highlighted *particular* identity categories that they were willing to see and name. Educators' associations of multicultural education with difference were related to either the socioeconomic status, the language background, or the refugee identity of students. Although none of these appeals to difference were explicitly about race, they were all coded for racial meaning. These difference discourses, then, ultimately rest on a colorblind ideology that ignores race and posits that race and racism do not matter in the lives of students or within schools. The way colorblindness allows teachers to avoid race is particularly important given the persistent racial achievement gaps in the Zion School District. Race clearly matters in this context, but even though educators at Spruce and Birch are making efforts to address the achievement gaps, they fail to consider how race matters in the very problem they are attempting to solve. Because race and racism form the core of whiteness, failing to acknowledge them also fails to challenge whiteness.

What distinguishes educators' difference discourse of multicultural education from their sameness discourse is that certain categories of difference are permitted in the difference discourse. Although colorblind difference is a subset of powerblind sameness, I discuss colorblind difference here separately in order to highlight the specific ways in which it was manifested at Birch and Spruce. Illustrating how educators sometimes equated multicultural education with colorblind difference highlights how they sometimes recognize that students may possess certain differences that impact the teaching and learning process. But engaging multicultural education as colorblind difference advances particular forms of niceness and thus protects whiteness just as engaging multicultural education as powerblind sameness does.

Difference Discourses at Birch

Birch teachers employed notions of difference in their claims that multicultural education was simply what they do every day *because* of the presence of "culturally different" students in their classrooms. This is different from the notion of sameness where teachers talked about multicultural education being for "all students" because in this case, although they were referring to almost all the students present at Birch, they were clear that they teach in a unique setting where almost all the students were from low-income backgrounds and were "different."

This theme was evident from my very first visits to the school when I introduced myself and explained that I was interested in studying diversity and multicultural education. Upon hearing this, one administrator said proudly that "we are the most diverse school in the state" and another told me that "this is a good school to do it [the research] in." A number of the teachers equated multicultural education with having a high percentage of culturally or ethnically different students in the classroom. During an interview, one teacher responded to my question about what multicultural education meant in the following way: "It's just coming from different backgrounds and probably the kid might have been born in the States but his heritage might not be from the States. . . . I have a lot of students [who] are Mexican. They are not from Mexico; their families are from Mexico. Many of them speak Spanish; some of them don't. But . . . um, it's just coming from a different culture. It doesn't matter if you've been born in the States, it's what your heritage is." In responding to my same question about what multicultural education meant, another teacher commented:

> Ms. Wendall: Um, multicultural education is teaching kids [who]
>   have very different . . . um, backgrounds, very different cultures . . .
> Author: Um hmm, so when you say kids from different cultures,
>   what do you mean by that?
> Ms. Wendall: I mean like, so for example, we have Hispanics here,
>   Samoans—
> Author: So like race or ethnicity?

Ms. Wendall: Ethnicity yes.

In these cases, the investment by Birch teachers in difference is evident in the way they characterized their entire student body as "different" from the students found in other schools. But the teachers I spoke with never named race; the difference to which they referred was always about social class, culture, or occasionally ethnic background.

Social class, and specifically ideas about poverty, played a significant role in the way teachers at Birch understood multicultural education. This phenomenon is at least partly explainable by the fact that 95 percent of Birch students qualify for free or reduced-price school lunches. Although 80 percent of the students are students of color, when referencing notions of difference, Birch teachers generally stayed away from the topic of race and instead focused on the socioeconomic status of the local community. Most teachers I spoke with relied on their understandings of difference related to poverty to shed some light on student behaviors and attitudes that the teachers otherwise could not understand. Teachers believed they could be more effective with students when armed with what they perceived to be accurate and helpful information about "the culture of poverty." Most of the ideas teachers at Birch had about "poverty" came from reading groups and workshops the faculty participated in related to Ruby Payne's *A Framework for Understanding Poverty* (1996). I provide more detail about Payne's work in chapter 4, but it is important to point out here that poverty was a popular way for Birch teachers to talk about difference.

I spoke with only one teacher—Ms. Ramirez—who questioned the general tendency among Birch teachers to blame the low-income backgrounds of their students for the educational struggles they faced. This teacher, who was also one of the few teachers of color at the school, explained a conversation she had with a White teacher:

> [The other teacher] said, "This is not a minority race problem; the one that we face here, it is a poverty problem. It doesn't matter what race, what nationality they are, but their real problem is being poor." And I just . . . I tried to understand her thinking, and I just tried to think of, you know, maybe minority students [who] were middle-class. And in a way, she is probably right, and in a way she is not. Because she is looking from her own, her own personal window that is a White, middle-class person, and she sees everything from just, you know, having money or not.

The White teacher's continual reference to the "problem" of poverty illustrates her deficit thinking about Birch students and reflects how Ruby

Payne's ideas have been embraced by many teachers. In analyzing why Ms. Ramirez might have disagreed with this dominant perspective, two factors seem important. First, as a new teacher, she had not yet been inculcated into the Ruby Payne way of thinking that was so pervasive among more veteran teachers at Birch. Although she certainly was exposed to informal conversations with teachers (like the one she described) and even various comments in faculty meetings, she had not yet attended an official professional development on this issue or read the book that so many of the other teachers had. Second, Ms. Ramirez was clearly relying on her own frame of reference as a person of color in the United States to justify her belief in the importance of race in addition to, and perhaps even over, socioeconomic status.

Equally significant at Birch were teachers' ideas about refugee status and particularly about the recently arrived Somali Bantu students. Some of my first encounters with teachers at Birch included them informing me about the "the new students from Africa." Later in the year, teachers again spoke frequently about the "Somalians" when a number of them were transferred midsemester from a local elementary school to Birch. Although Birch served a number of students classified as "newcomers" who spoke no English, the students from Mexico, Latin American countries, and East Asian countries were rarely identified in my conversations with teachers. Instead, many teachers were overly concerned with the Somali Bantu students, whom they perceived as troublemakers, uninterested in education, and academically low performing. One teacher who taught an ESL course with a number of Somali students voiced her frustration that they were being transferred out of the newcomer classroom and into hers before they were able to "read and write and explain things in English." She commented that "this is the mess we're dealing with" because the number of newcomer students was simply too high for the one full-time newcomer teacher to handle on his own. In describing the lack of success she had working with the Somali students in her class, she said, "It's at the point where I just want to give them paperwork; I don't even want to talk to them." Most teachers referred to these students as "those ESLers" and "the African kids" and presumed that I was interested in observing and helping with this particular group of students.

Birch teachers' discourses about their "culturally different" student body, low-income students, and the Somali Bantu students reflect both colorblind and deficit ideologies. In the numerous conversations I observed about the Bantu students, their identity as Black Americans was never mentioned, nor did teachers consider the possibility that race and racism mattered in the lives of students. Teachers clearly held deficit beliefs about these students' behaviors and academic abilities, and by limiting their analyses to the students' ethnic and cultural identities and difference, teachers were able to easily avoid (or code) race. Similarly, by equating multicultural education with the education of their predominantly "culturally" and "ethnically" different student body, Birch teachers could maintain their meritocratic, deficit, and colorblind ideologies and therefore remain uncritical of the racialized status quo.

Many of the deficit-oriented appeals to difference were not necessarily nice within conventional understandings of what niceness means. Indeed, there is something curious about the ways niceness breaks down in these instances. But even when niceness is not maintained by individuals or through interactions between individuals, niceness continues to function in service to whiteness. In other words, among a predominantly White, middle-class teaching staff, it is nice to protect oneself, one's colleagues, and the institution through which you all succeeded (i.e., school) from blame for the persistent failure of particular groups of "other people's children" (Delpit 1995). Whiteness is never not at work.

Difference Discourses at Spruce

At Spruce—a predominantly White, middle-class school with a small number of Latino, native Spanish-speaking students sheltered in ESL classes and a small but growing number of students (White and of color) from low-income families—language and, to a lesser degree, poverty were the primary forms of difference associated with multicultural education.

Almost all the teachers at Spruce made explicit connections between multicultural education and ESL—so much so that they seemed to equate multicultural education with the education being provided in ESL classrooms. This first struck me when I visited classrooms at the beginning of the semester to introduce myself, meet the teachers who had volunteered to participate in my research, and find out when they preferred me to visit their classrooms. Although they had all signed off on the letter I sent that described my research "on multicultural education" and were present at a faculty meeting less than one week earlier where I explained that my research was about diversity and multicultural education, almost every teacher at Spruce with whom I spoke initially assumed I was only interested in observing the periods during which they taught English-language learner (ELL) students. At least seven teachers told me about their ESL classes and then hurried through the rest of their schedules with comments such as "the rest is just regular." They believed that since I was interested in multicultural education, I would want to come to their ESL classes as opposed to mainstream classes during other periods. When I explained to these teachers that I was interested in a range of classes, they often seemed surprised.

Many teachers at Spruce did not teach ESL classes, but they did teach classes with a large number of ELL students who were tracked and sorted into the same classes. Even these teachers, however, believed that I was only interested in observing the ELL students in their mainstream classes. One teacher, for example, specifically pointed out who these students were and commented that "it might be interesting to see how they process differently" from the other students, and another teacher introduced a student to me by saying, "She's only been in the country a couple years, so she might be an interesting student for you to talk to."

Teachers also talked about the goal of multicultural education as being to "help" English-language learners gain better language skills and "get up to speed" with the mainstream population—thus still basing their understandings of multicultural education on ideas about the differences between students and what is needed to be effective with these "different" students.

> Ms. HOWARD: Even with my multiculturals, I still do a lot of writing (like vocabulary) because, yeah, maybe they don't get the vocabulary word, but they are practicing writing, they are practicing spelling—even if they are not consciously realizing it.
>
> Ms. CAROL: So you have to kind of get a different mind-set and kind of go, get to their level and be more, you know, explicit about the definition of things and actually show them. . . . So it's more hands-on things or bring in things to show them what it is and that type of thing.
>
> MR. ROBESON: Ah, a lot of it is fairly basic. I mean, paying attention to the kids; and if they have language problems and understanding and things like that, then you try to accommodate that. I mean, if I stand up and give a lecture and the kids speak Spanish and don't understand any English, that's totally zero for them. So you need to start seeing where the kids are and what they are doing and stuff like that. Things like group work or sharing or something like that. Pairing a student [who] is better with the language with a student [who] is not as good with the language. Those kinds of things pay great dividends. And he [the student who speaks English] can explain to him [the student who is not so good with English] what you just said, and he [the latter] will have a much better understanding.

In addition to the continual reliance on "teaching strategies," teachers consistently talked about difference as it related to language. There are at least two important points about this emphasis on language. First, the discourse around language was always isolated from any other diversity-related issues. In other words, teachers never referenced the ways language, race, social class, or gender intersected or the larger politics and contexts around language use in the United States. And second, discourses around language typically included an underlying thread of deficit thinking, so that language difference slipped into language-related deficiencies.

In addition to an emphasis on language, a number of teachers at Spruce also referenced "poverty" as an important difference that informed their ideas about multicultural education. Throughout the year, I heard countless remarks from teachers and administrators about "the neighborhood kids" and the kids who were "bused in." Although socioeconomic status was never explicitly named in these references, this was clearly what was meant and communally understood, since students who lived "in the neighborhood" were from middle-income and upper-income families in one of the most sought-after areas of the city, and students who took the bus to Spruce came from lower-income and less-desirable areas of the city. Another example occurred one day in the teacher lunchroom when I mentioned an article in the morning paper that talked about how the state legislature recently passed a bill that could make technology, life skills, and careers (TLC) courses optional in Utah schools. One of the teachers responded that she thought making TLC optional was "a terrible decision" because of the impact it would have on low-income students. She explained, "I feel bad for the kids who don't have any role models at home." She wondered who would teach them to "eat right and stay healthy" and concluded with "these kids need those skills."

Other references to socioeconomic status as it relates to multicultural education were more explicit. In a conversation with one teacher about how her incorporation of multicultural education has changed over the past ten years at Spruce, she explained, "When we weren't a magnet school anymore . . . we had a different population coming in . . . a lot more poor kids and um, there were kids coming in that hated teachers. Their parents hated teachers." The change in boundaries that accompanied the termination of Spruce being the district's ESL magnet school resulted in Spruce serving more students from low-income homes, and this particular teacher was candid about that transition and the difficulties she experienced. She called on this experience within the context of a conversation about why multicultural education is important for particular groups of kids and how that has changed over recent years. Much like this teacher's tendency to connect low-income status with "hating teachers," a Spruce administrator talked about "poverty" as the "biggest factor" in the school's recent decline in test scores and noted that "it's been documented that drug use and neglect correlate to poverty"—alluding to the problems she believes teachers now face among the student body.

Much like the discourse about a "culture of poverty" at Birch, the associations made by Spruce educators between low-income status and "hating teachers" and "drug problems" are understood as neutral facts. The presumed truth and neutrality is highlighted by the administrator, who prefaced her comment with "the research shows" and stressed that such associations had been "documented." This framing of neutrality and truth are acceptable ways to articulate otherwise not nice beliefs. Difference and deficit thus become a matter of fact and niceness continues to operate by erasing the role educators, schools, and other institutions play in creating and sustaining inequity.

Colorblind Difference in Practice

At both Spruce and Birch, a number of educational practices reflected educators' beliefs about multicultural education as colorblind difference and, specifically, the connection between difference and deficit. A deficit model posits a strong and inevitable or natural connection between low academic achievement and students' supposedly deprived family, economic, and social relations outside of school. For teachers who are well intentioned and truly believe they are doing all they can to "help" struggling students, the deficit model offers a kind of rationalization for the students' continued lack of success and the teachers' perpetual frustration. At both Birch and Spruce, tracking, lower expectations, and language practices grew out of notions of difference and deficit and prevented educators from pursuing equity.

At Birch, all students and teachers were divided into one of four "teams": English as a Second Language (ESL), Extended Learning Program (ELP), Resource, or Regular. Each teacher was assigned to a particular grade level and either the ESL/Regular team or the ELP/Resource team. Then each student was also placed on a team, with ELP being the higher academic level or equivalent to an "honors" program, Resource being the lower academic level and for students with minor behavior and/or disability issues, ESL being for students who were designated as not proficient English speakers, and Regular being for students who did not fall into any of the other categories and were simply "normal" or "regular." I never heard this placement system referred to as tracking among Birch teachers, administrators, or students—despite the facts that, first, their placement in one of these teams strictly determined the courses they took and, second, I was unaware of students moving between teams. Instead, they appeared to consistently take courses with the same general group of students.

Much like the use of the term *teaming* rather than *tracking* at Birch, some of the teachers at Spruce also seemed to deny the existence of tracking at their school. Upon learning that they were offering a "remedial reading" class the following year for students who needed extra help with their literacy skills, I spoke with one language arts teacher about how they would determine who should be in this class. After she explained that they were using a number of measures and trying to avoid it becoming a "dumping ground" for students "with behaviors," I asked her if that meant all the language arts classes would be tracked. She replied "No" but then added, "Well, there's ELP and honors and then all the rest." Then she said that next year they were adding the remedial class, so "they end up being tracked." Her response suggests that the school was not tracking students intentionally, but it just "ended up" that way because they offered four different levels of language arts courses—and actually five, if ESL is included. During another conversation with a different teacher, I was told, "You know how they're kinda tracked? Well, this is the more intellectual group." Although this teacher was more direct, she still displayed some reluctance in admitting that students were tracked and used the passive voice of "are tracked" rather than simply saying, "We track them."

These types of discursive strategies are nice ways to talk about the sorting and selecting mechanisms in schools. The niceness serves to deflect attention and responsibility away from the fact that schools and teachers are engaged in such processes. Only one teacher I spoke with at Spruce was explicit and unapologetic about the pervasive tracking of students, though he still used the passive voice: During my first observation of his advanced-level class, he explained, "These kids are tracked together all day long."

The presence of tracking at both schools was often accompanied by very different expectations for the "lower" and "ESL" tracked students. I regularly observed two Birch teachers, for example, say things to their ELP classes such as, "You guys can actually read so it makes it easier on me" and "I assume, unlike most of my periods, that most of you know how to spell your name and where you live." And in yet another class, the teacher regularly modified his teaching for his resource classes to such an extent that they were rarely required to think on their own or even listen and take notes based on what they heard. One instance of this occurred when he initially told the class that he was not going to "baby" them anymore, but he then proceeded to slowly dictate and write on the board exact sentences that the students were then supposed to copy onto a worksheet. The material included information that they had already read collectively and had listened to the teacher illustrate through a story, so the students should have been expected to do more than simply copy statements from the board. Unfortunately, these sorts of lowered expectations fail to prepare students for high school (let alone college) and only serve to perpetuate their low academic achievement.

The students certainly picked up on their placement in tracked classes, as was evident one day in a Resource math class when the teacher told her students that they were working on a problem that was more difficult than problems she had given to the ELP class, and a student replied, "We're in Resource; we're not supposed to do hard stuff." Student awareness of tracking placement was also apparent in a U.S. history class when the teacher told his Resource students that they were farther along in the text than his ELP classes, and one student complained, "I thought the whole point of Resource was that we got to go slower." Thus there was often a clear sense of difference between the classes and students in the classes.

A handful of teachers at both schools also appeared to hold different expectations for ELL students than for English-speaking, mainstream students (see also Lee 2005; Olsen 1997; Romo and Falbo 1996; Valdes 2001; Valenzuela 1999). I observed a number of examples in both Spruce and Birch classrooms of teachers not following through or being inconsistent in their directives and expectations regarding appropriate classroom behavior and engagement. I also sat in on too many periods when ESL classes seemed to "take the day off" and play soccer outside or do art projects rather than engage in subject-related lessons as the mainstream classes had done.

When I observed a Spruce teacher with her mainstream class early in the day, she distributed a handout and had one student read the directions at the top. The directions asked the class to imagine that they were Utah state legislators who had a number of concerns about practices in the workplace, such as child labor, gender pay discrimination, the absence of benefits for minors, and workers' compensation. She reminded the class that the day before they had learned how it took a long time for Utah to become a state because of their continued practice of polygamy, and she asked what document finally prohibited polygamy. After this quick review, she explained that the students needed to find one newspaper article related to a workplace issue in Utah. They were supposed to read the article, write a summary, then type the summary, and turn in a printed copy. She specified that students use 12-point Times New Roman font, double space their summaries, and use good sentence and paragraph structure.

The next period was the ESL version of this same core course, and although the teacher also instructed these students to find information related to Utah on the Internet, the assignment and criteria were quite different. She directed this class to the state of Utah's home page, and she asked them to copy three "quick facts" verbatim from the website on their paper. She then instructed them to find three other "facts" about the state, such as the official state flower, bird, or flag. Once they had copied six facts on their papers, the students were supposed to go into Microsoft Word and type these facts in a list using any font style in either a 12- or a 14-point size. This ESL class had between fifteen and twenty students, who were all at very different levels of English proficiency in reading, writing, and speaking. Two students were classified as "newcomers," had only been in the United States a couple months, and were probably a very good match for the modified assignment this teacher developed. However, at least five students in the class had very high levels of English proficiency, had already been mainstreamed in other core subject areas, and could have gained significantly more by being assigned the original project. This example is especially interesting because this teacher consistently held all her classes to very high behavioral expectations and was well liked among students and well respected among other teachers. I was often impressed with the creativity and more critical orientation of many of her lessons, so I was surprised when she, too, seemed to slip into the deficit assumptions about ELL students.

The pervasiveness of tracking combined with lower expectations resulted in the systematic delivery of poor-quality teaching and inequitable schooling for students at both Spruce and Birch. Tracking was evident at both schools and was often paired with lowered expectations for particular groups of students. There is a vast body of educational research on tracking practices in schools, and many scholars have critiqued tracking because it results in differential and unequal educational outcomes, limits access to the core curriculum needed for college, systematizes lower expectations for particular students, and is often characterized by an overrepresentation of students of color and students from low-income households in lower tracks (see, for example, Levin 1988; Lipman 1998; Oakes 1985; Wheelock 1992). In the Zion School District, and indeed across the nation, the students who were most affected by tracking and low expectations were those who have been historically and consistently ill-served by U.S. schools: low-income students, ELL students, and students of color. Each of these practices serves to differentiate and sort students along social-class, linguistic, and racial lines. The result is the reproduction of inequity.

Colorblind Difference and Whiteness

Most educators I talked with believed that the various foci on language, poverty, and refugees were a sort of natural outgrowth of the changing demographics throughout the district. The percentage of ELL students in the district had grown exponentially in recent years, and the number of students who qualified for free or reduced-price school lunches or who were refugees from various African and Eastern European countries had also increased significantly. Most educators claimed, then, that because these were the issues that were "front and center" in the district, it was "only natural" that they would be the focus of programming, professional development, and conversations about diversity. What this explanation misses, however, is that each of these identity categories also relates to race even though race is rarely ever named. I say more about silences around race in chapter 3, but my point here is that teachers have a strong allegiance to colorblind difference and frame multicultural education around this typically nice ideological construct.

The difference discourse among both Birch and Spruce teachers was wrapped up in colorblindness. Although teachers did recognize and strategize around language, social class, and refugee status, they did not do so when it came to the racialized identities of their students. While Spruce and Birch teachers could be credited for recognizing the salience of things such as the language, social class, and refugee status of students, they consistently failed to recognize the salience of students' racialized identities. A society in which race is irrelevant seems to be what many teachers strive to create in their classrooms—and many actually believe that this society already exists—given their hyperreluctance to see race. Although rooted in good intentions, colorblindness preserves racial inequity and whiteness (Frankenberg 1993). Although many of the teachers in this study were well intentioned in their allegiance to a colorblind perspective, colorblind ideologies are neither possible nor desirable (Omi and Winant 1994). Colorblindness protects whiteness by maintaining the belief that race does not matter. If race does not matter, then there cannot be inequity, privilege, or oppression based on race, and therefore whiteness neither exists nor is a problem worth examining and changing.

Furthermore, the difference discourse among Birch and Spruce teachers tended to illuminate a strong attachment to deficit ideologies. Cultural difference theory has been prevalent for at least the last twenty years and is positioned in the literature as one explanation of why certain children tend to do poorly in schools in the United States (see, for example, Au and Mason 1981; Erickson and Mohatt 1982; Philips 1983). The theory says that if a child's home culture matches the dominant culture in school, then that child is more likely to succeed in school. Conversely, if a child's home culture does not match that of the school, that child is more likely to fail and be disconnected from school. Shirley Brice Heath (1983) illustrates cultural-difference theory in her work with the Roadville and Trackton communities in the Piedmont Carolinas. Each of these communities has unique patterns of behavior around child raising and language use, and each also differs greatly from the Townspeople community's ways of being. As the children from each of these three communities enter the same school system, students from Trackton fall behind early on, Roadville students fall behind after the first few years, and the Townspeople's children generally succeed through school. Heath argues that each community's locally specific culture leads to the relative success of its children in school. Cultural difference theory, then, focuses on a group's language patterns, cultural beliefs, and expectations as causes for school success among the group's children.

The theory goes on to suggest that culturally specific adaptations in the classroom will directly impact students' likelihood of success. Lynn Vogt, Cathie Jordan, and Roland Tharp (1993) demonstrate the success of culturally specific classroom adaptations in their discussion of the KEEP project in Hawaii and the Rough Rock project on the Navajo reservation. For example, native Hawaiian children are accustomed to working together in peer groups, and they practice overlapping speech and have tough but warm adults in their home environments. Thus when teachers in KEEP classrooms made changes, such as implementing learning centers, giving indirect praise, and telling stories relating to everyday life, these students showed marked improvement in school. However, when teachers took these same adaptations to Navajo classrooms, it became clear that adaptations designed for one cultural group did not always work for other culturally distinct groups. According to this line of argument, in order for adaptations to be successful, they need to be culturally specific.

Like any other theory, cultural difference theory has strengths and weaknesses. Its strengths lie in the fact that there is plenty of ethnographic evidence that supports its accuracy. The theory seems to hold true especially when one considers the improved achievement that ensues when teachers make culturally responsive changes in their pedagogy. Another strength of the theory is that it provides motivation for educators to learn about various cultures; this increased knowledge is a benefit in and of itself. The theory has a number of weaknesses, however. While it seems fairly straightforward on paper, it can prove quite difficult to implement in practice, especially in culturally diverse communities. As we saw with the Hawaiian and Navajo case studies, what works for one group often does not work for another. This idea, taken to the extreme, could lead to a desire for culturally homogeneous communities and classrooms, since a uniform group would likely benefit from similar pedagogic adaptations. And finally, critics have charged that cultural difference theory fails to acknowledge the politics of difference—or in other words, how and why differences matter (Erickson 1993).

Although cultural difference theory was developed in response to—and as a critique of—cultural deficit theory, many teachers at Spruce and Birch had co-opted the language of cultural difference in order to talk about deficit in ways that are more acceptable and nice. While it is theoretically possible for a focus on difference to serve a positive function of decentering the norm and allowing for greater inclusivity, in practice educators' focus on difference too often slipped into a deficit framework. A deficit model posits a strong and inevitable or natural connection between low academic achievement and students' supposed deprivation outside of school. For teachers who are well intentioned and truly believe they are doing all they can to "help" struggling students, the deficit model offers a kind of rational explanation for the students' continued lack of success and the teacher's subsequent frustration (Lipman 1998). Tracking and lower expectations prevent schools from providing a high-quality education to all students and fail to work toward the promise of multicultural education. The deficit model that serves as a foundation for these educational discourses and practices protects whiteness by maintaining that inequity, privilege, and oppression are the fault of particular individuals rather than the result of purposeful structural arrangements.

It is in these instances where educators indicate their investment in cultural deficit models that we also can begin to see the coordinated functioning of whiteness. As a strategic mechanism of whiteness, niceness operates to prevent engaging multicultural education in ways that center power, inequity, or institutional agency. Niceness simultaneously operates to encourage safe, power-neutral recognition of difference and the placement of educational failure squarely on individuals and families. But although the boundaries of niceness allow some push-back around social class, language, and refugee status, the boundaries are firm when it comes to race.

The Ambiguity between Sameness and Difference

Although I have discussed teachers' understandings of multicultural education here as fairly distinct and falling under the broad category of either powerblind sameness or colorblind difference, it is important to remember that these appeals to sameness and difference were interwoven, simultaneous, and in constant tension. What is more interesting and significant than teachers' associations of multicultural education with powerblind sameness and colorblind difference was their persistent ambiguity and slippage between these two ideological investments. In other words, teachers very rarely understood multicultural education as *either* powerblind sameness *or* colorblind difference; instead, they shifted between these two frameworks. The very same teachers who talked about "all students" also singled out their low-income students. The teachers who talked about learning styles also spent much time talking about "the ESL kids," and those who referenced the importance of human relations also explained how teachers should include certain information in their curriculum depending on the "culture" of the students sitting in their classroom. One teacher emphasized different levels and styles of learning in her discussion of multicultural education, but she also repeatedly slipped into dialogue about students from other countries. Another teacher told me, "I mean, like some of the things we are doing now . . . are just a lot of little things that you can do that just help all the kids. In some ways it's more focused on multicultural, but in reality, it's going to help all the kids if they pay attention." Recall, too, Mr. James from the beginning of this chapter and the ways he shifted between sameness and difference in attempting to understanding multicultural education.

At Spruce and Birch, the ambiguity and tension between notions of sameness and difference was also regularly exhibited in the messages teachers sent about language to students. At times, the use of a language other than English was encouraged, such as when Ms. Ramirez spoke conversationally with her students in Spanish and even used Spanish to explain a concept that they did not seem to understand in English. Another example occurred when Ms. White was talking with a student and told him, "I beg you to teach your children Cambodian" and "Don't lose your family's language." She then addressed the whole class and noted how "great" it was to be able to speak more than one language and how important it was to hold on to, and pass down, your family's linguistic and cultural heritage. While this was the most explicit instance of a teacher advocating bilingualism I observed, it is important to note *both* that this was in the context of a predominantly White class *and* that the particular student she was addressing was a fluent English speaker who did not possess an accent and whose native language was not one that he used in school or that would be prominent in the community and thus perceived as some sort of threat to English. I never, for example, heard this sort of valuing of another language among classes with native Spanish speakers. However, a couple monolingual English-speaking teachers at Birch did make an effort to learn bits of Spanish from their students. Mr. James and Mr. Mecha, for example, both used an occasional Spanish word in casual conversation with their students. And yet at the same time, there were a number of teachers who clearly sent very discouraging messages about the use of languages other than English. One teacher, for example, told her students at various points during the year, "English only!" "If I wanted Spanish spoken I would have put you in a language class," "Your language is English in this classroom; remember that," and "We're not in Somalia; it's important that you understand that."

Thus, at both Spruce and Birch, the overall message seemed to be that it was appropriate to use a language other than English as long as you were fluent in English and predominantly an English speaker, but that only English should be used in all other circumstances. These multiple messages about language make sense given teachers' discourses about sameness and difference. English-only practices derive from an ideology of sameness and conservatism, whereas the encouragement of multiple languages in schools derives from an ideology of difference. Both sets of ideologies and practices, however, are couched within a framework of whiteness, where the status quo and the interests of the dominant group are protected.

The ambiguity between powerblind sameness and colorblind difference was also pervasive in professional development offered through the Zion School District. While attending a district workshop for teachers about using the Sheltered Instruction Observation Protocol (SIOP) model, I had a number of moments of confusion regarding who they were talking about, when the model should be used, and where they hoped it would be most effective. The workshop opened with the facilitator explaining that the model was developed for ELL students but that she would refer more generally to "diverse students." She seemed to link this shift in language with the fact that a number of special education teachers were interested in this model. So because the SIOP model was not just about ELL students, she would usually talk about "diverse learners." Nobody ever defined what "diverse learners" actually meant or *who* was referenced by this term. The facilitator consistently and sometimes explicitly implied that she was talking about ELL students, but there were also suggestions that this model was good for all students and should be used in all classrooms. And then still, at other times, she seemed to reference that the model should be used specifically in classrooms with "lower-end" or "less-proficient" students. Much of this language seemed to me to be coded for race and social class, but these categories were never named. And yet at the same time, I felt like the facilitator wanted to be able to sell the SIOP model to teachers in east-side schools with very little racial, language, or socioeconomic diversity.

Toward the end of the workshop, the facilitator talked about how it can be challenging for "these kids" in classrooms that do not utilize the SIOP model. In the next sentence, she finally indicated who "these kids" were: "English learners and special ed kids and diverse kids with needs." The field note I composed while sitting through this part of the workshop is indicative of the confusion I experienced:

> So I think this comes closest to defining *who* this is all aimed at.
> The book is specifically designed for just the English learners, but it
> sounds like [the facilitator] and I assume the district [is] . . . expanding it a bit to include special ed kids and "diverse kids with needs" . . .
> although, again, here I'm not sure what that means. . . . I mean,
> I think I do. I assume she means "others," i.e., kids of color and
> low-income kids who many teachers find "challenging". . . . Really,
> this might be it . . . basically, any kid who isn't White, middle-class,
> able-bodied, an English speaker, and a good student. So then, really,
> we're talking about the *vast* majority of the kids in Zion schools. So
> then maybe they really do see this as "good teaching practices" aimed
> at "all students."

Despite my own confusions, I did not observe frustration or confusion among the teachers at the workshop. Teachers did not ask the facilitator to clarify; they sat comfortably in their chairs, following along in their books, and nodding their heads in agreement.

When I asked teachers to talk about district professional-development and in-service practices, they echoed this ambiguity between sameness and difference.

> Ms. SEAN: Well, we did a lot of training in the district where the
> whole district would get together and do all of these breakout
> sessions. And it had to do with just good teaching practices. But
> [although] it was focusing on just good teaching . . . we knew it was

to bring out the lower kids. And, really, to help all the kids. And I don't know, I thought that was good because it addressed a different style of teaching. Not just the lecture, you know the teacher always talking to the students sitting there listening. Which I think is multicultural friendly.

AUTHOR: OK. So were the trainings framed as being for multicultural groups of students or for everyone? Or was it just framed as sort of good teaching in general no matter who you are teaching or who you are?

MS. SEAN: Well, it seems like that is what they would say a lot of times because I think some teachers didn't think they needed to be there. Because they would say things like, "I teach AP classes and all my kids are, you know, fine the way I teach." And so they [the district] would say, "Yeah, this is to fulfill our requirement to the State." You know, they are saying that all the teachers needed to be trained so they can teach ESL kids, but it's just good teaching [practice] anyway. And we would get bags and lanyards and have clothes that would say, "We Teach the World" and stuff like that.

In describing diversity-related professional-development sessions offered by the Zion School District, this teacher highlights the ambiguity between sameness and difference, between multicultural education and good teaching, and between "all students" and particular "other students." She also suggests that this ambiguity might have something to do with fulfilling policy mandates to train all teachers on certain issues and the subsequent desire to make the training and issues relevant to all teachers. This relates to the discussion in chapter 1 about the central office efforts around diversity and the way these efforts are largely a reaction to policy mandates. It also, however, highlights the danger in diversity efforts that attempt to be everything to everyone—in doing so, they often become meaningless and void of any real ability to address inequity. Whiteness, then, goes untouched.

Teachers and administrators did not indicate that they recognized the ambiguity between discourses of powerblind sameness and colorblind difference in their understandings of multicultural education. Because both of these ideologies serve as a kind of fortress that protects whiteness, it makes sense that teachers would subscribe to multiple articulations of powerblind and colorblind ideologies given the racially organized system in which we currently live.

Teachers do not recognize the inconsistency or tension between discourses of sameness and difference because it is generally believed that powerblindness and colorblindness are good things. Put another way, ideologies of powerblind sameness and colorblind difference are not viewed as contradictory, ambiguous, or problematic, because the ideology and institution of whiteness allows us to engage both simultaneously.

Sameness, Difference, and Whiteness

How do we make sense of the investments teachers have in both sameness and difference? And why is it significant that multicultural education is understood and engaged as both powerblind sameness and colorblind difference?

First, there appears to be a false tension in whiteness between difference and sameness, and this tension has implications for how educators understand multicultural education and issues of diversity in general. So while there is a strong tendency to erase any form of racial difference, there is also a powerful motivation to hold on to racialized dominance and White power. Another way to think about this is that teachers do not want to be perceived as racist, so they lean toward notions of sameness, and yet they are operating within a system of White supremacy that continues to subordinate people of color while benefiting White people. In her research examining White women's attitudes toward race, Ruth Frankenberg (1993) notes that we consistently articulate analyses of difference and sameness with respect to race. While Frankenberg found that White women often understand race in terms of sameness because of their tendency toward colorblindness, she advocates instead that we understand race in terms of political and social difference.

I am sympathetic to her call for difference over sameness, but it is important to recognize that the majority of teachers at Birch and Spruce did not relate multicultural education to political or social difference but rather to the essentialized notion of difference that Frankenberg rejects *and* to deficit ideologies. In the end, educators are caught in a bind between a tendency toward both sameness and difference because of the prevalence of whiteness within our schools and the larger society. What may seem like a tension (i.e., because sameness and difference are presumably opposites) is actually a dual system of support for whiteness. And what I've described as an ambiguity among teachers between sameness and difference is actually a powerfully entrenched dual discourse that maintains inequity and race dominance.

Second, the presence of two simultaneous discourses and sets of practices that primarily fall along liberal and conservative lines also helps make sense of teachers' investments in both sameness and difference. The words *liberal* and *conservative* take on a different meaning depending on the context and the issue being discussed, and they are not two discrete or neatly separated categories of ideology. But liberalism and conservatism tend to be essentialized in public discourse, and it is this essentializing and either/or dichotomy in which I am interested and that shapes how educators think about multicultural education.

Conservatives tend to stay away from the language of race, opting instead to talk about ethnicity when necessary, and they are more likely to gloss over differences entirely. They tend to adhere to colorblind philosophies and beliefs and thus maintain racial dominance and inequity by discursively erasing racial differences (Winant 2001). Liberals, on the other hand, sometimes talk about race to claim that racial differences ought to be celebrated, and sometimes they argue that the very idea of race is flawed and thus ought to be discarded (Winant 2001). At the same time, liberals advocate for the integration of people of color, while conservatives maintain that any focus on racial group membership simply serves to detract from our common identity as Americans (West 2004). Thus, while on the one hand we hear liberal praises of diversity, on the other hand we hear conservative fears about the "disuniting of America" and how any emphasis on diversity serves to balkanize our country (see, for example, Bennett 1988; Bloom 1987; Ravitch 1990; Schlesinger 1998). These competing discourses take on new and important meaning for educators because "schools are the primary institutional means of reproducing community and national identity for succeeding generations of Americans. This is where we first learn and where we are continually reminded with others of our generation . . . what it means to be an American" (Hunter 1991, 198). Teachers are certainly aware of, and engaged with, these competing discourses. Viewed in this light, the investments teachers have in both powerblind sameness and colorblind difference begin to make sense.

The result of this ambiguity between sameness and difference is that multicultural education protects whiteness by normalizing majoritarian perspectives and knowledge; obscuring or ignoring race, structural arrangements, and inequity; and failing to pursue social change. Figure 2.1 illustrates these mechanisms of whiteness vis-à-vis powerblind sameness and colorblind difference.

Because majoritarian perspectives and knowledge are normalized, particular kinds of niceness are valued (so dialogue and action related to power and race are avoided), social harmony and unity are valued (so anything that might disrupt those goals is avoided), and meritocracy and equality are valued (so oppression is ignored and reproduction ensues). In addition, race, structural arrangements, and inequity are obscured or ignored. This is achieved by centering the individual and by othering groups, perspectives, knowledge, and experiences that fall outside the

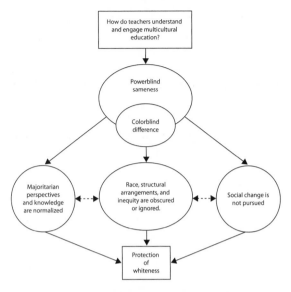

Figure 2.1   How multicultural education is operationalized to reify whiteness

norm. And finally, social change is not pursued because schooling is neither critically examined and critiqued nor seen as a politicized space. Here equity is not framed as a goal educators should pursue. Instead, assimilation to the dominant norm is pursued and potentially transformative philosophies and approaches are co-opted into nice ones.

Overall, the way multicultural education was understood and engaged in the Zion School District is void of any connection to structural dominance and oppression. This absence is paired with assumptions of meritocracy and therefore results in a schooling system that sees students as individuals acting freely within a society that provides equal opportunities to all. These beliefs about the basic equality of our society are intimately linked to the ways in which deficit assumptions about students are present throughout teachers' understandings of multicultural education. Ultimately, then, teachers' understandings of multicultural education reflect an ambiguity between powerblind sameness and colorblind difference that works to reify the status quo. Thus, when multicultural education is engaged by real teachers in real schools, it becomes both everything and nothing. It is everything because multicultural education is used to describe the "good education" that most everyone seems to be offering. But it is nothing because it is void of any meaning related to greater equity and systemic social change. Rather than working to dismantle whiteness, multicultural education ends up protecting—and thus perpetuating—whiteness.

Most educators are well intentioned and want what is best for their students, but whiteness is protected despite (and sometimes through) even the best intentions. Part of the problem is that most educators are not aware of whiteness. In addition to this lack of awareness, most educators are also invested in the status quo of whiteness (Lipsitz 1998). Educators' good intentions result in powerblind-sameness and colorblind-difference iterations of multicultural education—both of which privilege the individual; obscure or ignore race, structural arrangements, and inequity; and fail to work for social change.

CHAPTER THREE

Practicing Politeness through Meaningful Silences

One of the subtlest challenges we face . . . is how to relegitimate the national discussion of racial . . . tensions so that we can get past the Catch-22 in which merely talking about it is considered an act of war, and in which not talking about it is complete capitulation to the status quo.

—PATRICIA WILLIAMS, *THE ROOSTER'S EGG: ON THE PERSISTENCE OF PREJUDICE*

This chapter discusses some of the meaningful silences around—and silencing of—diversity in schools. Similar to the ways powerblind and colorblind iterations of multicultural education do the work of whiteness, educators also engage and reinforce whiteness by valuing polite interactions and schooling youth in politeness. To be polite means showing good manners toward others; being courteous, gracious, and poised; and not being rude. But being polite also refers to being "refined or cultured" and "well-bred" (dictionary.com). Politeness, like niceness, is a mechanism of whiteness. By defining the terms of engagement, politeness and niceness naturalize a particular sort of interaction, communication, and perspective that is void of any context, history, or knowledge of race and power.

The links between politeness, silence, and whiteness were vividly clear one day as I sat in a German-language class at Spruce Secondary School. A student's mother, who was White and from Germany, came to speak with the class. After she introduced herself in German, the students were instructed to ask her questions in the language. One of the few young men of color in the class asked what translated into "What is your color?" and the woman answered "Black" because she assumed he actually meant

"What is your favorite color?" The student was not satisfied with this answer so he asked the same question again, and when the woman gave the same answer, he said in English, "You're Black?" The mother then said in English, "Oh, you're asking me my nationality? You don't ask that. It is not appropriate." The student asked why it was not appropriate, and the mother gave a nervous chuckle, looked at the teacher, and simply said again that it was not appropriate.

The mother left shortly after this conversation, and the teacher was clearly upset with what had transpired. She reminded the students that they had "been in school for 165 days" and that they had "learned at least 100 questions." She explained that "one of the most cruel things you can do in Germany . . . is ask anyone what their race or ethnicity is." She then asked, "Is it polite here?" A number of students answered "Yes," to which the teacher retorted, "No, it's not!" The boy who originally asked the question noted that "they do it on the CRT[1] test," and a number of other students asked the teacher why she did not think it was OK to ask. The teacher simply said that it was not appropriate "in public" and "in front of everyone." She also said that the mother "was being kind" in her answer and that "in America it's not polite and in Germany it's worse." She added, "If someone came up to you and asked you about your religion or ethnicity or race, it's just not polite." The original student finally acquiesced to the teacher's position and said, "Oh, I get it, because you might get made fun of?" The teacher said "Yes" and seemed relieved to end the conversation with these last words: "It really doesn't matter because we're all humans." As the students were leaving the room, the teacher looked at me with wide eyes and put her hands to her cheeks in disbelief or possibly embarrassment.

This example illustrates a consistent pattern I observed at Spruce and Birch: Teachers encouraging students to be silent or otherwise avoid conversations about race. This veteran teacher was clearly flustered in the face of students' race talk, and her belief that such talk was "impolite" highlights what may be a critical motivating factor behind many teachers' silence and silencing of race. Educators are expected to school children in the social etiquette of the dominant culture, which includes knowing what particular issues to raise and when. As this chapter illustrates, students are consistently taught that silence is the expectation around issues of race and that they are "impolite" and "not nice" if they speak what is considered the unspeakable.

In addition to race, this chapter examines sexuality, homophobia, and heterosexism, and it suggests educators' silence around these issues perpetuates whiteness as much as, and perhaps more than, talking about them explicitly. Silences around race and sexuality are related in that they point to the ways in which diversity has been constructed as something safe and unthreatening to the dominant social order. Even though done with the best of intentions, these efforts at maintaining politeness end up sustaining the status quo rather than facilitating social change toward equity. The concepts of powerblindness and colorblindness are useful in making sense of these silences. The silences around race are clearly a manifestation of colorblind ideologies, and the silences around sexuality are manifestations of powerblind ideologies.

In order to build on the concepts of powerblind sameness and colorblind difference discussed in the previous chapter, this chapter layers notions of silence and politeness to offer an additional view of whiteness in action. Teachers, like many other people, are typically "put off" by words such as *race*, *racism*, and *White* because they assume that the words are imbued with personal and individual blame and guilt. Rather than attaching these words to structures and systems of oppression, most people attach them to individual action and feelings. As a result, the words become taboo. However, as Allan Johnson argues, by dispensing with such important words, we are merely making it "impossible to talk about what's really going on and what it has to do with us" (A. Johnson 2001, 2). "When you name something, the word draws your attention to it, which makes you more likely to notice it as something significant. That's why most people have an immediate negative reaction to words like racism, sexism, or privilege" (ibid., 11). Examining the silence around—and silencing of—race and sexuality in schools helps highlight the ways in which educational policy and practice related to diversity is not about social change but rather about maintaining inequity, practicing politeness, and protecting whiteness.

Silencing Race

In what follows, I examine how race-related silences operated in the Zion School District in three distinct ways: first, through the use of language that is coded for racial meaning; second, through the explicit ignoring of students' race talk; and third, through the active silencing of students around issues of race. It is important to note that the silence around race is part of teacher practice, but it is not a silence among most students. Many students are keenly aware of race and racism, so when teachers are silent on the topic, teachers end up silencing students as well. Part of being educated in whiteness entails knowing when, where, how, and with whom to engage certain issues. These rules of engagement constitute what it means to be polite. Nice teachers and students engage politely so as to not make others uncomfortable, nervous, or otherwise upset. Whiteness remains intact through well-intended efforts to school youth in the norms of politeness.

Racially Coded Language

Very few of the educators in the Zion School District explicitly referred to race in their discussions and student descriptions. Although both Spruce and Birch served a racially diverse student body and displayed racialized patterns in tracking and achievement levels, teachers very rarely named these facts. These patterns were highlighted in chapter 3's discussion of multicultural education as colorblind difference. At Spruce, *language* and *ESL* were particularly effective code words for race because almost all students of color at this school were classified as English-language learners and enrolled in ESL courses. Thus, by talking about "language minority" students, Spruce educators could talk about and around race in ways that were perceived to be safer and less threatening.

Like language, refugee status also served as a less dangerous way for educators to talk about race. And at Birch, refugee status was tied to race in complicated ways. Although students of color made up the overwhelming majority of students at Birch, they were primarily Latino and Pacific Islander.[2] Very few Black students attended Birch, and those who did were almost all Somali Bantu refugees. There were a smaller number of refugee students from other African countries, but I knew of only two Black students at Birch who were not refugees. Refugee status at Birch, then, was associated not only with race in general but, more specifically, with being Black.

At the district's central office, language, poverty, and refugee status all served as signifiers of race, and all these constructs were implicated in discourse around "east-side" and "west-side" schools and students. The west side of the Salt Lake Valley is typically where lower-income communities are located. All the students at Birch were from these communities, and Birch itself was physically located on the west side. At Spruce, students who were bused in from outlying communities came almost entirely from neighborhoods farther west than the east-side neighborhood that housed the school. Although the east-side and west-side concepts are defined in relation to race and social class, the usefulness of the labels lies in our ability to implicitly reference race and social class without ever explicitly naming them.

These code words were equally as pervasive in the local media and popular discourse as they were among educators in this study. So in their use of racially coded language, educators were acting in ways consistent with the patterns present outside of schools. District-level policies also contributed to the tendency to avoid race-based language. As chapter 1 highlights, the Zion School District allocated significant financial and human resources to "alternative language services," "refugee services," and professional development based on Ruby Payne's discussion of the culture of poverty. These efforts added to the dominant discourse in which these were the acceptable and commonly understood categories with which to describe students. Again, while issues related to language, refugee, and socioeconomic status are certainly important, my point here is that race is also important because it, too, shapes students' schooling experiences. Thus, although race always matters and racism is pervasive, educators have operationalized a number of "code words" that enable us to talk about race while never actually naming race (Delgado and Stefancic 2001; Ladson-Billings and Tate 1995; Solórzano and Villalpando 1998; Tate 1997; Villenas and Deyhle 1999). Use of such racially coded language is problematic for at least two reasons: first, it hides the reproductive practices in which schools engage related to race and inequity, and second, it allows educators to believe that they are not differentiating education based on deficit models of students' racial identities but rather delivering an education that is appropriate to what "east-side" and "west-side" students *need* (Buendia et al. 2004). It is clear, however, that although race was never named, how educators understood their students was still very much tied to ideas about race.

The tension, then, becomes how to view students as diverse individuals while at the same time protecting oneself from being perceived as racist, discriminatory, or unprofessional. Within schools, this tension is further shaped by things like policies, professional-development experiences, and the language that surrounds us. Teachers' racially coded language is a strategy for navigating this tension in a way that seems to be a win-win. But racially coded language allows racist views to be expressed without seeming to be racist (Bush 2004)—as such, racially coded language is nice. One of the ways whiteness operates is by concealing the power, privilege, and oppression that it perpetuates. Thus, by perpetuating racist beliefs through nice and seemingly nonracist, neutral, and "commonsense" language, whiteness is engaged and reproduced. Through the ignoring of race and power within schools, educators contribute to the hegemony of deficit thinking and meritocracy. These two ideologies are necessary for the rationalization of the status quo and business-as-usual schooling practices. Racially coded language is therefore one important way in which whiteness is both operationalized and legitimated within the Zion School District.

Teacher Silence

Just as educators' *talk about their students* was often coded for racial meaning and thus reflected a desire for safety and comfort, their nice *responses to race talk among students* also reflected a similar desire to maintain the legitimacy of the status quo. Through its politeness, teacher silence in the face of student race talk served to support and possibly perpetuate racist beliefs and actions.

At Spruce, most race talk and racist behavior from students went without response from teachers. One instance occurred while a small group of students were reenacting scenes from World War II in front of their social studies class. First they battled against Germans and repeatedly yelled, "Die, you Krauts!" and later they were Japanese military personnel and proceeded to have a "conversation" using very high-pitched noises that mimicked a stereotypical-sounding Asian language while using their fingers to pull the skin around their eyes out and downward slanting. The students in the audience found this all very funny, and the teacher also laughed a bit and described the skit as "good" and "entertaining." By laughing and calling such a clear exhibit of racism "entertaining," the teacher reinforced the idea that these types of displays are acceptable and that some (White) people's entertainment can come at the expense of others' identities. Rather than learn accurate and important history about the internment of Japanese Americans in their own backyards, these students instead left that particular class with the same stereotypical and racist assumptions about Japanese involvement in World War II as when they entered.

A similar example occurred when a teacher was teaching a lesson on some of the American Indian tribes in Utah. The teacher talked about various artifacts that have been found around the state, which archeologists and historians have used to piece together stories about both prehistoric and historic tribal groups. One student asked jokingly if they had "found a lot of Utah Ute flags" (the local university's mascot is the Ute), and then a group of White boys pretended to be "prehistoric basketball players" by making caveman-like grunting noises and moving their bodies in awkwardly violent ways. Later in the lesson, when the teacher explained that the Utes were a "powerful" group and asked what "advantages" they may have had over other groups, one of these same boys answered, "The first rounded rock." He then enacted throwing something with both hands from above his head while making a high-pitched shrieking noise.

These student behaviors were obviously imitating—and thus reinscribing—the traditional savage and uncivilized images of Indigenous peoples, but the teacher failed to intervene, question the assumptions that were being made, or provide more accurate information. The teacher's silence in this instance served not only to condone the behavior but also to miseducate students about Indigenous histories and peoples. When teachers do not interrupt students' racist behavior, they let an important opportunity pass and contribute to the perpetuation of racism. Rather than taken up as vehicles through which to disrupt the status quo, these instances were left as moments of entertainment for the class. The parallels with the racism involved in using ethnic groups as school mascots—as in the Ute mascot of the state's flagship university less than five miles down the road—cannot be overlooked. In both this classroom occurrence and the case of such mascots, the connections between individual's everyday practices and larger structural issues are clear: White privilege and dominance are left intact when these narratives of Indigenous peoples and tribal communities are passed on.

Another opportunity was missed in a language arts class. One morning after an announcement about a MESA[3] field trip to a local amusement park, a White boy from a very affluent family complained, "You know what bugs me about that—you have to be of ethnicality [sic] to go to that," and he explained that when he asked the MESA teacher if he could be in the group, "He told me 'no,' flat out." The teacher (and indeed the entire class) looked at the student as he said this but nothing was said in response. In this case, a student presented an opportunity to discuss issues of equity and why a program might exist that targets students of color, but again, the teacher's silence may have implied agreement with the assumptions the student made. Whether the teacher remained silent because she agreed with the student, did not want to engage the debate around affirmative action, or some other reason is less important than the fact that students were left with only the perspective of the popular White student who felt the program was "unfair." Whiteness is operationalized through the messages that are sent about what is fair, equal, and equitable.

Teacher silence in response to students' race talk is another important mechanism for legitimating whiteness in schools. Much like the effect of racially coded language, teacher silence around issues of race sends the message that race and racism are either nonexistent—figments, perhaps, of students' imaginations—or unnecessary topics of thought and conversation: something students use to try to divert attention or stir up controversy. Both of these possibilities are likely informing teachers' silence. Allegiance to colorblindness, equality, and meritocracy means that race can't possibly matter: If race and racism existed and held some significance in students' lives, then either our schools are not really colorblind, equal, and meritocratic, or teachers are not. Furthermore, the very topics of race and racism have historically been at the center of arguments, violence, and protest—all of which most nice teachers believe have no place in the classroom.

Educators have very few models of how such conversations might be handled differently. So why would we expect anything different from teachers who are already working hard to ensure that their students learn, behave appropriately, and pass standardized exams? But through this consistent denial of the systemic inequities, privileges, and oppressions associated with race, niceness is operationalized and whiteness is maintained. Students are being schooled in both the ideological and institutional aspects of whiteness—even when teachers do not say a word.

Silencing Students

When race talk was not met with silence on the part of teachers, it was usually met with teachers requesting student silence. An extremely common phrase I heard among the male ELL students at Spruce was "just because I'm Brown" and less often "just because I'm Black." This was generally used as a response to why these students were being disciplined by their ESL teachers.

One day after a boy was told, "Pull your pants up, and your belt shouldn't be hanging down," he made the requested rearrangements of his clothes while saying under his breath, "Just because I'm Black, man." In another instance, after a teacher started writing up a disciplinary referral for what she felt was excessive talking and failure to follow directions, another boy said, "Man, just 'cause I'm Brown." These Latino boys often equated their racialized identities with negative treatment by teachers, suggesting that if they had been White, they might not have been disciplined in the same manner or as frequently.

I heard at least one of these "just because I'm Brown" comments from the ELL boys every day that I was at Spruce, and most of the time, the teachers never responded. When the Spruce teachers *did* respond, it was with statements such as, "What'd I say about that comment?" "I don't want to hear it again," "Don't say that," and "That'll get you in [detention]." I never once observed an honest conversation between the students and teachers about what motivated the race talk, what it meant, or why the teachers thought it was problematic. Teachers were clearly bothered by these comments and were uncomfortable with the implication that they were racist, but rather than address these concerns and the concerns of the students in a forthright way, they simply exerted their teacher authority and White privilege by silencing the comments and pretending that they had no meaning—yet another operationalization of politeness and niceness.

Similar examples of teachers demanding student silence on issues of race occurred at Birch. But here, where students of color were the significant majority in the school, students' race talk was generally far more productive and less often racist than at Spruce. For example, on most of the days when I observed an art class at Birch, the students talked among themselves while they worked on their projects. On one particular day the conversation topic was race and racial labels. A Pacific Islander boy asked about the word "Spicket," and a Latino boy replied, "It's about your race." Another Latino boy related it to the word "Tonganos," and the Pacific Islander boy said to the Latino boys, "Your people say it in negative ways like 'stupid Tonganos.'" One of the Latino boys said that that was not true, and another countered that "some do."

At this point, the teacher interrupted the conversation and said, "Stop talking about race and ethnicity because it's making you upset" and "I want this to be a nice environment where everyone feels welcomed." From my vantage point, I did not sense that the students were getting upset; it seemed to me like they were having a productive conversation about race and language. The students continued the conversation a bit more quietly, and the teacher again interrupted by exclaiming, "Stop!" The boys explained, "We're just talking and playing around," and the teacher offered a perfectly nice response: "But other people can hear it and may get offended." The students switched to other conversations, and the teacher continued to walk around the room checking on the students' work. Unfortunately, as Beverly Tatum has noted, "Children who have been silenced often enough learn not to talk about race publicly. Their questions do not go away, they just go unasked" (Tatum 1997, 36). Thus, by silencing students' potentially productive race talk, teachers not only fail to answer student inquiries but also contribute to the likelihood that students will not voice such inquiries in the future. Both of these outcomes are part of the norms of politeness around race.

This, then, is another important way in which whiteness is legitimated in schools. When teachers silence students' race talk and students learn to avoid such talk in the future, they are not only learning how to engage issues politely; the likelihood of systemic change is also greatly reduced.

Without systemic change, achievement gaps persist, educational debts compound, inequities continue, and patterned privilege and oppression have the same material effects that have been true for decades. In other words, whiteness is reproduced, and through its reproduction, it becomes more normal, accepted, expected, and rationalized. Although students' race talk could create opportunities for critiquing whiteness, when it is silenced by teachers, it instead becomes another place for the legitimation of whiteness.

Some Exceptions: When Educators Do Engage Race

Two teachers I spent time with did provide exceptions to the otherwise strong pattern of race-related silences at Spruce and Birch. Both teachers were from Birch; both were also social studies teachers. Although they both engaged race with their students, they did so in different ways and, subsequently, engaged whiteness differently as well.

Ms. Manning, an older White woman, often brought up race-related issues with her students. In one instance, she initiated a conversation by asking about the frequent conflicts between students at the school, saying, "The usual suspects are Polynesian boys against Latino boys, but this year it's Latina girls against Latina girls . . . and that's really thrown people." She reiterated that "this has been new for this school . . . and why do you think that is?" Before they had a chance to answer, she added, "Look at all the colors in this room. . . . I would come to you people for being the least prejudiced and the least racist" and "of all the neighborhoods, I would think this would be the least prejudiced." One student called out, "This is a poor neighborhood," and Ms. Manning asked, "So is it the low income that makes you prejudiced?" Many of the students replied with an emphatic "No!"

The teacher then went on to talk about how she "hated it" the first two years she was at Birch, how she cried most nights when she got home, and how she thought she was "going to get shot." A student asked, "So why did you stay?" Ms. Manning replied, "That's a really good question" and "maybe I didn't have anywhere else to go." She continued, "I'm the White person from up on the hill [i.e., on the east side]. . . . I had to adapt to you. . . . I came into your hood; you didn't come into mine." She then said, "I've never thought of a person's color. . . . I never think about it until you bring it up." She then went back to her original question to ask why the Latina girls were fighting other Latina girls. One girl simply said that they "hated" each other, and the conversation shifted to what it means to hate. As the period was wrapping up, Ms. Manning concluded by saying the "bottom line" is that "you guys have to learn to get along."

The qualities of this classroom scene were repeated in many others during the time I spent in Ms. Manning's room. The conversation was prompted by something going on at the school and in the students' lives, and the teacher was clear about race and gender identities associated with the various players. She asked her students how they made sense of the phenomenon, and she referenced her own prior "prejudices" and growth in her perspective. Ms. Manning also maintained an individualized understanding of racism (i.e., through her assumptions that students of color would be "least racist" and by highlighting tensions between individuals as manifested through a fight), colorblindness (i.e., "I've never thought of a person's color"), and the value of niceness and human relations (i.e., "you have to learn to get along"). This type of engagement with race is consistent with whiteness because it does not question relations of power or challenge dominant ideologies. Instead, it strengthens key mechanisms of whiteness by privileging niceness, meritocracy, and colorblindness.

Another Birch teacher, Mr. James, who was a middle-aged White man, also regularly included race talk in his lessons and informal conversations with students. A typical example occurred when he was collecting homework assignments one day and dramatically grabbed them from students. One Latino boy countered, "Don't take papers from a Brown kid like that," to which Mr. James replied, "Yeah, you know how us White guys are"; a number of the students called out, "Yeah!"

On another day while this same teacher was lecturing about the establishment of the original thirteen colonies, he explained that his students could not understand the history of New Jersey without understanding the history of New York, which they had already talked about on a previous day. He explained how the Duke of York realized he had too much land to handle, so "he calls his hommies and says yoooo." The students laughed at his exaggerated impersonation of how many of them interact, and he said, "Yeah, I know us White guys can't pull that off." He continued on with his lesson in a seamless fashion, indicating that such incidents were commonplace in his classroom, that they need not disrupt the flow of teaching and learning, and that Mr. James had a particular comfort level with the students that most of his White colleagues did not.

On another day while the students were filing into his classroom, a Latina walked up to Mr. James and looked closely into his eyes until he noticed that her eyes were a bright green color and asked, "What happened to the big brown eyes I remember?" She explained that she bought colored contact lenses, and Mr. James launched into a tirade about how "Americans have this assumption that beauty is something blonde and blue-eyed" and that if you do not meet those criteria, we have a "false assumption" that you aren't beautiful. He added, "It seems a little silly to operate on the assumption that what American advertising is feeding you is what's really beautiful," and he encouraged his students to read Toni Morrison's *The Bluest Eyes.*

Like Ms. Manning, Mr. James displayed a similar comfort in talking about race with his students and engaged in efforts to establish friendly relationships and a certain degree of in-groupness with his students. But as highlighted in the last example with the girl who changed her eye color, Mr. James also consistently critiqued elements of whiteness explicitly. In this case, he challenged whiteness in the beauty and media industries and the impact of dominant norms on his students. I also observed him challenge racialized patterns in education, racial disparities in the justice system, and oppression related to capitalist ventures around the globe. His engagements with race thus had a very different quality than those of Ms. Manning.

Though different, these two teachers were anomalies in the otherwise strong pattern among Spruce and Birch teachers to avoid talking about race and to remain silent regarding the ways race might impact schooling. Late in the school year, I shared the patterns I was seeing regarding an overwhelming silence around race with Mr. James and mentioned that he and Ms. Manning were the only two teachers who did not fit this pattern. I asked him why he thought that might be. His first response was that it probably had something to do with "students" and "content." By students, he meant that almost all his students were "Brown." He said, "It's not a big surprise for these kids to find out they're Brown." When I pushed this explanation by noting that this is the case for all Birch teachers and yet the vast majority still suppress race talk, he explained that that's why "content" is important. "Topics in social studies lend themselves to talking about that stuff," he said. Indeed, Mr. James and Ms. Manning were both social studies teachers and their core curriculum included some explicit references to issues of diversity and various racialized groups. Further, because social studies was not yet tested by the district, they likely did have more leeway to discuss topics of interest and to depart from the standardized curriculum.

Mr. James then added that his willingness to talk about race is likely related to his "reluctance to deal with the political correctness stuff" and that "I don't really buy into dancing around it." He noted that "you owe them [the students] the truth" and "talking about race is the truth." This points to another crucial explanation for the race-related silences at both Spruce and Birch. "Buying into political correctness" is directly related to educators' allegiance to particular forms of politeness and our fear of being considered racist. Noticing or talking about race is considered a bad thing and something that nice people do not do. Educators are certainly not immune to these dominant ideologies and cultural norms, and thus they act in ways that are consistent with them. While teaching students of color in a subject like social studies might present more opportunities for race talk, many educators fail to take up those opportunities (or to create them in other spaces) because they believe they are not supposed to do so within the context of whiteness.

Another likely explanation for educators' silence relates to the discomfort that most White people feel around issues of race. Perhaps acknowledging the race of their students might also entail acknowledging their own race and their role in systemic racial inequities. In describing a discussion of White privilege in a university course, one Birch teacher of color explained how this discomfort often shut down conversation.

> MR. MECHA: I do remember doing some ESL core courses where
> people were kind of challenged about their beliefs. I mean, I noticed
> a lot of, well . . . I mean, a lot of our teachers here are Caucasian.
> Um . . . they were very resistant to some of the . . . ah, I can't
> remember what it was called. They were offended by, ah . . . I think
> it was White privileges is how it was, ah, termed.
>
> AUTHOR: Was it related to Peggy McIntosh's work, maybe?
>
> MR. MECHA: I think so. We didn't really; we didn't really do enough
> reading on it. I think it got too . . . too many people got offended
> by that. . . . I thought interesting things came up, but we kind of
> just glossed over them because they offended people or they got,
> you know, they wouldn't accept that is the way things are. They
> said, 'I'm not like that.' And that wasn't the point; it wasn't that
> they were like that, it's the point that you have to understand that
> is how some people feel.

Whiteness is operating here in both Mr. Mecha's analysis of his White colleagues' discomfort and his own belief that White privilege is about "how some people feel." Not accepting the reality of White privilege stems from an understanding of race and racism as individually based, related solely to identity, and void of systemic and patterned uses of power. But even Mr. Mecha's own understanding of White privilege as being about how some people feel relies on a purely individualized and psychologized (rather than also structural) framework of race and power. Whichever way the issue is framed, politeness, niceness, and whiteness are employed.

This theme of discomfort and White people objecting to race talk because they "aren't like that" also came up in one of the Zion School District REACH sessions I attended. During the second day of the three-day training, the facilitators initiated a discussion about stereotypes by explaining that "prejudice happens" when "aspects of collective identity are given a negative connotation." In order to highlight how this occurs, the Latino male facilitator asked the group to list all the positive and negative stereotypes about "the Hispanic male collective" that came to mind. Nobody said anything. The facilitator encouraged them by saying things like "Let's have fun with this" and "You don't have to be responsible for what you say." He offered a few common stereotypes, and then two participants offered a few as well. One of the White female participants interrupted and said, "I don't like this," and another White woman added, "My guy isn't like this." In response to these White women's concerns, the facilitator relented and said, "We're going to push through this." In other words, the group was stopping the activity and moving on to something else. A number of the White women said "Thank you," breathed a sigh of relief, and turned the page in their books.

These examples further illuminate the hyperreluctance of most teachers to engage in race talk and our strong desire to maintain the polite nature of interactions that whiteness encourages. Through both teacher silence and demands for student silence around issues of race and racism, teachers exhibit an overwhelming aversion to acknowledging that race exists or matters. This aversion is, of course, consistent with the niceness and colorblindness that are effective mechanisms of whiteness. Through their discursive appeals to culture, equality, and meritocracy, teachers further erase race and engage whiteness. This is significant because through these silences, educators are able to maintain the legitimacy of meritocracy, which serves to protect the status quo and the interests of White people and communities. In other words, by denying race, educators are able to also deny the ways in which we participate in the legitimation of whiteness.

Silencing Sexuality

Similar to race, issues of sexuality are also constructed as dangerous, impolite, and not nice, and thus they are not part of the accepted discourse within the Zion School District. At the national level, recent incidents related to sexual orientation and gender identity have been framed around the generic notion of "bullying." Websites and information abound linking homophobia and heterosexism to bullying, including, for example, the Safe Schools Coalition, Mental Health America, stopbullying.gov, and even the White House via a summit on antibullying initiatives. However, "by using vague terms such as bullying and name calling, scholars and educators avoid examining the underlying power dynamics that such behaviors build upon and reinforce. When policies and interventions do not name and explore systems of power and privilege, they effectively reinforce the status quo" (Meyer 2009, 11). Conversations about bullying and harassment often frame the problem as one of individual problem students, but this is another iteration of powerblind sameness. By remaining silent about the homophobia and heterosexism underlying specific instances of bullying and harassment, educators engage in powerblindness and whiteness. As a result, we are unable to examine the larger cultures of schools or the ways in which power maintains patterns of inclusion and exclusion.

A comprehensive report issued by Human Rights Watch in 2001 found that the most common theme running through the stories of lesbian, gay, bisexual, transgender, and queer (LGTBQ) students and educators they interviewed was "isolation and the almost total failure of the public school system to take seriously the human rights of these students" (Human Rights Watch 2001, 4). The report is based on interviews with thousands of youth and educators in a number of states, including Utah, California, Texas, Georgia, and New Hampshire. Silence around issues of sexuality in schools is well documented, and Lisa Loutzenheiser argues that this silence is generally more acceptable than silences around race or other identity categories:

> Voicing one's negative feelings about homosexuality is one of the last bastions of socially acceptable prejudice. In most public forums, it is no longer acceptable to use racial epithets or sexist slurs. Yet, when it comes to gay men, lesbians, and bisexuals, there is little hesitation to demonstrate bigotry without concern for who might hear or be offended . . . In most schools, we, at least, tell students that it is not acceptable to make sexist or racist comments, even if we do not always follow through or "walk the talk." Yet, when it comes to gay, lesbian, and bisexual issues, we hold back in fear. By allowing antigay harassment to be voiced without reprimand, schools are sanctioning and even encouraging bigotry. (Loutzenheiser 1996, 59)

Allowing antigay harassment to continue also, perhaps ironically, maintains politeness, niceness, and whiteness, since the mere mention of sexuality and gender identity is potentially uncomfortable.

But schools are clearly unsafe spaces for LGBTQ youth. According to the 2009 National School Climate Survey, almost 90 percent of these youth heard *gay* used in a negative way frequently at school, more than 72 percent heard other homophobic remarks frequently at school, more than 62 percent heard negative remarks about gender expression often at school, more than 60 percent felt unsafe at school because of their sexual orientation, and almost 40 percent felt unsafe at school because of their gender expression (Kosciw, Greytak, Diaz, and Bartkiewicz 2010). Despite the extent of this violence, only about half of school antiharassment policies across the United States specify sexual orientation or gender expression as a protected category (Harris Interactive and GLSEN 2005). Further intensifying the problem is that school staff rarely intervene on behalf of LGBTQ students.

Homophobia and Heterosexism at Spruce and Birch

Homophobia was rampant among students at both Spruce and Birch, and I observed only one teacher who attempted to address this student behavior. In most instances, teachers either ignored student homophobia, responded to it in limited ways, or perpetuated it by engaging in heterosexist behavior themselves. The silence around sexuality sustains the illusion that either sexual orientation does not matter or difference in sexual orientation does not actually exist. The result of either is the same—the heterosexual norm and homophobia are left intact and the status quo is unquestioned.

Throughout my field notes, I had almost fifty references to incidents when students made homophobic comments and there was no response from the teacher. Most of these examples involved students calling out "That's gay" or "Don't be gay" or something similar within the classroom setting. In one class, for instance, the teacher made a reference to Snow White, and a boy called out, "She's gay!" In another class, the teacher asked the class to imagine if everyone in the world were exactly the same, and a student called out, "Hell, no; that'd be gay!" And in still another classroom, a student walked in singing a song, and another student yelled, "You sound gay!" The use of the word *gay* as a "put down" was definitely the most common homophobic comment, although there were also comments referencing *faggot* and *queer*—always in negative and derogatory ways. Again, the vast majority of these student comments went unquestioned and uncorrected by teachers. They were also usually followed by laughter from other students but never a critique from students.

One example of teacher silence occurred when I was observing in a Spruce classroom. While students were working quietly at their desks, a student whose gender presentation was ambiguous entered the room and delivered something to the teacher. As she was waiting near the teacher's desk, a boy whispered multiple times, "Hey, dude?!" Then as she walked across the front of the room and toward the door to leave, another boy whispered, "Are you a boy?" and laughed as she left the room. The teacher, who was at the front of the room, did not respond to any of what had happened. After the students left, I asked the teacher if she knew the student who came in earlier. When she said "Yes," I asked if the student got harassed often and explained what I observed earlier. The teacher did not indicate that she was surprised by what I said and simply responded, "She's told me she wants to be a boy" and that "when she first came here [to Spruce], I couldn't tell if she was a boy or a girl." She added, "I don't think she gets teased a lot" and "she has friends; I don't think she really cares." Silence perpetuates and supports a transphobic school environment. Voicing issues of sexuality and explicitly addressing the students' confusions could have led to a safer and more accepting school climate for all students.

Occasionally, homophobic comments from students did elicit a response from teachers, but these comments were always limited in nature. The most common responses from teachers included, "I don't want to hear that word," "You know I don't like that word," "Noooo!" "Hey!" "Be polite," and "Don't use that word." I found little rhyme or reason to when homophobic comments elicited such responses from teachers, and I did not find that certain teachers generally responded while others did not. In other words, the exact same comments from students were sometimes ignored by teachers and sometimes responded to in a limited way by the very same teachers.

One Spruce teacher seemed to only respond when students said negative things about gay people but not when they said that something or someone was gay. One day, for example, the students had said that things or people were gay multiple times with no response, but when someone said something about how gay people were "dumb," she replied, "No, don't say that!" She replied in exactly the same way on another occasion when a student said that "GPS" stood for "gay people suck." Similar to the ways in which teacher silence results in the silencing of students around issues of sexuality, these directives to be silent also do little to teach students anything beyond that certain topics should not be spoken about in school. As noted before about race, however, although such silencing does not make the questions, assumptions, and issues go away, it does school youth in the norms of politeness and it maintains an impression of niceness.

Niceness is maintained in multiple ways, but it is always in service to whiteness. Silencing sexuality completely is nice because it avoids conversations that could be uncomfortable, awkward, or divisive. Responding to homophobic discourse with silence is nice because it avoids confronting the issue. In this case the individual is not called out (which is nice to him or her) *and* the presence of homophobia is not called out (which is nice to heteronormative structures of power). Niceness is not maintained toward queer youth and communities, but this is presumably a small price to pay for maintaining the status quo. Any time injustice is perpetuated (in this case, heteronormativity), whiteness is engaged and legitimated.

The niceness of heteronormativity is also exhibited in instances when teachers engage conversations with students that assume a heterosexual norm. For example, when one teacher defined the word *flirt* to her ESL class, she said, "Flirting is when a girl tries to get romantic attention from a boy, or the other way around." Similarly, when teachers referenced romantic partners of students, it was always in reference to the gender opposite of the person to whom they were speaking. So when talking to a boy, teachers consistently referenced "your wife" or "girlfriend," and when talking to a girl, it was always "husband" or "boyfriend." In these seemingly benign interactions, straight gender identities and sexualities are presumed universal, normativity is reinforced, and whiteness continues to function.

Teacher silence around issues of sexuality might be explained in part by a lack of awareness and knowledge of the issues. It is also possible that teachers may *choose* to remain uninformed and avoid issues of sexuality because of their own moral objections to homosexuality. As Loutzenheiser has noted, "The threat or the possibility of religious or community disagreement is often enough to stop conversations before they begin" (Loutzenheiser 1996, 59). This is especially likely in conservative states like Utah and in self-described nice communities like the Salt Lake Valley.

A Single Exception

These patterns of student homophobia going unchecked or responded to in a limited way, and of teachers exhibiting heterosexist bias, were present in all but one classroom I observed at both Spruce and Birch. This pattern was so pervasive that I started to wonder if I would ever witness an educator respond differently. Toward the end of the year, I started observing a teacher at Birch who proved to be the one exception to this particular rule. A small group of students in Mr. Mecha's classroom often made the same homophobic comments that I had observed in other classrooms, but Mr. Mecha never let any of them go. Although occasionally his responses sounded like the limited ones I described before, he coupled these responses with more meaningful ones.

One day, for example, a girl shouted to a boy sitting across the room, "Shut up, gay guy," and Mr. Mecha said, "Watch it or you'll find yourself down in the office." When the girl asked, "What for?" he replied, "Sexual harassment." I regularly observed this teacher get visibly angry when students repeatedly made homophobic comments. He sometimes spoke with these students individually, and at other times he addressed the entire class.

One day during a discussion about who had lived in Utah their entire life, a student called out, "Utah sucks," and then another yelled, "Utah's gay." Mr. Mecha became visibly upset and raised his voice to say, "That's the third time I've heard that word today!" He explained that if he heard it one more time, they would be sent to the principal's office, which prompted a couple students to say that their parents did not care if they said "that word." Mr. Mecha explained, "We use different words" in different settings: "There are two different languages you use—one is for at home and with friends and one is for at school and work. We're at school right now, and you don't use that word." He went on to say that "it's [using the word 'gay' in that context] just a way of saying you don't like something; so don't use it" and "to some people it's bad." Mr. Mecha was the only teacher who took time to talk to students about the language they were using and why it was inappropriate.

While his discussion of the "two languages" and various contexts for using language was helpful, Mr. Mecha stopped short of explaining to students why they might want to reconsider using such language in all contexts. His explanation that "to some people it's bad" fails to acknowledge the social, political, and historical context of heterosexism and homophobia in this country. On the other hand, this teacher obviously faced an uphill battle considering how little consistency and support he got from other teachers in the school on this particular issue. His frustration over this issue was only intensified when he asked me if I had seen similar instances in other classes. I shared with him that I often observed students making very similar comments but that I never observed other teachers attempt to correct students or explain to them why homophobia and heterosexism were problematic. He seemed relieved to hear that his was not the only class in which students made such comments, but he was surprised and disappointed that he was fighting this battle alone.

Other Systemic Silences

District and school policies around nondiscrimination and school library holdings also point to ways in which sexuality was silenced. The district's nondiscrimination policy, for example, did not include sexual orientation as a protected category. The policy only provided protection from discrimination for "any person or group of persons because of race, color, creed, national origin, sex, mental or physical capacity, or economic status." In addition, Utah state law prohibited the teaching of "alternative lifestyles," which was commonly understood to mean LGBTQ issues. In describing this law, one Zion School District administrator explained, "It is quite clear in that we really cannot teach about sexual orientation at all. Teachers are not to support any alternative lifestyles and basically are required to refer students to their parents with questions regarding most things." Similarly, a teacher told me (via e-mail), "We are specifically instructed *not* to discuss homosexuality. I guess 'they' think that would be promoting the lifestyle. It's so unfortunate, as there are LGBT kids and kids who know LGBT people, including family members. . . . We're limited on any kind of sex education." I conducted a keyword search of Spruce and Birch's online library card catalogs, and Table 3.1 conveys the results.

As these numbers indicate, there are clearly very few resources for students to access information about LGBTQ issues, people, and histories.

Table 3.1 Library Holdings Related to Issues of Sexual Orientation

Keywords	Spruce	Birch
"Sexual orientation"	0	0
"Gay"	0 (7 items came up but none were relevant; in most cases "gay" was an author's name)	0 (10 items came up but none were relevant; in most cases "gay" was an author's name)
"Lesbian"	0	0
"Homosexual"	0	1 (A book titled *A History of Intolerance in America*)
"Homophobia"	0	0
Total library holdings based on this search	0	1

Although I did not do a systematic evaluation of the inclusion of LGBTQ people and issues in the textbooks at Spruce and Birch, it is highly unlikely that they included any information on this topic. In another study of multicultural education, Christine Sleeter asked teachers to evaluate the texts used in their own classes and found, "Gay and lesbian people were completely invisible in the texts teachers analyzed. Although a few people in the texts were gay, they were not identified as such" (Sleeter 2005, 86–87). Although it is not as commonly analyzed as race, ethnicity, and gender, sexuality has been found to be invisible in textbooks in other studies as well (Hogben and Waterman 1997).

Given Utah's conservative culture, the district's prohibition of teaching about "alternative lifestyles," and the state's legislation defining marriage as a union between a man and a woman, the silences around sexuality in the Zion School District are not surprising. Unfortunately, as Donald Fraynd (2004) explains, the lack of accurate information about homosexuality during adolescence leads LGBTQ youth to internalize negative self-images and to struggle to accept themselves. Loutzenheiser adds:

> They hear few positive reflections of themselves. School curriculum rarely mentions gay, lesbian, or bisexual people or issues. When included, it is often a dismissive comment in a health book causing snickers and groans by other students. The students rarely have role models because gay, lesbian, and bisexual teachers are afraid to come out in the classroom for fear of harassment or of losing their jobs. The end result is greater isolation for the students and more internalization of the sense of Other. The Othering and silences are often interpreted by students as a confirmation that homosexuality is shameful and bad; otherwise, it would be acceptable to bring up as part of the school's curriculum. (Loutzenheiser 1996, 62)

Furthermore, Fraynd elaborates that a "culture of fear exists for those who advocate for, or are thinking about advocating for, GLBTQ youth" (Fraynd 2004). This culture of fear is well justified in Utah, since local teachers have lost their jobs simply for "admitting" to students that they were lesbian or gay. Unfortunately, such fear results in a lack of role models for LGBTQ students.

Spruce and Birch are clearly not ideal environments for LGBTQ youth. These youth have to endure daily verbal harassment (whether directly aimed at them or not) and expectations about "normal" gender roles, and they lack appropriate and accurate information about themselves in the curriculum and library materials. Kevin Kumashiro explains that fighting heterosexist and homophobic oppression is especially complicated because the curriculum "is already too full" and the political climate "is often silent, if not hostile, toward any mention of sexual orientation" (Kumashiro 2004, 111). This is especially true in places like Utah where a conservative religion is predominant and shapes politics, including school policies and curriculum. According to James Sears, "There is a great need for a healthy, frank, honest depiction of the fluidity of sexual behavior and sexual identities. Yet, too many educators are partners in a conspiracy of silence" (Sears 1991, 54).

The fact that I only observed one of twenty-four teachers address students' homophobia is striking. This systemic silence by teachers, combined with the lack of information about sexual orientation through either the curriculum or library holdings, results in a huge absence around a topic that is obviously present in students' lives and impacts their schooling experiences and, in some cases, academic performance. The GLSEN 2005 annual report found that unchecked harassment of LGBTQ students correlates with poor academic performance and diminished aspirations, but that supportive teachers can make a difference: While 24.1 percent of LGBTQ students who cannot identify supportive faculty report that they have no intention of going to college, the figure drops to just 10.1 percent when they can identify a supportive teacher (GLSEN 2005). Remaining silent on a topic does not make it disappear. Indeed, the opposite may actually occur—by being silent about issues of sexuality, these issues come to matter even more.

Thinking through Influence, Intentionality, and Implications

Spruce and Birch students, like students around the country, had many ideas about race and sexual orientation. Through teacher silence and acts of silencing, students learn rules about what can be acknowledged, publicly recognized, and discussed (Polite and Saenger 2003). But if schools hope to advance equity and dismantle whiteness, they must take on the difficult task of talking to students about issues like race and sexuality. When we fail to explicate the ways in which racism, heterosexism, and other forms of oppression are operating within our schools, educational inequity is left to be understood as resulting from individual deficit (Gillborn 2005). Thus meritocracy and whiteness are mutually reinforcing of one another. When meritocracy is assumed, our focus is directed away from systemic inequities and toward individual success and failure. Meritocracy allows us to see ourselves as "innocent bystanders rather than participants in a system that creates, maintains, and reproduces social injustice" (Applebaum 2005, 286). Teachers' participation in this system clearly carries a significant influence over our nation's youth.

The educators at Birch and Spruce were, for the most part, well-intentioned individuals who wanted their students to succeed and who wanted to provide a welcoming and fair educational climate within their classrooms. Indeed, most of the silences and silencing I observed were motivated by teachers' desires to "keep everyone happy," "not offend anyone," and protect students from "getting upset." The general belief was that talking about race and sexuality was too conflict laden, tense, and hurtful and, perhaps more important, implied that one is racist, heterosexist, or otherwise prejudiced (Bush 2004; Solomon, Portelli, Daniel, and Campbell 2005). But even when it is with good intentions that we silence or avoid responding to students' inquiries about race and sexuality, we are engaging in practices that perpetuate whiteness within our schools. This is, in fact, the brilliance of the way whiteness operates—just like any other hegemonic ideology and institution, it is most successful when the majority of its adherents are least aware of it and its power.

The silencing of race and sexuality in the Zion School District thus serve an important purpose: They feed the cycle in which meritocracy is justified, business-as-usual schooling is rationalized, and inequities are sustained. The cumulative impact of this cycle is the legitimation of whiteness. The cycle helps illustrate why it is so easy to continue: It is not a very big step from one point to the next, but the cumulative effect is quite troubling.

Schools are clearly institutions that reflect—and are shaped by—the larger societies in which they find themselves. The silences and silencing we see among teachers at Spruce and Birch are not isolated to these schools—nor to schools and teachers broadly speaking. Indeed, we have trouble interrupting racist, homophobic, and other oppressive discourse and interactions all the time. Given the ethos within schools to get students through, to stay on task, to work in isolation, and to prepare students for the status quo, it is even more difficult to interrupt these discourses and interactions among students in classrooms. Because the daily grind of teachers' work and the rhythm of schooling frames so much of what teachers do and do not do, it would be a mistake to place blame or sole responsibility for silences and silencing on teachers.

Teaching is a difficult job, and this is especially true currently—given the context of high-stakes testing, standardization, weakening unions, and the corporatization of schools. Many educators suggest that teaching is no longer an intellectual endeavor and that it is getting more mechanistic each year. This context means it is more difficult to do the kind of equity-driven, critically oriented work I'm suggesting. In other words, this work is structurally and institutionally silenced just as much as it is silenced through individual acts and interaction.

The silencing of race and sexuality and the subsequent legitimation of whiteness have multiple and varied implications for students. The politeness associated with race-related silence works for—and to the advantage of—students at schools like Spruce. And the politeness associated with sexuality-related silence works for—and to the advantage of—straight students. Engulfed in a system meant to benefit us, straight White people may have much to lose by explicitly addressing race and sexuality. But conversations about these issues would likely resonate with the everyday experiences of students, which could, in turn, lead to improved academic achievement through the development of critical thinking about real-world issues. These discussions are also important for working toward structural and ideological social change—a move that contradicts the entrenched nature of whiteness but is necessary if we hope to bring about greater equity in schools and the larger society. Indeed, when educators fail to address race and sexuality, they fail to address students' needs (Pollock 2004; Thompson 2005). Within a framework of whiteness in which the status quo is desirable and beneficial, silence truly is golden. But within a framework of equity in which social justice and fairness are sought, silence suggests indifference and is highly problematic.

CHAPTER FOUR

"It Isn't Even Questioned"

Equality as Foundational
to Schooling *and* Whiteness

In the conversation on race, there is the danger that we merely
reproduce a liberal ideology of racial containment . . . What we
don't need is the crass and deceitful politics of toleration that masks
the sources of real power, that conceals the roots of real inequality,
that ignores the voices of the most hurt, and that is indifferent to
the faces of the most fractured.

—MICHAEL E. DYSON IN CHENNAULT, "GIVING
WHITENESS A BLACK EYE"

As has been alluded to in previous chapters, most teachers, principals, and
other educational leaders share a steadfast belief in meritocracy—that is,
that the worth and success of an individual is based solely on the merits
of his or her work. Meritocracy assumes that a level playing field exists in
society and its institutions and that everyone has access to the same opportunities to get ahead in this world. Meritocracy's foundation is rooted in
notions of the individual, competition, and neutrality. Indeed, our entire
system of schooling is based on the notion of meritocracy. Grading, grade-
level advancement, standardized forms of assessment, and admission to
selective schools all rest on the assumption of meritocracy, and meritocracy cannot be divorced from the concept of equality. Equality must exist
for meritocracy to function; otherwise, we cannot be sure that rewards are
really being earned as a result of effort and achievement.

Equality and meritocracy are foundational ideologies for diversity-
related policies and practices. They are also central to the "politics of
toleration" that engages niceness and sustains inequity. This chapter
explores how equality, as a mechanism of whiteness, operates in the

diversity-related efforts at both Birch and Spruce Secondary Schools. Although educators at the two schools subscribe to different understandings of equality, both ultimately result in the reification of whiteness.

So What Is Equality?

Equality is a long-standing and largely unquestioned American value, but equality is not the simple or obvious concept that it is often assumed to be by those who casually accept it. Critical race theorists draw our attention to the difference between *restrictive formal equality* and *expansive substantive equality*. Whereas restrictive formal equality is based on the sameness of a rule or policy, expansive substantive equality looks to the results or outcomes of rules and policies. Another way to think about this is to consider the difference between inputs and outputs in a given situation. In her analysis of antidiscrimination law, Kimberlé Crenshaw (1988) explains the distinction between a restrictive and expansive view of equality: "The expansive view stresses equality as a result and looks to real consequences for African Americans. . . . The restrictive view, which exists side by side with this expansive view, treats equality as a process, drowning the significance of actual outcomes. The primary objective of antidiscrimination law, according to this view, is to prevent future wrongdoing rather than to redress present manifestations of past injustice. 'Wrongdoing,' moreover, is seen primarily as isolated actions against individuals rather than as societal policy against an entire group" (Delgado and Stefancic 2001, 38). Restrictive formal equality focuses on sameness in treatment between and among individuals and groups who share similar characteristics. As Crenshaw highlights, restrictive formal equality assumes that equality previously existed, so the move is back to the starting point (i.e., an assumed equality), rather than to correct a previously existing inequality. Ideally, restrictive formal equality would produce overall equality, but this is impossible because it rests on the faulty assumption of an equal starting point. Expansive substantive equality recognizes that cases are very rarely alike because of the historical and persistent differences in social conditions between and among various groups. Thus expansive substantive equality stresses results and outcomes that are fair or just— qualities that are not always easy to determine or agree on.

Restrictive formal equality is the equality typically meant in popular discourse and policy, but critical race theorists have critiqued the standard of restrictive formal equality on a number of grounds. These critiques include that its focus on sameness is limited because of the persistent and pervasive social construction of race, class, and gender; that although it can remedy the most extreme and shocking forms of inequality, it can do nothing about the business-as-usual, everyday forms of inequality that people experience constantly; and that it masks expansive substantive and pervasive inequality. In most educators' appeals to equality, we privilege equality of opportunity over equitable outcomes, processes over results, colorblindness over race consciousness, and individual freedoms over group experiences. Furthermore, as Derrick Bell reminds us in his analysis of the *Brown v. Board of Education* decision, "The danger with our commitment to the principle of racial equality is that it leads us to confuse tactics with principles. The principle of gaining equal educational opportunity for Black children was and is right. But our difficulties came when we viewed racial balance and busing as the only means of achieving that goal. At a much earlier point than we did, we should have recognized that our tactic was making it harder rather than easier to reach our goal" (Bell 2004, 189). In a similar way, most educators' commitment to restrictive formal equality shapes our daily policies, practices, and discourses and thus limits the pursuit of expansive substantive equality.

This distinction between restrictive formal equality and expansive substantive equality builds on my discussion of equity in the introductory chapter. The restrictive formal equality talked about here is what is typically understood as simply "equality." And expansive substantive equality is very similar to what I've been calling equity—or, in other words, that which is fair and just (Brayboy, Castagno, and Maughan 2007). That which is fair is typically not the same as that which is equal. Genuinely pursuing equity often requires unequal distributions of resources in order to address long-standing and persistent inequalities. Returning to Bell's point about the *Brown* case, when we confuse tactics with principles, we also confuse equity and equality. If our ultimate goal is equity, we cannot continue to emphasize simple equality.

Equality is both ahistorical and acontextual, and as such, it is unable to address inequity. An ahistorical and acontextual understanding of student achievement, for example, fails to account for the ways in which achievement was initially measured through racist exams and normed against particular groups. It also fails to recognize the importance of the differential access youth have to good schools, high-quality teachers, appropriate and challenging texts, and culturally relevant education. The ahistorical and acontextual nature of equality is highlighted in Gloria Ladson-Billings's distinction between "achievement gaps" and "the educational debt" (Ladson-Billings 2006). Thinking solely about a current gap in achievement between different racialized groups is very different from thinking about the multiple historical, economic, health, political, and cultural factors that contribute to both how we understand and how we measure achievement in schools. These different ways of thinking about achievement lend themselves to different approaches and strategies for moving forward. The pursuit of equity requires an understanding of the historical, persistent, and structural nature of oppression and dominance. Losing sight of history and context results in a skewed—although much nicer—perception of the problem. But it is exactly this nicely skewed perception that obscures whiteness and hides the need for equity.

Equality in Action: Ruby Payne and the Culture of Poverty

Ruby Payne's popularity among teachers across the nation illustrates the degree to which meritocracy and equality form the foundation of educators' ideas about youth, communities, schooling, and opportunity. Teachers in the Zion School District participated in reading groups and workshops on Ruby Payne's book *A Framework for Understanding Poverty* (1996). Payne's book starts out by defining poverty as "the extent to which an individual does without resources" (Payne 1996, 16). According to Payne, the resources that are unavailable to youth living in poverty include "choosing and controlling emotional responses," "believing in divine purpose," and "having frequent access to adults who are appropriate" (ibid.). Payne goes on to explain the difference between "generational" and "situational" poverty; she is concerned with the first and notes that generational poverty "has its own culture, hidden rules, and belief systems" (64) that may "surface at school" in students who "are very disorganized, frequently lose papers, don't have signatures"; "bring many reasons why something is missing"; "don't do homework"; "are physically aggressive"; "only see part of what is on a page"; "can't seem to get started"; "cannot monitor their own behavior"; "dislike authority"; and "talk back and are extremely participatory" (78).

In her discussion of how to improve the academic achievement of children who come from "generational poverty," Payne highlights a number of "cognitive deficiencies" these children have. Her claims are bold and far reaching. She says, "These students have no consistent or predictable way of getting information. They only see about 50 percent of what is on a page. . . . They simply do not have the cognitive methodology for doing tasks or a systematic way to finish tasks" (123). Payne goes on to claim that children from low-income backgrounds have an "inability to hold two objects or two sources inside the head while comparing and contrasting" and have an "inability to know what stays the same and what changes" (124). She argues that "problem solving and other tasks are extremely problematic because students from poverty seldom have the strategies to gather precise and accurate information" and that "they have neither the vocabulary nor the concepts for spatial orientation" (123). Payne also makes claims about what low-income children value: "I find among students from poverty that time is neither measured nor heeded. Being somewhere on time is seldom valued. And time itself is not seen as a thing to be used or valued" (123). Overall, Payne suggests that educators are no longer able to "conduct school as we have in the past" because of the rising numbers of students who fit the characteristics she outlines.

Teachers at both Birch Secondary School and Spruce Secondary School relied heavily on Payne's model and described their own work as needing to "build the cognitive capacities" of children from low-income backgrounds. Mr. Mecha, for example, explained that he had recently "read and learned much more about how living in poverty affects students." He noted that this information has "helped me let things the students say go in one ear and out the other because they can say those things at home, and that's related to their low-income backgrounds." In a similar conversation, another teacher commented that "there's the culture of poverty, and that's a lot of what's going on here at [Birch]."

The Zion School District is not unique in its use of Ruby Payne's work. Her book has sold more than a million copies, and her company has offered workshops and presentations in every state and in ten different countries (ahaprocess.com). Indeed, I have encountered educators from at least six other districts in two additional states who have been introduced to Payne's ideas through either district-led professional-development programs or courses in colleges of education. In every instance, educators were encouraged to engage Ruby Payne's ideas as a way to more effectively serve "diverse students."

Like most well-intended diversity efforts in schools, Payne's work advances a "compassionate conservative approach" (Gorski 2006) that positions youth as victims of their family circumstances and thus in need of remediation at school. Payne's work clearly rests on a deficit model and perpetuates deficit assumptions about youth from low-income communities and youth of color. The manifestation of her thinking can be seen in the teacher quotes in the previous paragraphs. This framework positions educators as "saviors" who "fix" students. In none of this thinking do we see recognition of structural or ideological dominance or a plan to address patterned inequity. Payne's line of thinking and its operationalization by educators is indicative of—and results in—the reification of our education in whiteness.

The popularity of Payne's framework among K–12 educators also highlights the insidiousness of our allegiance to meritocracy and equality. The rationale at work here is that if teachers focus on the "inputs" they are able to control—including the knowledge they impart to students, the teaching styles they employ, the communicative norms they establish in their classrooms, and the disciplinary approaches they engage—then equality has been achieved and meritocracy can function effectively. Then when there are winners and losers at the end (i.e., when certain students leave school without graduating and others collect awards and AP credits), we need not question why, who, or what won or lost, because our responsibility was fulfilled at the beginning of the race. The implied neutrality of schooling obscures what is actually a stacked competition. Further assumed in this model is that there will be losers—that is, educational reform is a zero-sum game in that some win at the expense of others. Although never named, whiteness thrives when meritocracy and equality are held in such high regard.

Distinct Engagement with Equality

Ruby Payne's work and its embrace by teachers at Birch and Spruce highlight the powerful appeal of equality and meritocracy as well as the danger in relying on these ideological workhorses of whiteness. It also, however, should raise questions about the extent to which equality and meritocracy are engaged similarly in very different school contexts. We know, for example, that schools are differently positioned in relation to mandates for standardized measures of success and accountability, so we might also expect some distinct articulations of, and engagements with, equality and meritocracy. This chapter explores how diversity-related efforts at Birch and Spruce rely on distinct understandings of equality. One central office administrator in the Zion School District begins to unpack some of the distinctions:

> I think it goes back to east-west. If you look at our district demographics, there really is an east and west. I think the west side is really aware of the need [for diversity initiatives] and are running as fast as possible to be educated and to be aware and to know and not to be insensitive or to break someone's cultural mores or whatever it might be. On the east side of town, I don't think there is a sense of urgency. And I don't think there is a real feel of need. . . . I really think it has to do with need. If there is a pressing need, then you make the effort and you . . . try to adjust your behaviors or your

thought patterns. If you don't, then I think it's just too comfortable to stay where you are.

This administrator foreshadows some of the different issues at Birch and Spruce. The histories of the two communities, the contexts in which they are located, and their relationships to calls for accountability and standardization all contribute to distinct pressures related to diversity. As previous chapters have highlighted, whiteness operates in both schools. But here I explore the Spruce and Birch contexts independent of one another in order to illustrate how equality is engaged differently in the two schools.

While the distinction between restrictive formal equality (i.e., equality) and expansive substantive equality (i.e., equity) is important for understanding more obvious differences in diversity-related policy and practice, I want to suggest that restrictive formal equality actually takes multiple forms that are not immediately visible under this dichotomous framework. In fact, thinking about equality as *either* restrictive formal *or* expansive substantive leads to an analysis in which some diversity-related policy and practice may appear more equitable because it does not look like the obviously inequitable policy and practice seen in other places.

This is the case when examining some of the unique elements of Birch and Spruce Secondary Schools. Although restrictive formal equality shapes policy and practice at both Birch and Spruce, teachers at the two schools engage equality in distinct ways. These different manifestations of restrictive formal equality result in unique articulations of equality, power, culture, and merit, but both schools ultimately continue to educate for whiteness. Spruce educators employ a powerblind, colorblind formal equality; this is the restrictive formal equality that is articulated by critical race scholars. Birch educators employ a more race-conscious and power-conscious formal equality, but it falls short of engaging the systemic, institutional, and ideological nature of race and power. As such, it fails to educate against whiteness. While both ways of engaging equality are consistent with niceness, the race- and power-conscious formal equality undergirding Birch's efforts begins to push the boundaries of what is typically understood as nice among educators.

Shaping and Maintaining Spruce's Reputation

The Zion School District at one time had a magnet model for its secondary schools, and Spruce served as the district's magnet for English-language learner (ELL) students and services. Thus, although Spruce is located in an

overwhelmingly White and middle-class to upper-middle-class neighborhood, for many years ELL students from around the district were bussed
to Spruce and schooled in a setting with a critical mass of teachers who
were both trained in and committed to the education of linguistically and
racially diverse students. Five years prior to my research, and only after
many heated conversations and much advocating on the part of the district's more elite constituencies, the magnet model was disbanded, and
the district's secondary schools reverted back to "neighborhood" schools
where students attended the school that was nearest their homes. This
shift resulted in a number of dramatic and immediate changes to Spruce,
including a significant drop in the numbers of ELL students and students
of color, a significant drop in the number of teachers who were knowl-
edgeable about and committed to diversity-related issues, and a (re)newed
focus on the "neighborhood kids" who were largely White and middle
class and who came from families with parents who had higher educational credentials.

The rationale behind the change from a magnet to a neighborhood
school centered ideologies of equal opportunity, colorblindness and powerblindness, and individual rights. The predominantly White, middle-class
parents who advocated for this change relied heavily on the appeal of providing all students with the same educational opportunities close to home,
and they critiqued the magnet model as infringing on these opportunities
and therefore on individual students' and families' rights to good local
schools. This discourse is intimately tied to colorblind and powerblind
perspectives that view students as individuals with few, if any, distinctions
that have any relevance to the schooling they are offered. If students are
simply viewed as students, not as students of color or English-language
learners, then it follows that the schools to which they are assigned should
simply be schools—not specialized schools designed to meet particular
and specific needs. Furthermore, the restrictive formal view of equality is
clear in its emphasis on the process of schooling that assumes neighborhood schools will serve all students equally well—as opposed to critically
examining the results and outcomes that follow from this process to determine whether the process is moving toward greater equity.

Equality shaped many other aspects of schooling at Spruce. In what
follows, I highlight some of the ways Spruce educators rely on what I
call powerblind, colorblind formal equality. In this classic engagement
with restrictive formal equality, Spruce educators were firmly rooted in
meritocracy and assumed equal opportunity existed both within and
outside of their school. They also operated within a deficit framework
regarding the ELL students at Spruce. A handful of teachers who did

recognize problems with the way ELL students were educated did not assume any responsibility to voice their concerns or act on their concerns. In every instance, niceness and whiteness were operating through policies and practices that privileged powerblind, colorblind formal equality as the driving ideology.

The Meaning of Excellence

In its more recent role as an "east-side neighborhood school," Spruce was widely regarded as one of the top secondary schools in the district, and Spruce educators were committed to providing what they perceived to be an excellent education to their students. What this meant in practice was that students were exposed to a fairly traditional curriculum that emphasized core curricular areas but also included creative outlets and diverse pedagogies. Although this "excellent education" seemed to be appealing to and meeting the perceived needs of the majority of White, middle-class students at Spruce, it was not meeting the needs of the English-language learners, nor was it moving toward greater equity within or outside of the school. Instead, excellence seemed to be defined by educational practices that maintained the status quo—a status quo that privileged the majority of White, middle-class families served by Spruce.

The mark of excellence among Spruce educators was an education that is both academically oriented and creative. During most of my classroom visits, I witnessed what appeared to be fairly typical lessons: graphing linear equations in a math class, discussing tectonic plates in a science class, conjugating verbs in a language class, writing poetry in a language arts class, and discussing westward expansion in a U.S. history class. The majority of the teachers I observed facilitated their classes with a high level of organization and order, and students were engaged in activities such as reading from texts, completing worksheets, note-taking, group work, and correcting homework. Most teachers also maintained a high level of consistency from day to day through the use of the same general schedule.

The classes I observed appeared to closely follow the state's core curriculum and their assigned textbooks, but there was a fair amount of creativity in how lessons were taught and the types of educational activities in which students were engaged. Social studies classes, for example, regularly worked on projects such as writing "historical fictions," designing imaginary "road trips" through Utah, and constructing newspapers for a particular historical period. A math class designed restaurant menus to learn about combinations and proportions, a language arts class wrote letters to students around the country, science classes researched the biographies of scientists to learn about their lives and discoveries, and a world language class designed and carried out interviews in Spanish with native Spanish-speaking students and staff at Spruce.

The frequency of creative assignments and class projects was mirrored in the extracurricular activities offered at Spruce. This focus on creativity and the arts highlights an important component of Spruce's understanding of what counts as an excellent education. The arts were a major extracurricular focus among most teachers and administrators at Spruce. This was particularly salient when the Parent-Teacher Association and a select group of educators from Spruce decided to produce a "Broadway musical." Although almost two hundred students were involved through either orchestra, drama, dance, or choir, I only observed six students of color and no students who were in the English-as-a-secondary-language (ESL) classes.

The absence of Latino, Spanish-speaking students in the musical production was not an isolated occurrence, but it went unquestioned in Spruce's drive to shape its identity as an "excellent neighborhood school." From its general curricular focus to its choices about engaging the arts and its overall décor, everything about Spruce exuded White, middle-class, and English-speaking norms. There was little overt awareness that these particular cultural norms permeated the school, and there was no discussion around the expectation of assimilation to those cultural norms that students likely experienced.

At Spruce, powerblind, colorblind formal equality shaped the way students were viewed and the way schooling was done. There was an assumed norm that centers students as individuals unaffected by particular identities and who, as a result, ought to be equally impacted by what is perceived to be a neutral and high-quality educational experience. As long as Spruce educators maintain the excellence they believe forms the foundation of their school, any student who enters through the school doors has the same opportunity and likelihood of success as any other student. This understanding is connected to deficit beliefs because when students do not succeed, it is they, their families, and their communities who are assumed to be at fault (Gorski 2006; Hyland 2005; L. Powell 1997). There was a shared understanding at Spruce that "what is excellent for one student is excellent for all students." It is the simultaneous belief in the "normalcy" or "commonness" of what Spruce teachers do daily alongside the assumptions of meritocracy and equal opportunity that characterize the powerblind, colorblind formal equality seen at Spruce.

Normativity in the Presence of Difference

Though rooted in sameness, formal equality does allow recognition of, and some remediation around, difference. Recall that Spruce teachers did engage difference as it related to the language and social-class backgrounds of their students. These engagements were similarly framed by a powerblind, colorblind formal equality—a pattern that is highlighted in the ways Spruce teachers discussed and employed the book *Seedfolks* in the language arts program. This book is fairly explicit in addressing issues of language, culture, race, and social class, but teachers at Spruce engaged it under a powerblind, colorblind formal equality framework that emphasized meritocracy and equal opportunity. During an interview with a teacher who taught the ESL language arts class, Ms. Scott described this book and why she believed it was a particularly effective text with her ELL students:

> One example of the books that I use in class is *Seedfolks,* and each chapter is different. Nearly everyone is a different person from a different country who has come to the United States to live; and if they haven't come from another country, they've at least come from different parts of the United States, and so they are from different ethnic backgrounds. And we read that book and talk about all these different people. We talk about their traditions and a little bit about their culture; and again, I don't think I do a great job with it, but it's a nice book to start out the school year because some of the issues that are addressed in the book are issues that I think these kids are dealing with.
>
> For example, there is a kid from Guatemala who says something to the effect of, "When you're old and come to the United States, you come to be like a baby, and the babies or the kids turn to adults." And he says that because he's in eighth grade, and he has to do all the translating for his dad or his mom when they go to the store, or when they pay the rent, or when they have a problem with a landlord. Well, so many of my kids, that's very familiar to them; they know what that's like. The kid in the story says he learned English from watching TV. You know, my kids always get a big kick out of that because they say that really helped them. So they can relate to it more than something that's totally just Western American. So, I see them liking it and enjoying it more, and I think maybe getting more out of it than maybe some other books.

Like her teacher colleagues, Ms. Scott understood the importance of using curricular materials that might strike a chord with students. As an ESL teacher, she believed *Seedfolks* was an especially important text for her recently immigrated students, because they could relate to some of the characters and stories found in the text.

But engaging texts with some relevance to students' lives may still result in youth being educated in whiteness. If such texts are framed around notions of powerblind sameness, colorblind difference, equality, and meritocracy, they do little to question dominant power relations or disrupt the status quo. In fact, because they are embraced as "multicultural literature" or "diversity-related curriculum," such materials actually engage whiteness even more dangerously than the Eurocentric canon. Because they are understood as diverse, multicultural, and relevant to students' lives, they shelter schools from accusations of not providing an inclusive education. Including texts like *Seedfolks* means Spruce is being inclusive and "welcoming of diversity," which in turn means they are providing an "equal education." And providing an equal education is what schools and educators are supposed to do. Again, we see how whiteness works through good intentions and nice people.

Another language arts teacher at Spruce also used *Seedfolks* with her mainstream, predominantly White class. She began the book by reading the first few chapters aloud to the class. After a number of pages describing people who lived in poor, urban high-rises, she stopped to ask the class, "If they [i.e., the characters in the book] were living in a country club, how would it be different?" Some of the students responded with "less crowded," "wouldn't be gangs driving by," "nicer," and "more sophisticated." The teacher broached the topic of social class by asking her students to compare a fictional low-income "project" and a "country club," but she did not pursue an analysis of why some of those differences exist, how they are maintained, or what they indicate about social class in the United States.

Even a text that offers explicit opportunities for critically oriented and transformative learning is able to be framed in ways that fit educators' beliefs about meritocracy and equality. Using a book like *Seedfolks* in a predominantly White school like Spruce may result in sensitizing students to the experiences of people who are different from them and in exposing students to multiple perspectives, but it falls short of critically examining current social realities and thinking through possibilities for social change when it is grounded in a colorblind, formal equality framework. This is an appropriately nice operating framework because it highlights how we might be more individually compassionate, but it does not suggest the presence of dominance or injustice. Acknowledging differences between people while simultaneously subscribing to an assumption of equality and the myth of meritocracy results in the general belief that the status quo is acceptable and those who are poor, unemployed, unhealthy, or uneducated have simply not taken advantage of the many opportunities available to them. Educating youth about differences between groups and communities without situating this knowledge within a larger context of how power, institutions, and everyday actions create and maintain those differences is a common practice that educates for whiteness.

ESL: Seeking Equality while Assuming Deficits

Although ELL students made up a small percentage of the overall student body at Spruce, they offer another illustrative space for seeing power-blind, colorblind formal equality at work. Spruce had four teachers, and only a few more actual classes, that were designated as "ESL sheltered" and served the entirely Spanish-speaking, predominantly Mexican-origin students who qualified for these "services." In general, the teachers who were ESL endorsed and worked with the small group of ELL students at Spruce felt that although they were doing what they could to support these students, there was a significant lack of support from other teachers and administrators at the school. Consistent with my observations at Spruce, many ethnographies of immigrants' schooling experiences illustrate how most immigrants are exposed to a Eurocentric education that separates and marginalizes them, subtracts their rich cultural knowledge, and replaces it with "American" culture. Eurocentric education also fails to require high academic achievement and the development of a critical consciousness (see, for example, Gibson 1988; Lee 2005; Olneck 2004; Olsen 1997; Valdes 2001; Valenzuela 1999). Furthermore, powerblind, colorblind formal equality shapes the education provided to ELL students at Spruce. The value placed on meritocracy, the assumptions of deficit, and the concomitant absent sense of responsibility among teachers provide a fruitful context for an education in whiteness.

At Spruce, the four designated ESL teachers provided academic and social support within an ESL framework for this particular group of students. Spruce's approach to educating its ELL students was aimed at facilitating the students' rapid acquisition of English. None of the ESL teachers were fluent in a language other than English, and all instruction occurred in English. These teachers did allow students to converse in their native languages during "free time" and when a student helped to explain a concept to a peer who did not understand the English explanation, but the overwhelming emphasis was on English-language learning—with little or no effort made to ensure that students maintained or improved their literacy in their native language.

In Ms. Carol's ESL math class, she developed word problems using students' names and experiences that were relevant to them, such as figuring out their grade based on a number of exam scores or using various sports-related examples. This teacher also regularly asked the class things like, "So what does that mean [in everyday English words]?" She encouraged risk taking by suggesting that students guess if nobody knew an answer. If a student gave an answer that was true but not necessarily what Ms. Carol was looking for, she often said something along the lines of, "Yeah, I know where you're getting that, but let's think about it . . . [in some other way]." Although the ESL teachers recognized their own limitations in being able to communicate effectively with students given their own monolingualism, they explicitly supported the ESL model of education. These teachers cared deeply about their students and wanted to provide them with a high-quality education, but they clearly saw their goal as mainstreaming ELL students into the English-speaking dominant culture of the school. This is, of course, consistent with the school's reputation and mission of preparing students for higher education, but it relies on a deficit model of ELL students rather than on an additive bilingual model.

Colorblind, formal equality is manifested in Spruce's reliance on an ESL model and a focused goal of mainstreaming ELL students who are proficient in English. Like the previous examples, this approach to education privileges sameness and perpetuates the ideal of equal educational opportunity. The assumption is that if ELL students learn English as quickly as possible and are mainstreamed with their native-English-speaking peers, they will have all the privileges of the high-quality education Spruce offers, and thus they will benefit from those opportunities in the same ways their peers do.

Notions of equality and meritocracy are so entrenched here that it is difficult to see how they operate: If you believe that equal opportunity exists and that individuals will be rewarded for their success within an equal system, then it follows that you would want every individual to enter that system. Educators at Spruce certainly subscribe to ideologies of equality and meritocracy, and they see no reason every student at Spruce would not be able to equally enter the meritocratic world of school. But the ESL model relies on a cultural-deficiency framework that assumes students whose first language is not English are lacking and need remediation (Valdes 2001; Valenzuela 1999; Yosso 2005). Formal equality and deficit models are therefore two sides of the same coin. Since ELL students at Spruce are not succeeding like their White, English-speaking Spruce peers, it must be because they are deficient. It cannot be the result of anything systemic or structural within the school because Spruce offers a high-quality experience regardless of who a student is.

Equality through Assimilation

Alongside their own efforts to integrate ELL students into the Spruce fold, most of the ESL teachers had some concerns about how their students were treated outside the ESL classrooms. An issue that arose late during spring semester highlights their concerns. Although the school was once the district's magnet secondary school for ELL services, the population of ELL students was only 15 percent of the total student population the year I conducted research. These changes in student demographics were accompanied by changes in personnel and course offerings. In 2006, Spruce offered sheltered ESL courses in language arts, math, science, and social studies at each grade level, but this list was significantly cut for the next academic year. Although I heard various explanations, which ranged from lack of funding to low enrollment numbers to an unwillingness to modify the master schedule to accommodate these classes, the end result was that the following year Spruce would only offer grade-level ESL language arts courses, and the ELL students would be "mainstreamed" for all other subject areas. When the ESL teachers found out about this change, they were upset and scheduled a meeting with the school administration and the district's English Language Services Director. They learned that Spruce was only required to offer two courses in sheltered language arts in order to be in compliance with federal and state laws.

Although this was the ultimate plan for the following year, there was still some unrest among the small group of ESL teachers, who felt that their school was overly interested in offering more honors-level courses for "the neighborhood kids" at the expense of serving ELL students who were, for the most part, "bussed in." In speaking about this incident and other similar examples, one teacher conveyed the following:

> There's a feeling sometimes that the administration isn't as supportive
> of the ELLs and [is] . . . more interested in focusing on the, you know,
> neighborhood kids. And so I think a lot of people, including me,
> were uncomfortable with that. I felt like there really were some times
> when neighborhood kids got priority . . . I would like to feel more

supported and a little more interest like from the principal and from
the counselors. I'd like to have them in the classroom more often. I'd
like to have them know these kids better—all my kids but particularly
my ELLs. I'd like to have them know more of their concerns and, you
know, maybe I need to be stepping up and expressing that more. But
I just think we've gone a little bit back to focusing so much on neighborhood kids and mainstream kids and, you know, the top kids—the
kids [who] . . . don't cause problems—and we kind of lose sight of
some of the other kids.

This ESL teacher was speaking against the strong pattern at Spruce to
cloak assimilative schooling in a veil of formal equality. Powerblind, colorblind formal equality is operating in the desire to offer the same general
classes to all students at Spruce and in the belief that focusing on the
process of schooling (i.e., which classes are offered) is the best approach.
What is really happening here is that White, English-dominant, middle-
class students are the universal norm that Spruce organizes around. This
approach fails to address what students really need from school, and it
fails to acknowledge what school is actually doing to students. There
exists no focus on the outcomes of whether all students are succeeding.
Privileging assimilation to the dominant, mainstream norm at Spruce is
understood by administrators and most teachers as an appropriate and
effective way to school youth *because* (at least, in part) it builds on an
ideological foundation of equality.

Although the "focus on neighborhood kids" is certainly consistent
with the way Spruce positions itself as an "excellent east-side school,"
its appeal to equality is actually a cover for unequal schooling. Cutting
course offerings for ELL students while simultaneously adding course
offerings that are inaccessible to ELL students and thus really only for
White, English-speaking students is neither equal nor fair. If Spruce was
working to ensure the honors courses were available to ELL students
and these students were proportionately represented in them, then we
might applaud the school's efforts. But this was not the case. It is striking
that the addition of courses for high-achieving White students was not
viewed as offering "added benefits" to this group of students. Instead,
these courses were largely understood as the "right" thing to do and the
obvious approach for a school like Spruce. Offering additional courses
to ensure the success of ELL students, however, was viewed as "pouring
resources into a small group of kids at the expense of our other kids."
This contradiction was lost on most Spruce leaders and teachers. The
sorting mechanism embedded in these decisions is not uncommon in

schools. Whiteness is reinforced through these sorting mechanisms, but the harm is veiled behind ideologies of equality and meritocracy.

Accepting Whiteness

There are countless examples of similarly racist, marginalizing, and inequitable schooling for ELL students across the nation, but what is less talked about, and more insidious, are the ways the ESL teachers understand their own responsibility in these instances. The ESL teachers at Spruce subscribed to a "hands off" approach with their colleagues and administration. In reference to the majority of teachers, one ESL teacher said, "I just think that there is this wall—that they just want to teach the students [whom] . . . they want to teach." Another teacher recalled an incident when an electives teacher approached her about one month into the school year and told her, "I gave this test to so and so, and I don't think he understood it at all." The ESL teacher went on to explain that "the student [this teacher] was referring to had been in the country just since summer; he read English a little bit but I hadn't been able to have a conversation with him at all. He just had no, or very limited, oral language skills. And it kind of made me smile that here we were like four weeks into the term, and this teacher was just realizing that this kid doesn't speak any English." Not realizing that your student does not speak English is clearly unacceptable and an extreme example, but I include it here to highlight the pervasive nature of the powerblind, colorblind equality that is employed at Spruce. While teachers need to be held accountable for this sort of obvious lack of engagement with ELL students, teachers also need to be cognizant of the ways in which their allegiance to equality and meritocracy results in less obvious harm to students.

Consider one ESL teacher's narrative about the recent changes to Spruce's demographics and the role of teachers in advocating for students: "When we had a bigger population of students from different backgrounds, there were more teachers and there was more pressure from the district. And, I think . . . that maybe there were some teachers and some people [who] . . . were more . . . um, vocal and maybe a little more adamant in their, you know, expression of the need for multicultural education. I don't think I'm that way. I think sometimes I'm pretty willing to just do my own thing. I'm not political at all." In saying that she was not "political," this teacher meant that she was not one to "rock the boat" or bring up concerns to her colleagues or the administration—even when she believed that her students' needs were not being met in the best possible way. In other words, she was a nice teacher. Another teacher talked about how she used to be involved in planning the annual "multicultural assembly," but when she and a few other teachers could no longer lead that effort, Spruce simply stopped having the assembly because nobody else took on the responsibility. And still another teacher described how there had been a significant decline in dialogue about issues of diversity among teachers—especially at faculty meetings. This teacher noted how they rarely talked about multicultural education or diversity "unless someone brings it up, but usually nobody ever does." Indeed, there appears to be an unspoken assumption that diversity and excellence do not mix. This makes sense when we consider how entrenched powerblind, colorblind equality is at Spruce.

Although some of the ESL teachers were well aware of the school's weaknesses related to meeting the needs of ELL students, they did not see themselves as either part of the problem or part of the solution. This is not unlike White teachers in "liberal Lakeview" (Kailin 1999) who ascribed racial problems to others (whether children, parents, people of color, and/or their colleagues) and also believed it was the purview of educators of color to address the problems that existed. What is happening here is that inequality and discrimination are understood as individually perpetrated within a system that is fair and equal. At the same time, the White ESL teachers are abiding by cultural and professional expectations of niceness. Also at the same time, there is a school-wide belief in the excellence, goodness, and neutrality of the education offered at Spruce. Taken together, the conditions are ripe for whiteness to be maintained and strengthened. For educators at Spruce, their ideas around race—which are also the dominant ideas in most predominantly White settings (Frankenberg 1993; Lewis 2003; Morrison 1992; Perry 2002)—led them to focus their energy and resources on providing a high-quality and creative education that primarily appealed to the White, middle-class families in their immediate local community. Colorblind ideals and believing in the irrelevance of race justified what was perceived to be a neutral and "good" education for "all students." These ideologies and practices, however, were neither meeting the needs of ELL students nor cultivating equity or educating against whiteness at Spruce.

Birch's Contradictions of Success

Given the student population, school leadership, and pressure from the district, Birch teachers and administrators were far more likely than Spruce educators to exhibit interest in and commitment to issues of educational equity and cultural diversity. Birch educators were involved in a number of efforts to improve their students' academic performance and to embrace and celebrate the students' ethnic diversity. Although Birch educators were more likely than Spruce educators to see themselves as activists concerned with educational equity, they were constrained by No Child Left Behind (NCLB) regulations and a context in which tests define success. As a result, teachers were only able to see their activist role in terms of standardized achievement. Their efforts were also constrained by their reliance on restrictive formal equality and meritocracy as guiding principles. These workhorses of whiteness guide policy and practice at both Spruce and Birch, but the work is very different and produces very different results within the two schools—an outcome wholly consistent with whiteness.

Although restrictive formal equality was the operating framework for Birch educators, there existed elements that approximate expansive substantive equality (or equity) as well. At Birch, there was a concerted effort to look at the outcomes of schooling for Birch students. Indeed, the principal and some Birch teachers were well aware of the problematic educational outcomes for their students. The response, however, was (primarily) to change the inputs and then assume that the outputs would also subsequently change. This sort of response falls short of addressing the systemic nature of inequity and the ideological and institutional workings of whiteness. Birch educators were also still reliant on a framework that attempted to prevent future wrongdoing, rather than on one that attempted to explicitly address present manifestations of past injustice. They did not assume equality of opportunity like their colleagues at Spruce, but they did restrict their understanding of competition and success to notions consistent with whiteness. This occurs, in part, because of the way NCLB regulations and the context of standardized schooling forces schools like Birch into a stacked competition. But it also occurs because equality and meritocracy do the work of whiteness—so any engagement with them means whiteness is also engaged and reified.

An Academic Focus to Level the Playing Field

Birch educators were involved in a number of efforts to create a strong academic culture within the school. This was evident in a school-wide poster contest during the advisory period, which had the theme "It's cool to be great in school." Each advisory class was directed to make a single poster with this theme, and the winning class earned a pizza party. Similarly, one of the art classes created a number of posters displaying various students reading and quotes from the students about why reading was important.

The school employed a full time "Title I Director" whose primary responsibility was the reading program, and she worked hard to ensure consistent fidelity to the reading curriculum, pedagogical strategies, and assessment schedules. She modeled lessons, shared effective teaching techniques, and kept teachers informed about students' reading progress or lack thereof throughout the year. Every student spent first period in a reading class with peers who were homogenously grouped according to their reading level. Students were tested every eight weeks and assigned to new reading classes based on their new reading level. The gains in student reading levels were impressive: The school averaged almost a two-year reading-level increase in just one year's time. This is significant because at the time of my research, the average reading score for students entering Birch was three grade levels below their actual grade. The challenge facing Birch was also obvious in the fact that less than one-third of Birch students were reading at least one grade level below their actual grade.

Each reading class chose books based on their reading level and worked through a standardized curriculum that included individual, partner, and group reading; vocabulary words; discussions to check for and improve reading comprehension; journaling about the text; and weekly assessment exercises. All teachers were trained in this teaching model, and I observed two midyear faculty meetings in which the Title I Director talked about the reading program, encouraged teachers to continue working hard, and stressed that they needed to "lovingly bust" those students who were clearly not doing their nightly reading homework. Reading gains were often displayed on school bulletin boards and talked about over the morning announcements, and administrators regularly visited reading classes to support individual teachers, observe lessons, and talk to students about their progress and the room for improvement. In addition, mailings in multiple languages were sent to each student's home every eight weeks that informed families about their student's current and past reading scores and the progress the student was making, as well as offering suggestions for supporting the child's continued reading improvement. Every student was expected to read a minimum of twenty minutes at home each night, and most students were required to ask an adult to sign a form indicating that they completed their daily reading. The school went to great lengths to ensure that parents were informed about the importance of reading, the expectation that students read at home, and the reading progress their children were making. In addition to the regular mailings, one administrator organized a group of multilingual people to circulate during parent-teacher conferences and talk to every parent about the reading program.

During class discussions, teachers encouraged students to "use your resources" and avoid random guessing when they were unsure of an answer. One teacher instructed his students: "Here's what I should be seeing—I should see you opening the book to look for something when you don't know [the answer]." In another class when the group was trying to decide which book to begin reading, a student asked if they could "vote" on a book that they had already read. The teacher asked the class, "Is it OK to read a book more than once?" The students said "Yes," after which the teacher explained that they were "still increasing . . . [their] reading skills." She went on to tell her class that reading and writing were important to improve literacy and that she expected them to work hard. She explained, "These are the things that are going to bring your grades up and your reading skills up."

Birch teachers worked to cultivate a strong academic culture in their other classes and through other school responsibilities as well. One teacher worked on a committee during the summer that was charged with developing strategies for increasing the number of Birch students in advanced classes. He related this work to his efforts in his classroom, and he stressed that his students would "leave knowing how to write a thesis statement." He also worked hard to "cultivate an attitude" in his students that "I can compete with anybody," and he was joined by others who talked explicitly about preparing Birch students for higher education. One teacher emphasized the skills needed to format papers on the computer; she talked about how papers should be left-justified with the title centered, and she explicitly illustrated how to do these tasks on the computer. She further explained that instead of writing "by" and their name at the bottom of their papers, they should make "a header" in the top left corner that listed their name, date, period, and assignment and that "it's a good habit to get into." And finally, another teacher required students to develop Power Point presentations on a topic of their choice. He emphasized that the students were required to "keep it interesting" and create "presentations that we actually want to see!" He explained that the idea was to introduce students to the technology and to help students practice public speaking on a small scale.

While these academic skills may seem obvious, most Birch teachers recognized that in order for their students to be successful in their later years of schooling, they would need to know particular information that is generally not taught in school. Because these expectations are often assumed, many Birch teachers made a point of actually teaching these skills and explaining when and why students would need to know the information.

This practice is not unlike Lisa Delpit's suggestion that teachers must expose low-income students and students of color to the "culture of power" in order to truly provide a high-quality education (Delpit 1988, 1995). She explains that this culture of power includes the rules and norms (i.e., the "codes") that reflect the dominant group, and that if you are not already a member of this group, being told explicitly about the codes will make acquiring power easier. In other words, efforts by Birch teachers to explicitly convey information about academic expectations, norms, and rules facilitated the acquisition of greater school success and potentially increased access to power among their minoritized student body. This type of training is important and admirable work, but it also buys into the myth of meritocracy and fails to challenge the structural imbalance of resources and rules that frame schooling.

Many Birch teachers did not assume equal opportunity existed. Rather, they knew their students started out academically behind their east-side peers, and they knew their students faced additional obstacles as they moved through the school system. This is an important difference from the powerblind, colorblind formal equality operating at Spruce. In many instances, Birch teachers exhibited a more race-conscious and power-conscious allegiance to equality. They recognized unequal playing fields, and they believed that a pointed academic focus would result in a more level playing field. But they also still operated under the belief that once the field was made level, meritocracy would be fairly applied and equality would thus be achieved.

In some ways, then, Birch was pushing the boundaries of the niceness exhibited in Spruce's reliance on powerblind, colorblind formal equality. Acknowledging inequality and talking to students about specific strategies for succeeding in the face of disparities is like treading on the outskirts of potentially choppy water. But any allegiance to formal equality maintains some degree of niceness. Here even Birch educators kept a safe distance from the waters of inequity by not specifically and explicitly addressing the structural impossibility of equality given patterned and systemic inequity.

Although it was more race conscious and power conscious, the restrictive formal equality framework driving Birch's focus on academics and reading provides a poignant illustration of how Birch is educated in and educating for whiteness. What could be wrong with emphasizing academic success and literacy? Indeed, such an emphasis is what has for decades been missing from schools serving primarily low-income families and youth of color. It is a risky venture to go down the path of critiquing a school like Birch that is actually doing many of the things schools are supposed to be doing. But consider the line of thinking involved and the implications. The assumptions at work here are that if students maintain a diligent focus on their academic responsibilities, they will learn the material, learn how to read, earn good grades, and go on to be successful students and members of the community. If teachers remain faithful to the process outlined for them—including precisely outlined lesson plans, time-defined learning tasks, and frequent assessment, then equal opportunity has been embraced, and we can go home feeling good about our work. In this way of thinking, when students do not succeed, we do not need to worry that their lack of success is the fault of the system, the school, or the teacher, because we covered those bases by ensuring that the educational inputs and processes were "right." Meritocracy helps us make sense of the outcome because, in fact, not everyone is supposed to get ahead, and one's merit explains whether one will succeed or fail. This reasoning places primary focus on the individual, which fails to acknowledge group experiences of success and failure and systems' roles in these successes and failures.

To be clear, the work Birch was engaging to improve the academic success of students is absolutely necessary. Teachers must maintain high expectations for their students and provide them with the knowledge and skills they need to succeed in school. But although this work is necessary, it is not sufficient to undo the damage of whiteness and bring about equity. This work needs to be paired with informed and pointed critiques of the unfair systems embedded in schools *and with* work that changes those systems. Engaging solely in efforts that target the individual and maintain the myth of meritocracy, and thus protect the system, cannot ultimately challenge whiteness, which is by definition ideological and institutional.

A Standardized Academic Culture

Although Birch educators strategized around how their students could achieve greater success in the system as it is currently arranged, they were not equipping those students with the knowledge and skills necessary to change the system. Because their ideas about what constitutes success and achievement were defined by NCLB regulations, standardization, and accountability, Birch educators stopped at the point of improving their students' academic skills. So although these teachers exhibited an impressive focus on academics, this focus was limited and still grounded in a restrictive formal understanding of equality. This is why context and history are so important. Without an understanding of the historical and contextual factors that impact east-side and west-side schools differently, we are left believing that all schools are the same and that all students will thrive under the same approaches. Standardized educational approaches fail to account for the vastly different histories and contexts of schools, students, and communities and, as such, naturalize patterns of success and failure. When these patterns are naturalized and made to seem normal, whiteness thrives and students get left behind.

No Child Left Behind regulations place increased burdens on schools like Birch that serve low-income students and students of color, and these schools subsequently feel pressure to "teach to the test" by focusing on standardized knowledge. The math and language arts classes at Birch were routinized, seemed to strictly follow the core curriculum, and tested students often. Carl Grant and Christine Sleeter found a similar pattern at a Midwestern junior high school: "The teachers rarely considered student interests; activities that promoted critical and analytic thinking; or the experiences and perspectives of different racial groups, social classes, and disability groups, and of both sexes" (Grant and Sleeter 1996, 127).

One Birch math teacher organized her classes according to previous years' standardized math tests; so rather than following the textbook or an order that made logical sense based on the concepts to be learned, she taught topics that were covered on the tests and spent more time on topics that were covered extensively on the tests. All Birch math teachers were also required to test students every Friday using standardized tests that the district provided. These tests were shorter versions of the test used to comply with NCLB regulations, generally covered a handful of particular topics, and were meant to simulate the "real" test given at the end of the year. Teachers could track their students' progress on these tests, and teachers whose classes did not demonstrate appropriate levels of achievement on the tests were given support in the form of a "math coach" from the district.

Another practice that occurred in the math, language arts, and science classes was to begin these classes with one to three "problems of the day" or "warm ups." While a similar practice also occurred in a number of Spruce classes, the problems at Birch were of a different nature and were often taken directly from previous years' standardized tests. So while Ms. Carol at Spruce developed problems using her students' names and describing activities in which they might reasonably be involved, Ms. Ramirez from Birch took problems from old standardized tests that were often about fictional and unfamiliar topics. Such standardized and routinized patterns at Birch are clearly the result of pressures imposed by NCLB regulations. Given that Birch students have historically underperformed on standardized tests, and given the imperatives for the school to improve performance, it is understandable that Birch teachers would resort to standardized "teaching to the tests." This is one of the consequences of the No Child Left Behind Act that disproportionately affects schools like Birch.

Even within Birch, some students had to bear the burden of standardized measures of accountability more than others. The school added a series of language arts classes in 2005 targeted specifically at what it called "the bubble kids." Eighth-grade students who had scored just below the passing mark on their seventh-grade language arts tests were assigned to this class with the intent that they would be able to pass the test in eighth grade "with a little extra help" from the school. It is significant that this class was made available to a very particular group of students rather than all students who didn't receive a proficient score on the language arts tests. School leaders believed their resources should be focused on a small group of students who were within a close enough range that passing seemed like a realistic goal. Indeed, the students in this class showed marked improvement on their reading scores and language arts scores when tested throughout the year—far more improvement than similar students who were not in this "extra" language arts class. So students who were not identified as "bubble kids" were truly "left behind" *because of* the pressures felt by NCLB regulations. As Mr. Mecha noted, the No Child Left Behind Act "has thrown the baby out with the bathwater."

Some teachers, like Mr. Mecha, were critical of the "bubble kids" approach, but others were supportive of it. In both instances, however, we see the ways equality and meritocracy act as mechanisms to sustain inequity. Teachers who critiqued this approach did so on the grounds that students who were not in the bubble were being denied equal opportunities to succeed. These teachers thought it was "unfair to single out some of our kids for special treatment" and suggested that "every student at Birch should get this kind of special treatment." This is a clear manifestation of equality—all students should have access to the same opportunities—paired with an appeal to fairness. The problem here is that when sameness and fairness are collapsed into the same thing, it is impossible to enact differential approaches (because that would be unfair) even if that is what is needed to ultimately achieve equality. Teachers who supported the "bubble kids" approach acknowledged that there were limited resources, and they believed those resources were best spent in ways that would "bring up the scores for the whole school." But even this motivation to make the school more equal to those across town is problematic because in the race to make Adequate Yearly Progress (AYP) and improve the reputation of the whole school so that Birch appears more like Spruce, students who need more resources actually get less.

My point here is to demonstrate the multiple ways in which Birch's curriculum, pedagogy, and services were shaped by accountability measures and a desire to meet AYP and show improvement on standardized tests. Indeed, Birch met these goals in large number and was slowly changing its reputation within the district. Although Birch failed to meet AYP just three years prior, in 2006, it not only met AYP goals but also posted higher test scores than other schools in particular subjects. It would be fair to say, then, that many of the school's efforts paid off. The strict emphasis on testing and resources going toward students who seemed "within reach" did, in fact, result in higher overall test scores from previous years. But what might be lost in this "drill and kill" educational approach? What are students not getting when Birch teachers report spending 40 percent of their time on mandated practice tests? My findings are consistent with other research that shows that teachers are feeling tremendous pressure not only to plan curriculum explicitly around state content standards but also to draw curricular emphases directly from anticipated test items. This is even more likely to occur among new teachers (Kauffman, Johnson, Kardos, Liu, and Peske 2002) and teachers in schools like Birch that serve primarily low-income students and students of color (Lipman 2004). The result, as Sleeter points out, is that teachers tend to "turn the standards into the curriculum itself. Doing this, however, is likely to result in boring, superficial teaching that favors memory work over understanding" (Sleeter 2005, 44). Thus, at Birch, although test scores were rising, it is useful to consider what this means in the context of whiteness.

Because schools rest on a foundation of meritocracy and equality, schools like Birch are forced to engage in very different behaviors than schools like Spruce. There is a differentiated effect of NCLB regulations operating in the schools. Spruce can essentially ignore its small ELL population and pour time, energy, and resources into the White and middle-class students who make up the majority of the student body. Birch is held captive by tests that are biased and not normed on its student population. Equality, which is the espoused goal of the No Child Left Behind Act, and closing the achievement gap, is clearly not equal. Furthermore, the standardized accountability system under NCLB defines the quest for equality as being solely about test scores. *Even if* tests scores on state exams were equal across schools and between minoritized students and their White peers, what about patterned inequities across other measures both in and out of school? As long as diversity-related policies and practices in schools are narrowly defined and built on a foundation of restrictive, formal equality, success and merit will be understood as individual traits within a fair and just system.

Broaching Systemic Change

A handful of educators at Birch, most notably the principal, did engage policies and practices that have the potential of disrupting the individualized focus on formal equality and meritocracy. Mr. More recognized that the entire educational *system* often works against Birch students and thus, in order to be truly effective, Birch needed to collaborate with its feeder elementary schools and the high school most Birch students attend. Mr. More was clear with the local elementary schools that he expected to see improvement in the reading levels of students entering Birch, and he was clear with the high school that he expected to see more Birch students in honors and advanced placement (AP) classes and on their graduation rosters. The principal spoke at length about his efforts to ensure that Birch students were successful in high school:

> With [the high school], we've worked this year in a couple different ways to see, ah, to make bridges for—specifically to make bridges for minority students, but all of our students. Build bridges for our minority students to be successful and take full advantage of the things [the high school] has to offer them. . . . For example . . . in September, when we realized we had thirty college-level readers in the school and all but two were minority students, I met with their parents, the [the high school] principal, and the [high school] counselor and shared with the parents what they need to do to take advantage of AP courses while their child is at [the high school]. Because these parents, not always, but many of the parents didn't know about AP classes. For different reasons they are unfamiliar with how the system works and so . . . we know if the parent wants something to happen, that's a good influence. It's a great influence. And of course, we're not over there [in the high school], but the parent will still be with the child, and hopefully the parent is realizing, "Oh, great, this is a great way to get essentially free college." One of the parents, after that evening said, "I wish I would have known this for my other kids." . . . So, we're educating the parents on how to take advantage of the system if they don't already know. And that's an easy thing to watch the numbers on, isn't it? . . . We can watch to see. Each year we can run numbers to see how many former [Birch] students were in

AP classes. And we've met with [the high school] faculty three times and shared with them the reading growth with our low kids, and we showed them where they start and where they end. And they, ah, they can't help but like us after that because they are realizing, you know, we're not being lazy over here. We are actually moving the kids, but we're just getting a third of our kids reading on a third-grade level or lower. OK, so . . . we've shared with the [high school] faculty that we're looking for those AP numbers to go up. So we are giving them gentle but firm pressure. We'd like to see those numbers go up, and we are asking them for feedback on what our kids don't know that they need to know so that we can be training them to be able to take advantage of the cool things and life-changing things that they could be a part of at [the high school]. So it's not adversarial but it's tough. I mean, we're sending a clear message.

Mr. More identifies a step-by-step process in which he engaged to begin to break down the systemic inequity impacting his students. He first recognized that the system is broken: He wondered about the "college-level readers" from Birch and the missing "bridges" to ensure Birch students succeed at every point along the educational pipeline. He continued working to change the broken system, and he did so through multiple points of entry and strategies. He talked to educators, educational leaders, counselors, and parents, and he was armed with clear and convincing data. He also named specific structural pieces that were broken when he pointed to the number of students in AP courses and the lack of information provided to parents. Mr. More recognized that this work is not a one-shot effort; instead, it requires constant reminders, soliciting feedback, and sharing potentially uncomfortable information with various institutional actors. And finally, he pressed for change in the outcomes—noting that his work was "not adversarial, but it's tough."

These efforts are especially important given the context of Birch and the Zion School District. All Birch students attend the same high school unless they move out of the school's boundaries or complete a bureaucratic process requesting to attend another district school. Although this high school has a good reputation among White, middle-class families from east-side communities, the graduation rate at this high school for students from Birch is an abysmal 25 percent. High school officials have noted that a very high percentage of their school's overall tardies come from students living in "the [Birch] zip code," and it is well known that teachers at the high school regularly comment on the "problems" they face with "those kids from [Birch]." So Mr. More was engaged in what he called a "focused PR [public relations] campaign" to change the perception of his school, his students, and the communities Birch serves; his efforts were largely aimed at his Zion School District colleagues.

Mr. More's efforts illustrate a particular kind of nice approach to engaging systemic change. He noticed patterned unfairness and strategized about how to effect change within his district, but his efforts were carefully shaped around clear data and straightforward messages connected to the educational mission of schools. Mr. More did not call out racism as such, and he did not point to specific people or groups of people who need to be held accountable.

The work Mr. More explained highlights the importance of the entire system of schooling and that a systemic approach is needed to truly bring about change. Advocating for students throughout their educational careers within the district can still be linked to notions of equality and meritocracy, but it is work that begins to create an equitable system rather than just relying on an assumption of a mythological equal system. Unfortunately, this work was limited by ever-present commitments to restrictive formal equality and pressures of standardized accountability. These limitations are highlighted by a Birch teacher: "All we're doing [at Birch] is teaching the kids who will help our scores, and it isn't even questioned by anyone because it's so much the culture of the school. It's talked about all the time in meetings and nobody even questions it. . . . But you don't have time to have those conversations . . . Our funding is related to [improving test scores], and if we lose, we lose money. But if other schools lose, they just lose a little reputation." So even with a principal who articulates and engages strategies for reversing patterned and systemic inequity, the "culture of the school" defaults to the lure of meritocratic competition.

Equality, Success, and Whiteness

As the cases of Birch and Spruce illustrate, diversity-related policy and practice in schools is typically framed by notions of meritocracy and equality. The ways educators engage equality can take many forms, but as long as it centers individualized sameness at the expense of structural power mechanisms, equality will never allow equity. Put another way, it is impossible to achieve equity through equal means (Brayboy, Castagno, and Maughan 2007). Indeed, "remaining faithful to the racial-equality creed enables us to drown out the contrary manifestations of racial domination that flourish despite our best efforts" (Bell 2004, 188). We cannot continue to privilege restrictive formal equality, in any of its forms, if we hope to achieve justice and fairness for every student, family, and community. When using the standard of equity, we should ask ourselves what characteristics or circumstances are significant, what results or outcomes are fair and just, and what specific strategies are most likely to lead to the desired results or outcomes. Some of these criteria were beginning to drive the work at Birch, but the allegiance to restrictive formal equality continued to operate just below the surface.

In addition to the distinct but shared allegiance to equality and meritocracy, Spruce and Birch Secondary Schools also shared a focus on targeted public relations campaigns and building particular reputations. In both cases, educators strove for what they believed to be an excellent, high-quality education that would, in turn, foster success among their students. The meaning of excellence and success was different in each school due to their varying contexts and the associated pressures of standardized accountability under NCLB. But although the drive for excellence and success looked different in each school, it operated in service to the same end. Although excellence and success are cast as neutral pursuits that benefit all students equally, they actually function to normatively sort students. This normative and sorting mechanism, hidden under the guise of equality, is a powerful tool of whiteness in schools.

In 2006, the stakes involved in these efforts around excellence and success were very different than they are now with the massive increase in choice initiatives in the Salt Lake area and across the country. Public schools can no longer rely on a given enrollment based on their catchment areas. Schools are now in competition with other schooling options; they are also competing against one another for federal grants and philanthropic funds. These added elements of competition, liberalism, and neoliberalism are additional manifestations of whiteness. Given the ideological and institutional nature of whiteness, there exists a zero-sum game in which there will be losers and there will be winners. Competition assumes a level playing field and fairly executed rules, and the structure of the game reinforces the myth of meritocracy and allegiance to equality. These themes are explored in the following chapter, but they have been lurking just below the surface for some time.

CHAPTER FIVE

Obscuring Whiteness with Liberalism

Winners and Losers in Federal School Reform

We may have reached a moment in which theoretically, empirically, and strategically it's time to shift gears (or multiply). If institutions are organized such that being white (or male, or elite) buys protection and if this protection necessitates the institutional subversion of opportunities for persons of color in policies/ practices that appear race-neutral, then liberal strategies for access are limited. By that I mean that those who have been historically excluded may disproportionately "fail" to perform "to standard." Some will drop out. A few will go nuts. A handful will survive as "the good ones." The institutional mantra of deficit and merit will triumph.

—MICHELLE FINE, "WITNESSING WHITENESS"

Birch Secondary School experienced a number of changes between 2006 and 2010, including the departure of Mr. More, the principal; the completion of a brand-new school building; the arrival and departure of another principal; and the arrival of yet a third principal, who started when Birch was awarded a federally funded School Improvement Grant (SIG) in 2010.

This chapter asks readers to fast-forward five years and take a look inside Birch during the implementation of a federally funded school-improvement effort. I recognize that the time lapse may cause readers to wonder what happened in the interim, but my point in jumping ahead to 2010–12 is to examine whether, how, and to what extent whiteness continues to operate given the current school-reform moment in which we find ourselves. Although some of the specific tools look different, the larger mechanisms of whiteness have not changed. There continue to be structural and institutional barriers standing in the way of equity, and there continue to be explanations and efforts that center the individual. Perhaps even more so than previous efforts to address diversity and equity in schools, SIG policy and practice highlight the power of policy to solidify racially patterned success and failure and, simultaneously, to obscure the work being done to entrench those patterns behind ideologies of individually based deficit and merit.

Reflecting on the School Improvement Grant at Birch, a veteran teacher explained that "this is supposed to be an effort that is supposed to bridge the achievement gap, make things more equal; but right now what's happening is it's just making us more different, way more different." This teacher identifies the good intentions behind the SIG program but simultaneously points out that the reform effort is not actually doing nice things within his school. Indeed, exacerbating "differences" and missing the target on equality are not nice outcomes within schools. As the teacher points out, themes from the previous chapters continue to be evident at Birch. The way sameness and difference come into contact in educators' narratives, their appeals to equality, and their well-intended efforts to advance equity—all these elements of whiteness continue to operate in the new federally driven school-reform movement. But mapped onto these themes is a pointed allegiance to classical liberal ideas about the individual and social change.

Liberalism, with its steadfast protection of the individual and individual rights, has been a recurring theme in the previous chapters. This chapter centers these concepts and illustrates how liberalism and individualism are at work through a federally driven effort to improve academic achievement in schools serving youth of color and those from low-income communities. I suggest that analyzing SIG policy and practice through a lens of liberalism highlights how current federal school reform results in a neoliberal transformation of schools in which the individual is held staunchly responsible for failure that is institutionally predetermined, inequity is further entrenched, and the outcomes are understood to be both natural and acceptable.

The first half of this chapter analyzes SIG policy, and the second half examines the actual experience and impact of the School Improvement Grant at Birch Secondary School. Before exploring SIG policy and practice, it will be helpful to understand some fundamental tenets of liberalism. The preceding teacher's quote highlights the tension between efforts to advance equality in the face of stark differences and patterned inequity. Building on the previous chapter's discussion of equality, this chapter examines current school-reform efforts in order to illustrate the trouble in relying on classical liberal tenets and corresponding tropes of *the individual* and *social change* absent a commitment to justice. Liberalism maintains educators' focus on individuals so that structural barriers and institutionalized patterns remain invisible.

Classical Liberalism, the Individual, and Whiteness

Classical liberalism is characterized by a number of ideas and values that might otherwise be understood as wholly American. Three tenets of classical liberal thought are individualism, egalitarianism, and meliorism (Cochran 1999; Dawson 2003; Locke 1986; Mill 1982; Olson 2004; Starr 2008). *Individualism* asserts the ethical primacy of the human being against the pressures of social collectivism. In other words, the individual is the main concern within a liberal framework. *Egalitarianism* assigns equal moral worth and status to all individuals, so each individual is the same within the liberal framework. *Meliorism* asserts that successive generations can improve their sociopolitical arrangements. Individuals can improve, and individuals can also improve society, through hard work. Meliorism implies that progress is important and that the betterment of society is dependent on both individual and societal progress. These three tenets of liberalism cut across what we tend to think of as "liberal" and "conservative" ideas in the United States; rather, they are nice values to which most Americans subscribe regardless of political affiliation. In the following sections, I employ these three liberal tenets to analytically unpack SIG policy at the federal level and SIG practice at Birch.

Examining the School Improvement Grant through a liberal framework also highlights the ways public education is currently undergoing a neoliberal transformation. Classical liberalism and neoliberalism are certainly linked, and both enjoy such prevalence as to be considered an "ideological monoculture" with no other alternatives (Ross and Gibson 2007). Although rarely used in mainstream U.S. discourse, neoliberalism describes the current economic, and increasingly social, policy perspective embraced by most Americans. As Wayne Ross and Rich Gibson (2007) note, "The free market, private enterprise, consumer choice, entrepreneurial initiative, deleterious effects of government regulation, and so on, are the tenets of neoliberalism" (2). Both classical liberalism and neoliberalism minimize the relevance of context, relationality, and community. This overlap between liberalism and neoliberalism exists because of the primacy of the individual—an emphasis that is firm, resilient, and unfriendly to equity. Many current conversations in education revolve around neoliberalism and its impact on schools, youth, and communities.

This chapter advances these conversations by introducing the ways liber-alism, neoliberalism, and whiteness intertwine with devastating effects on youth of color, low-income youth, and communities like the Zion School District.

The energy and focus of SIG reform efforts are centered on issues that divert attention away from the inequity and injustice so prevalent in schools and are therefore consistent with niceness. Struggles over policy implementation, the rules of competition, divisions between players, and the meaning of reform all result in an absence of struggle over whether all youth are actually learning, what the nature of schooling is for various groups of students, and the extent to which schools are engaging commu-nities in healthy ways. Liberalism shapes the issues and struggles that get our attention, effectively glossing over the students and communities most harmed by these phenomena. Liberalism, then, is an important iteration of whiteness in the U.S. context, and it provides an extremely effective vehicle through which whiteness operates.

SIG Policy: Schools Take Your Mark, Get Set, Go!

Since 2009, the U.S. Department of Education has authorized more than $4.5 billion for School Improvement Grants and made these funds avail-able only to Title I schools whose achievement records are in the lowest 5 percent within their state. This federally funded school-improvement effort is related to the more commonly known Race to the Top program, but it is specifically aimed at and only available to schools identified as the lowest performing in each state. The SIG program was initially conceived as a policy under the 2002 No Child Left Behind Act. It was not funded, however, until 2007—and even then, it was only awarded minimal funds. In 2009, the SIG program was transformed and expanded through the passage of President Obama's American Recovery and Reinvestment Act.

The SIG reform model is part of "a long, historical trend in which the federal government has increasingly leveraged its comparatively small financial contribution to public K–12 education to bring about highly specified changes in school organizations and practices" (Dee 2012, 3). This reform model includes elements of teacher and principal effective-ness, instructional reform, extended learning time, increased community engagement in schools, operational flexibility and support, and the use of various community services needed by youth (Dee 2012). These are changes advanced by school-reform movements at various points over at least the past thirty years. Although the reform model is not new, what goes unnamed and unarticulated in the SIG program is the primacy of individualism and specifically defined calls for social change. As long as educators remain invested in liberal, and thus individually based, ideologies, persistent structural inequities also remain intact.

In what follows, I analyze SIG policy at the federal level and suggest that its foundation in liberal notions of the individual and social change encourages schools to compete under assumptions of equality and meritocracy. But the scales are unevenly weighted, so educational debts continue to compile against schools like Birch, while successes at schools like Spruce appear to be the result of individual effort and merit.

Why the School Improvement Grant? Why Now?

Among educational leaders and social commentators, one interpretation of this federal school-reform effort is that the SIG project is designed to close the persistent achievement gaps not addressed through the No Child Left Behind Act. This rationale positions School Improvement Grants as advancing equity. Another interpretation is that the SIG project is designed to advance the privatization of education and further entrench a market model among schools. There is a complicated, and yet also simple, line of reasoning at work here on both sides of the debate. On the one hand, liberalism criticizes government involvement, and so the SIG effort can be constructed as too interventionist, overly micromanaging, and overstepping the federal role in education. Under this framework, government should back off and let individual schools step up to the plate and compete in the open market for customers (i.e., students) by proving their value. And if schools are unable or unwilling to engage in this competition, or if they simply do not make it, the subsequent consequences (school sanctions, closures, etc.) are well deserved. On the other hand, government involvement is welcomed if it is aimed at protecting or even advancing individual rights and entitlements. So School Improvement Grants are an acceptable intervention if they help build a structure for competitive individualism among consumers (i.e., students and schools themselves). Either way, we can see how liberalism, individualism, and neoliberalism are engaged but also naturalized.

Alongside these debates, the SIG program is framed at the federal level as a much-needed response to the stagnantly poor education offered to youth of color and students from low-income backgrounds. School Improvement Grants are publicly linked to the economic well-being of the nation and to ideologies of meritocracy and individualism. In May 2012, responding to a study of California schools receiving SIG funds that showed academic improvement in the state's lowest performing schools after just one year of SIG funding, U.S. Secretary of Education Arne Duncan noted, "Educators and school leaders cannot give up on making far-reaching improvements in student learning in our lowest-performing schools. Children only get one shot at a good education. And Dee's new study reminds us that poverty is not destiny" (Duncan 2012). The discourse here is steeped in notions of individualism, helping, paternalism, and urgency. Teachers are implored to "not give up." The assumption is that individual teachers do make a difference and that student success is largely dependent on educators' efforts and determination. While individual teachers certainly matter, my point here is that teachers can only make limited gains with students as long as the system continues to rely on inequity as its foundation. Duncan further invokes the liberal trope of the individual by remarking that "poverty is not destiny." In other words, one's socioeconomic standing, which is unequivocally tied to one's access to resources (i.e., healthy food, good schools, quality medical care, etc.), does not actually impact one's likelihood of success. Within this framework, change is the result of individual work and results in individual success. Furthermore, the SIG effort is framed as a good, and a decidedly nice, effort to improve education for youth of color and those from low-income communities. As such, it is potentially dangerous to critique the SIG program. But it is precisely this framing that masks the institutionally sanctioned inequity and whiteness that continue to operate through this well-intended educational policy.

States award SIG funds to eligible schools based on a competitive application process, so schools that have consistently struggled to serve students compete against one another for a limited pot of money. This is typical of the zero-sum game implied in liberal ideologies and, by extension, in whiteness. It is not possible for everyone to access much-needed resources. When resources go to one entity, they must be withheld from another. This pits entities (in this case, schools and districts) against one another in a competition that belies the actual problem—that is, that the entire system of education is structured inequitably and that that inequity is the foundation of whiteness. Race is central to the competition for SIG funds because it is primarily students of color who reside in schools eligible to compete. Awarding funds to schools struggling to serve students of color is the sort of unequal approach that might be needed to advance equity. Unfortunately, there are other mechanisms at work that thwart this possibility.

The goal of the SIG program is "turning around the nation's lowest performing schools." Even in the program's name, we see an appeal to social change: "improve" schools and "turn around" our worst schools.

Implied here is that such change is both necessary and possible, and that it is possible through strategies outlined by the federal government and carried out by individual districts, schools, principals, and teachers. Schools that are awarded SIG funds must undergo significant reform under one of four models outlined by the U.S. Department of Education:

1. *Transformation model.* Replace the principal, reform instruction, increase learning time, and provide "flexibility and support."
2. *Turnaround model.* Same as transformation model, but also must replace at least 50 percent of the staff.
3. *Restart model.* Close the school and reopen it as a charter school.
4. *School-closure model.* Close the school and reassign students to a higher-performing school.

Of the schools awarded SIG funds thus far nationwide, 74 percent have adopted the transformation model, 20 percent have adopted the turnaround model, 4 percent have adopted the restart model, and 2 percent have adopted the school-closure model. In other words, the model requiring the least drastic measures has been adopted by the most number of schools. This is not surprising when viewed through a lens of whiteness: Acquiescence to the status quo allows inequity to go unquestioned and unaddressed.

Inequity also thrives because, within the SIG reform model, there is a mismatch between the location of power and the location of responsibility. As one Birch teacher described, "So the district says, 'Here's how you're going to do it.' The school implements it, it doesn't work, and then it feels like it's the teachers' fault or the school's fault." The power of the purse strings and decisions with broad impact lie at the federal and state levels and, to some degree, with districts. But the responsibility for change and blame when things do not go well lies with schools, principals, and teachers. The federal government holds the funds, defines the options for school-improvement models that schools can adopt, and determines eligibility requirements. The states then distribute funds based on competitive applications, and they monitor the implementation of school-improvement efforts. But the principals and teachers ultimately carry out the hard work and, more important, take the blame when efforts do not produce the sought-after results. Thus the schooling of youth is determined by policies and decisions made far removed from their immediate space and place. This mismatch is not unlike the patterns I described in chapter 1, whereby responsibility for equity is displaced, making accountability for equity almost impossible. The tendency to relinquish responsibility is consistent with both niceness and the liberal privileging of individual autonomy because it can be framed as allowing others to self-actualize and take leadership. The problem, of course, is that if leadership and accountability for equity are relinquished by everyone, then no one does anything about it.

The Individual: A Liberal Distraction from Structural Problems

Recall that a central tenet of liberalism is a focus on the individual. Liberalism posits that the individual is of utmost importance: Individual rights are to be stringently protected, and individuals are autonomous agents acting within the world. It is easy to think about students and teachers as individuals, but under the SIG program, schools are also made into—and treated like—individuals. This is not unlike the notion that corporations are individuals, with the ability to enter and enforce contracts, sue and be sued, and exercise and protect certain rights and entitlements. If an entire school is an individual, it now has its own identity, agency, and culpability. This has important implications for the ways schools get talked about, managed, and assigned both rights and responsibilities. For example, a school can be sanctioned and even shut down as a result of persistently low test scores. Lost in this consequence is the way academic failure is institutionally patterned across the entire educational system. As individuals, schools' presumed autonomy justifies their responsibility for decisions and outcomes. But the decisions are actually made elsewhere. And the outcomes are largely dependent on *both* resources that they have little control over *and* larger structures of schooling, race, and power.

The competition inherent in the SIG program highlights the way schools are viewed as individuals. Competition among individuals is acceptable, and even encouraged, within a liberal framework, and under the SIG program, struggling schools enter into a competitive game for a prize that they cannot all be granted. The fact that there is a \$4.5 billion payout for this game diverts attention away from the stadium in which the game is being played. But this stadium is fraught with legacies of race and power dominance, including health disparities, justice inequities, economic liabilities, and educational debts. Liberalism—and its concomitant individualism, egalitarianism, and meliorism—averts our gaze to the game and the trophy so that we lose sight of the conditions under which we are playing. In other words, we know that our system of schooling has historically worked to the advantage of some at the expense of others. We also know that schooling is political and holds high stakes for students, families, and communities. But the liberal emphasis on individual competition allows these facts to fade into the background as we get wrapped up in making sure we get the money, spend it in a timely fashion, and maintain an honorable score. This avoidance of the larger context of the competition is an effective mechanism of both niceness and whiteness.

Competition is one place where we can see how schools are made into individuals, but we also see how schools are framed as individuals through the discourse of "school improvement" and "school turnaround." Just as educators once talked about remediating at-risk students, policy makers now talk about remediating at-risk schools. This is important because of the way it lulls us into compassion and empathy for schools. Schools are no longer institutions that we must work to ensure are serving all people equitably. Instead, schools are the individuals that now need our care and compassion. Again, it becomes easy to lose sight of actual people, relationships, and communities when our focus is turned to the school as an individual. When schools become individuals, it masks the real issue—that students are not being served equitably. This distraction cloaks the needs of individuals and groups of students within the larger "reform effort."

Alongside this individualism of schools, we see the meliorist element of liberalism played out in multiple ways within SIG policy. At the school level, the thinking goes that if money is funneled into a struggling school, the school should be able to "turn around." The federal government provides schools with extra money in an effort to level the playing field and ensure equal opportunity. SIG policy tells schools to pull themselves up to the level of the schools across town. And if they cannot meet that standard, even with the extra funds, then surely schools either have not tried hard enough or are simply unable. Under this framework, equal opportunity is a code for maintaining the status quo and ignoring the structural issues at play. Although the SIG policy positions itself in stark contrast to the punitive argument that says, "If we take money away from failing schools, they will be forced to improve," the end result is the same. In both cases, schools, as individual entities, are assumed to be solely and independently responsible for their own fate. But inequity is a structural problem that cannot be addressed by engaging either schools, students, or teachers as individuals. Instead, schools should be treated as part of a larger whole in need of systemic change. This sort of change can only occur when we are able to reframe and reorient the conversation around patterned inequity, ideologies of dominance, and unjust institutions.

At the teacher level, the thinking goes that if the SIG program mandates more instructional time in core subject areas and more professional development, the teacher should be able to "turn around." The policy implies that professional development and ten extra minutes in math, language arts, and science will result in better teaching. The operating assumption of the SIG program is that teachers were not doing a good job previously but that with these imposed remediations, their practice will improve.

At the student level, it is the same story. If youth have "more time on task" in their core academic subjects, test scores will improve, and we can conclude they are being better educated. This is a story line of educational reform that we all know. It is also a nicely packaged meliorist discourse about improvement through hard work and the open possibilities for improving one's lot.

Thus the SIG program locates the problem of "underperforming" schools with individual students, teachers, and schools and therefore masks structural problems that are actually about power and race. It relies on assumptions that meritocracy will prevail and that equal opportunity exists given the added resources awarded to "failing schools." Under this model, emphasis is placed on discrete units that need assistance and remediation, rather than on larger patterns that are housed in systems and ideologies. This masking of structural and institutionalized phenomena is a consistent feature of liberalism. Through its design and implementation, SIG policy holds tight to individuals as the central unit of analysis. Something is not working, so fix it. If the attempted fix did not work, try again—and keep trying a few more times. This model keeps energy and attention on the individual, since that is what is broken. Attention is not spent on the structures and systems of dominance. And it is very difficult to change something that is not obviously broken.

But what if the individual is never actually meant to be fixed? This, in fact, is the suspicion of many teachers working within the SIG context at Birch. As one educator shared with me, "It's almost like they're setting us up for failure." And another explained, "I feel so demoralized right now. I feel like this grant is destroying me, and it's destroying the school. It's destroying all my teacher friends, and it's destroying the kids." Teachers suspected that SIG policy assumes that individuals—whether they are students, teachers, or schools—are expendable. This is a word teachers used frequently in our conversations about the School Improvement Grant. One clearly noted, "I feel that I'm expendable," and this feeling extended to others in the school community as well.

Students were believed to be expendable in the sense that they are the ultimate "guinea pigs" for current educational experiments. Teachers were believed to be expendable in the sense that they are fairly easily removed and replaced within SIG schools. Birch teachers explained that they were repeatedly told by district leaders, "If you don't like it, you can leave." Principals were most certainly believed to be expendable, since replacing them was a condition of accepting SIG money, and they are often relocated if they do not produce the desired results. And finally, schools were believed to be expendable because if they are not completely closed through the School Closure Model, they are closed as public institutions and reopened as publicly funded private institutions through the Restart Model. And if they are not subject to one of these conditions, they are expected to "turn around" or "transform" into something new. As one teacher articulated, "I think the purpose of the grant is to somehow restructure the school." Indeed, most teachers I talked with were keenly suspicious that the SIG program was a cover for something larger—some sort of bigger agenda in which their participation was not genuinely designed for their betterment or the betterment of their students or the local community.

This notion of the expendable individual is a bit of a paradox within my data and, I think, within liberalism. On the one hand, the individual is of central importance and matters greatly. But on the other hand, individuals are expendable. This is precisely why an analysis of race and power matter. The primacy versus expendability of individuals is not random or coincidental. Particular individuals matter a lot. Particular other individuals do not and are expendable. Consider the fact that policy makers never set up SIG-like programs in their own children's schools. Nor do they treat their own children as guinea pigs for the latest round of school-reform efforts. Their children are safely ensconced in schools that do not need the "help" offered through programs like the School Improvement Grant. Their children are protected from the casualties that result from such efforts. Children of color and those from low-income communities are the obvious casualties. But still, every student, educator, and community is harmed when whiteness is reified through liberalism.

Reifying Whiteness through Policy

Critical race scholars have convincingly argued that the discourse of liberal individualism has at times served as a cover for coordinated collective group interests. In other words, the courts, policy makers, and anyone with power can easily and effectively employ liberalism to rationalize decisions. In the case of School Improvement Grants, the framing of schools as individuals, the ensuing competition, and the appeal to social change are all attractively packaged within a classical liberal paradigm. It is difficult to argue against this neatly bundled reform model.

Why, for example, would one want to question additional funds being funneled to schools serving youth of color and those from low-income families? Similarly, why would we be critical of a program that asks educators to provide traditionally ill-served students with better instruction and higher expectations for academic achievement? Indeed, to raise these questions seems to position one as antiequality, antiopportunity, and even anti-American. This is the seductiveness of liberalism.

But it bears repeating: The liberal discourse has often served as a cover for coordinated group interests. So whose group interests are being protected here? What group interests are being at once obscured and reinforced through SIG policy? In other words, if certain individuals are expendable within liberalism and under SIG policy, we should ask ourselves what the system gains by expelling them. The gain is the erosion of a public commitment to the good of the whole. Or, put another way, the gain is the erosion of community. Without a public commitment to what is good, equitable, and just for everyone, we become even further committed to the individual. Individualism—and the ideologies of meliorism and egalitarianism that correspond to individualism—is both normalized and legitimized. Liberalism, then, is validated and further entrenched.

If everybody matters, and matters equally, then the call for equity and for real reform against whiteness would be easy to make. Instead, under a liberal framework, individuals matter, and certain individuals matter a lot more than other individuals. This is foundational to our economic system, and it plays out in countless instances in our nation's history. Manifest destiny is a prime example of the way liberalism privileges certain individuals over others and over the good of a community; it is also a prime example of the meliorist element because "progress" was viewed as necessary and morally right. The SIG effort is similarly positioned as necessary and the obviously right thing given the failure of many schools and students across the nation. But the moral expediency of liberal approaches often masks the loss incurred.

Within the SIG reform model, there will be both winners and losers. A few will succeed, and many will fail. The successes provide evidence of an effective system. They allow educators and reformers to say, "See, it IS possible to turn around a school given these conditions!" The failures, however, also serve an important purpose. They provide a target; they give us something to keep working on, to keep feeling good about our efforts, because at least we are trying. We have a project, and liberalism thrives on projects. Remember that meliorism is the idea that we can improve society, society's institutions, and our individual selves with a little hard work and determination. If we just keep at it, surely change will occur. The appeal of change and the assumption that progress is always good masks the casualties that occur. Equally problematic is that liberalism does not implore us to ensure equity now. Instead, it encourages us to just keep trying to slowly chip away at what is actually systemic, institutionalized, and pervasive.

These concerns are exacerbated because not just any teachers and students are impacted by SIG policy. The teachers who are impacted are those in schools serving youth who have been the least well served for generations. Also impacted are the communities whose educational debt (Ladson-Billings 2006) has yet to be repaid and is, in fact, compounding daily, monthly, and annually. Liberalism structures this arrangement so that it seems natural, commonsensical, and even ethical. Schools that have been awarded SIG funds are most often urban high schools serving youth of color and those from low-income communities. Consistent with this trend, Birch serves more than 90 percent students of color and 80 percent students who qualify for free or reduced-price lunches. This is not insignificant.

Engaging in a liberal project like the federal SIG program in schools that house students of color and those from low-income communities maintains patterns of inequity within our system of schooling. These youth are not gaining access to the kind of schooling provided to privileged White youth. Instead, they are meant to feel lucky to have been given the opportunity to improve their lot. They are meant to feel hopeful that the playing field really is leveling out. They are meant to believe that their hard work will prevail. And they will be held responsible for the end result.

But the end result is not really within any individual student's, teacher's, or school's control. Instead, the results are largely influenced by our ideologies and systems of race dominance. By centering individuals, SIG policy nicely obscures structural arrangements, maintains an ideology of goodwill, and accepts the ensuing snail's pace of reform. As a system of racial dominance, whiteness is therefore not only engaged but actually reinforced through School Improvement Grants. Whiteness maintains power and privilege by perpetuating and legitimating the status quo while simultaneously maintaining a veneer of neutrality, equality, and compassion: This is precisely what we see happening with School Improvement Grants. Whiteness encourages people to behave in particular ways that then reify whiteness; the result is that youth, families, communities, and educators are all buried in the toxic soil of whiteness.

The SIG Effort at Birch: Pursuing "Truth" at the Expense of Equity

So what happens to SIG policy in a real school? What happens when liberal tropes of the individual and the social change embedded in the SIG policy hit the ground and intersect with actual people and communities with varying interests and investments? In the first round of funding for the federal SIG program, Birch was awarded monies to embark on a three-year reform project. As an external evaluator hired by the district to provide feedback on the SIG efforts,[1] I visited the school and conducted lengthy interviews with the majority of Birch teachers, staff, and administrators on four separate occasions over the three-year grant. The following sections look squarely at Birch educators' narratives about their experiences with the School Improvement Grant over the course of two years. Birch is typical of the vast majority of schools that have been awarded SIG funds across the United States in terms of student demographics and achievement levels, so it is important to examine how this common educational reform effort is educated in and educating for whiteness.

Data from my school visits and conversations with teachers and administrators highlight a tense environment with multiple contests for control, struggles to make meaning, and intersecting allegiances. In the end, the ensuing divisiveness diverts educators' energy away from what really matters—teaching children and ensuring that they learn. So the contests for control and struggles over meaning are, perhaps paradoxically, nice diversions. Equity gets lost in the shuffle, and whiteness continues to reign.

Contests for Control

Implementing the School Improvement Grant at Birch was fraught with ongoing contests of power, struggles to determine authority, and negotiations over meaning. Both teachers and administrators readily articulated these dynamics and some of the problematic outcomes they produced within the school. Contests for control began with the introduction of the SIG program to Birch teachers, advanced through the first two years of implementation as teachers and administrators continued to butt heads, and culminated in the departure of half of the teaching force and the principal after the second year of funding. Every player in these contests for control relied on liberal tenets of individualism, meliorism, and egalitarianism. The contests were only possible because students of color become objects of the struggle. The active players (here, teachers and administrators) obtained their sense of self, their identity, and their individual agency through the dismissal of students and communities of color as having any role within the SIG efforts. In the end, liberalism ultimately collapsed in on itself within the walls of Birch.

Almost every teacher at Birch expressed significant concern over the initial application for the School Improvement Grant. The grant application was written by central office personnel and shared with teachers after the grant had been secured. Reflecting on the application, one teacher explained, "There's a lot of negative stuff about us teachers that [isn't] . . . even true. This person who wrote the grant didn't even ever talk to us personally and has never been in my classroom." In another conversation, a second teacher echoed the same frustration: "It almost sounded like they had to write something to get the grant. So they had to prove that we are incompetent and unable to handle things when that is an outright lie . . . it was inappropriate." Another shared, "We had no confidence that any of it had any sense of reality. It was just put in there to get this federal grant . . . and it didn't really reflect the school," and still another noted, "I would say there are misrepresentations. And that is angering." Absent from the Birch teachers' discontent were the students and communities Birch is meant to serve. The struggle here is over the right to determine how teachers (primarily, though not exclusively, White) are represented. Are they competent, highly qualified, and effective? Do they know their students and the local community? Are they able to deliver the kind of education that is needed at Birch? These are the kinds of questions teachers felt were at stake. Whiteness is employed vis-à-vis the liberal investment in individual autonomy and authority to define oneself.

On the other side of this struggle over the SIG application sat the central office administrator who wrote and secured the grant for the district. A middle-aged White woman, Ms. Floyd articulated a staunch commitment to the need for change at Birch. Her commitment was framed around the need for individual teachers who share the Zion School District's "vision that every child will succeed" and who are "able to get the results we need to see at [Birch]." She was not unique in her assessment that many Birch teachers had "not gotten the job done" and were more interested in union solidarity and the mantra of site-based leadership than they were in student learning and success. Ms. Floyd admitted that the initial SIG application could have benefitted from greater input from teachers, but she also pointed out that the application was due under a very tight time frame and that teachers were off contract for the summer when she was working on the application.

Central to Ms. Floyd's perspective is the call for change and an appeal to particular outcomes at Birch. Standing in the way of progress is the teachers' union as well as the often-heard critique of veteran teachers who are "stuck in their ways." Ms. Floyd appeals to meliorism and the notion that change and progress are good and necessary. Here again we see a White actor determining the meaning and processes of change; still absent are youth and communities of color who recede into the background as objects of the change.

The ways the application represented Birch teachers and Birch as an institution was extremely troubling for teachers, but they were also troubled by the process through which the application and initial implementation were handled. There was a strong feeling among teachers that the grant was "imposed on the school" by central office leaders, and that it failed to build on successes the school had experienced in the past and current strengths in the school. Many teachers shared one colleague's sentiment: "We have this grant because it was imposed on us. The reason that the school was picked was because it had a history up until last year, the year before the grant, of not making Adequate Yearly Progress. But basically it was imposed on us."

Two years into the grant (which was funded for a total of three years), most Birch teachers continued to resist buying into it. One teacher reflected on the grant at the end of the second year of funding and shared that it "has a very punitive feel . . . instead of like, 'let's get in this together,' instead of inspiring leadership . . . 'If you've been here and you're inside the building, you don't have professional knowledge; we're going to bring it to you from the outside' . . . It makes you not have confidence in even yourself sometimes." The ongoing struggle teachers identified to determine the direction of SIG implementation was a direct assault on their individual autonomy, sense of purpose, and right to control the education offered in their school. These things are entitlements under a liberal understanding of what it means to be "American." Attempting to (re)gain them is a natural response of self-determined individuals.

On the other side of this contest for the natural rights of individuals sat the Birch principal, who was hired by central office leaders (primarily Ms. Floyd) and brought to Birch as a condition of the School Improvement Grant (recall that replacing the principal is a requirement when accepting SIG funding). Mr. Layton was a popular and, by all accounts, effective principal in another west-side school before being recruited to Birch to lead the SIG efforts. A tall White man with a quiet voice, he walked a fine line between articulating his ultimate role as the school leader and the value of teacher leadership. Mr. Layton had spent years navigating the Zion School District's context of site-based leadership and a generally powerful union, and he knew the challenges involved with taking the top position at Birch when the School Improvement Grant was awarded in 2010. After struggling during the first year of the School Improvement Grant's implementation to "bring everyone on board," he entered the second year of the program with a vocal "good riddance" to the many teachers who continued to voice discontent. In an ironic twist, he was relocated after the second year of the grant by central office leaders. On this moving stairway, individual leaders get bypassed by other individual leaders. Still lost are the students, their families, and the larger community.

These contests for control resulted in an absence of solidarity between teachers and the school administrative team. This divisiveness emerged in the initial days of the grant when teachers were upset about and resisted what they called a "top-down approach to the SIG leadership and implementation." As the grant progressed, some teachers began to feel like teacher input was more valued, but others did not, and the lack of trust and cohesion between teachers and administrators persisted. As one teacher explained, "We have no input on what is going to happen. Now we're starting to get a little input, but at first it was just what somebody else thought we needed. And it's still for the most part true." Another shared, "We are being listened to, but I don't feel like that matters. . . . The follow-through is 'Thanks for sharing; we understand a lot of you feel this way, but we're going to go ahead and do this other way anyway' . . . it's not impacting decisions." And still a third noted,

> I personally don't feel safe. I think other people feel less safe than I do. So, yeah, there's not a lot of trust in the building right now, not [in] . . . the administration here, not [in] . . . the administration downtown . . . there was sort of like a turnaround in the middle of the year where it went from only top down to "hey, you guys could have done what you wanted, this is all up to you, nothing is up to us." And, you know, we had a big one-day meeting about that, which did not instill any confidence for me because it was a complete turnaround from the way things were, and we're already in the deep, you know.

Considering the overall impact of the SIG program, a fourth teacher suggested, "I think the psychology of the grant needs to flip from teachers feeling like they're being punished to teachers feeling like they're being supported and valued."

The entire first year of the SIG program at Birch was spent negotiating these contests of control. Were teachers or administrators right in their interpretation? Whose grant was this? Who decided how implementation was going to look? How would disagreements be handled? In some ways, the answers to these questions do not really matter. What matters is the way in which whiteness operates and gets strengthened through teachers' and administrators' investments in liberalism. The resulting anger, distrust, lack of buy-in, and divisiveness was palpable each time I entered the front doors of Birch. These contests for control and struggles to make meaning left little room for the Birch community to strategize about how to shape the School Improvement Grant into something genuinely useful and powerful. This, in fact, demonstrates how liberalism is a well-functioning mechanism of whiteness. Absent an effective use of the SIG program to dismantle structural inequity, patterns of success and failure become acceptable and rationalized through ideologies of meritocracy, equal opportunity, and individualism.

Liberal notions of the individual and social change facilitate these struggles for control, the ensuing divisiveness, and the value placed on individual autonomy and empowerment. On the one hand, we have an abstract, idealized notion of the individual. This is the individual we find referenced in policy, heralded in success stories, and employed in appeals to individual rights and protections. On the other hand, we have real, actually existing individuals—individuals who do not always conform to the trope operationalized in liberal discourse. These individuals struggle to achieve the autonomy, rights, and protections espoused in liberalism's idea of the individual. These individuals enter contests that they cannot all win—contests that result in divisiveness rather than solidarity. What does this have to do with whiteness? The tension between the individual as liberal trope and the individual as a material reality is racialized. The idealized notion of the individual is figuratively, and often literally, White, while the material reality of the individual is not.

The Meaning of Merit (Pay)

The awarding of SIG funds mandates that schools employ some system of merit-based pay for teachers. Linking one's compensation to specific job-related outcomes is a long-established practice in many industries, but it is a relatively new device being employed in schools. As the name suggests, merit-pay systems are perhaps a logical outcome of our society's allegiance to meritocracy. Merit pay is also consistent with the liberal notion that individuals work to maximize pleasure and are thus motivated by rewards for their labor. But critiques of employing merit-pay systems in schools include that it is difficult to directly link student learning solely to teacher practice, that student test performance may not be an accurate measure of either student learning or teacher effectiveness, that teacher quality is impacted by multiple factors not easily measured, and that teachers are not (or should not be) motivated by financial rewards. Because one of the primary mechanisms for using the SIG funds at Birch was to award merit pay to teachers, I want to explore what merit pay came to mean for teachers, how it maps onto the themes of liberalism, and what its implications are for whiteness.

At Birch, merit pay was composed of two strategies. All teachers could earn a bonus if the entire school met certain achievement levels on the state's standardized math, language arts, and science tests. In addition, teachers who taught the "core assessed subjects" of math, language arts, and science could earn another bonus at the end of the year if their particular students met certain achievement levels on the state tests. The first set of bonuses was figured and awarded to the school based on school-wide test performance. The additional bonus was figured and awarded to individual teachers based on individual student test performance. Whether at the school level or at the teacher level, this merit-pay system is a clear iteration of individualism, since it measures individual performance and rewards individuals. Through the merit-pay system, the School Improvement Grant presumes student achievement on standardized tests is solely an individually based act. Within this framework, test performance has no connection to systemic patterns of race dominance or power.

Teachers felt strongly that the merit-pay system resulted in a division of the teachers at Birch. As one teacher shared, "They divided the teachers big time. Some teachers are more important than others." The administrative team concurred, but they voiced only minimal concern over this outcome. Almost every teacher with whom I spoke expressed concerns about the divisiveness of the merit-pay system. They were concerned about the impact these divisions had on the sense of community within the school, the absence of collaborative relationships between teachers from different content areas and grade levels, and the resulting feelings of stress and isolation among teachers and throughout the entire school. Most teachers felt there was a division between the teachers who taught "core assessed" subjects (i.e., language arts, math, and science) and those who did not (everything else—from social studies to art, physical education, and so on). Most teachers and administrators attributed the divisiveness to the merit-pay system, since core-assessed teachers had the opportunity to earn a bonus that was twice as large as the bonus noncore, nonassessed teachers were able to earn.

What is ironic in all this is that the SIG model, and particularly the way merit pay was implemented at Birch, sorts teachers just as schooling sorts students. Through the operationalization of individualism via merit pay, Birch teachers are sorted and judged based on factors that largely lie outside their control. Although teachers see this sorting mechanism and its problematic outcomes among themselves, they do not see how schooling sorts their students every day. This irony illustrates the primary role of whiteness: critiquing sorting among a largely White teacher population does not call dominance into question, but critiquing racialized sorting among students does. In other words, merit-pay systems and the larger SIG reform model are structured so that students are lost while the focus centers on individual teachers and appropriately liberal issues.

An ongoing struggle related to the merit-pay system at Birch revolved around the meaning of the potential bonus at the end of the year. Teachers, with strong union support, made elaborate arguments about the additional time required in their work day and the corresponding absence of compensation for that time. Given the additional minutes they figured entered into their day, week, and year, they argued that if they were awarded the bonus, it was essentially compensation for the added time. If they were not awarded the bonus, however, they were "working for free" for many additional minutes, hours, and days throughout the year. Central office leaders and Birch's administrative team had a very different perspective. They argued that teachers were paid an annual salary, not an hourly wage, and that they "signed on to the additional responsibilities of [SIG] at the beginning." Administrators believed that teachers knew that the longer school days and additional days in the year would not be compensated under the "typical structure in which teachers are paid" but that the work was "needed to see the kind of results we want to see" and that it was "a requirement of the grant." They added that Birch teachers had the opportunity to earn "far more than teachers in other schools in the district" if they got the merit-pay bonus.

Linked to the concerns around the additional time required by the grant were concerns among teachers and counselors that their time was used very differently and was highly structured by the school's administrative team and central office leadership. The entire school counseling staff, for example, told me that they spent a majority of their time on scheduling and other administrative tasks. The counseling staff was concerned about how their time was being used under the SIG program, and they felt these changes were not to the students' benefit. As one school counselor noted, "This [the School Improvement Grant] takes counselors away from kids and away from contributing to the school in positive ways." Another counselor shared, "The [new, incoming students], especially, see us as schedulers, not as counselors." Teachers also talked about how their work day was far more structured. Most days there were school-wide or area-wide meetings before school and other committee responsibilities and professional developments after school. In thinking about the impact of the School Improvement Grant on their work, teachers noted, "SIG has impacted my time," and "my day is successfully structured." Perhaps more important, teachers and other school staff felt they had very little input into decisions about how to best use time before and after school. These were issues that were decided at another level—either among the school's leadership team or by the central office. Perhaps unsurprisingly, this is yet another contest of control prompted by liberal tenets of autonomy and individual self-determination. Educators, as individuals with particular rights and entitlements, have strong investments in their time and the sense of control over that time.

The fallout of this merit-pay system was that time and money became central. Whether symbolically or literally, time and money figured prominently in teachers' discourse and the ways both teachers and administrators understood the nature of SIG work and how that work should be rewarded. Teacher after teacher told me in our conversations that "I'm not doing my job better because I think I'm going to get a bonus at the end of the year; I'm not motivated by that. . . . If anything, I'm put off by that." And yet, the majority of my conversations with teachers somehow related to merit pay and teacher time.

In addition, student placement was affected because if a student was moved from one teacher to the next, it was difficult to determine which teacher should be credited, or docked, with his or her test scores. After the first year of the School Improvement Grant, district and school leadership decided to develop a system to award merit pay that employed a formula based on how long students had been at Birch and with which particular teachers. Students' bodies and learning were commodified into a particular point value, and then percentages were assigned to different classes and teachers based on where students had spent their time during the school year. Because the SIG program places so much importance on two areas—increased learning time in core tested subject areas and merit pay for teachers—school became almost solely about time and money. But time and money were diversions from the real issues at play. Just as the contests for control serve as liberal mechanisms of whiteness, so, too, do the attachments to time and money.

Losing Sight of Equity

What were the consequences of these contests for control and negotiations of power within the Birch community? How were Birch students, largely youth of color and youth from low-income communities, impacted by the School Improvement Grant? Since the SIG program is framed as an effort to improve student achievement and defines student achievement by standardized test scores, the good news is that test scores did rise for many students at Birch. The school made adequate yearly progress in both math and language arts after the first year of the grant, and scores improved slightly again after the second year. The bad news, however, is that relationships, community, climate, and health were all significantly compromised at Birch. The most striking pattern in my conversations with Birch teachers over the course of two years was the low morale and toxic climate throughout the school—a climate that was strikingly different than what I experienced five years earlier.

The divisiveness among adults at Birch, combined with the exhaustion experienced by many teachers due to the longer school days, additional meetings, and subsequent increase in the amount of work they took home, led to extremely low morale among the majority of teachers at Birch. By most accounts, morale was "the lowest it's been in years." Teachers described the morale in a number of ways, and these descriptions were consistent during the entire first two years of the grant:

- *Teacher 1:* "Teacher morale is at the lowest that I have ever seen it. Teachers are tired. They're burned out. They're stressed."
- *Teacher 2:* "I'm so demoralized right now. I feel like this grant is destroying me, and it's destroying the school. It's destroying all my teacher friends, and it's destroying the kids."
- *Teacher 3:* "I just think it's like being in a pressure cooker, and that's not conducive to having the kind of positive, supportive, and energetic atmosphere you need to raise student achievement."
- *Teacher 4:* "It's not easy to work here, and it is draining at times, but when you feel like you are going nowhere, when you don't have goals, you don't have a vision, you see things are not going anywhere, you're working hard but where's it going? And it's like on an emotional level, it's a lot more draining."

In addition, teachers believed that the morale was impacting the entire Birch community, and they pointed to support staff and substitute teachers as evidence of this. A number of teachers shared that they had observed substitute teachers "walk out in the middle of the day" and "refuse to come back" to Birch; this was not something teachers had witnessed in prior years. Additionally, teachers shared that the "support staff" was "very unhappy" at Birch; the janitors, for example, were extremely frustrated at the condition in which students left the school and the lack of behavioral expectations both during and after school.

Many teachers commented on the escalation of problematic student behaviors; as one Birch veteran noted, "I have never seen the kids so rude or act so entitled, and the graffiti is just getting worse and worse, and the damage too." Teachers explained that their students said that graffiti, fights, student absences, and other problematic behaviors had escalated because "they [the students] are angry; they don't want to be here longer than everybody else; they feel like they're being punished." When students are talked about, it is largely in the context of their "bad" behaviors from the perspective of teachers. Administrators were quick to counter these representations of students; instead, they invoked "bad" teachers as the root of most behavioral problems at Birch.

Never articulated in these contests for control and alternate meanings among teachers and administrators are the complexities of schooling, the role of schools as sorting institutions, or the social reproduction embedded and reified in our educational system. These factors are the fuel for structured, patterned, and pervasive inequity. This fuel and the subsequent inequity provide the soil in which whiteness thrives. It thrives, in part, because of the way liberal tenets are naturalized, and the resulting struggles and divisiveness are understood as the normal course of events. In fact, when I talked to school and central office leaders about these patterns, I was repeatedly told that it was "part of the process" and that "SIG schools across the country are experiencing similar challenges." But if we are able to remove the assumption of normalcy and instead center the pursuit of equity, we might be more compelled to educate against, rather than for, whiteness.

Another measure of the impact of the School Improvement Grant can be seen in teacher attrition. After each of the first two years of the SIG program, somewhere between one-quarter and one-third of the teaching staff left Birch. In other words, after two years of the reform effort, at least half, and potentially two-thirds, of Birch teachers were replaced by new teachers. Most of these departures were by veteran teachers who had spent the majority of their teaching careers at Birch. Most of them also explained that they had purposely chosen to teach at Birch because of the community it served, that they hoped to return to Birch "when this mess is straightened out," but that they had to leave to maintain their own physical and mental health. Most of the newly hired teachers were in the early years of their careers, and all of them were on provisional contracts at Birch. Clearly, the loss of veteran teachers and the introduction of newer teachers are not necessarily or always problematic. Indeed, it is often the case that newer teachers facilitate greater student learning and improved test scores. But an exodus of teachers to the extent seen at Birch should at least raise some red flags and prompt conversation. I saw no evidence that this was what happened at Birch.

Students were also lost through the School Improvement Grant because they either became passive objects or were entirely absent in teacher and administrator narratives about the School Improvement Grant at Birch. Through the contests for control, the struggles to make meaning, and the displays of autonomy, we rarely saw students or an indication that this work was really about students and their communities. Part of what happens when schools are made into individuals is that real individuals get lost. In the case of the SIG program, the transformation of schools into individuals obscures the role of students (and, to some extent, teachers) as individuals. But the other thing that happens—and this was evident at Birch—is that students are not really privy to the status of individuals within a racialized, liberal framework. As students of color, they do not factor into the idealized notion of the individual as a free-acting, autonomous, self-determined consumer with rights and entitlements worth protecting. While this may seem antithetical to liberalism's central concern with the individual, it is actually wholly consistent when viewed through the lens of whiteness. Race and power are never not at work.

Who Wins? Who Loses?

Returning to the teacher's quote that opened this chapter, we can see that his comment about the School Improvement Grant "making us more different" despite being aimed at "closing the achievement gap" is significant on multiple levels. First, given the policy itself, the reform model advanced, and the liberalism undergirding the SIG framework, it is questionable whether the mandate is to really extinguish the proverbial achievement gap. Surely the intent is to see some schools "turn around," but the intent also seems to include the failure of many schools and many students. This is the natural outcome of equal opportunity and meritocracy. Second, differences were actually exacerbated when SIG policy entered Birch. Contests for control, struggles over meaning making, and the ensuing divisiveness should not be underestimated as an insignificant "part of the process." Students were lost in all this and literally left behind. Indeed, these outcomes may be a natural part of the process when liberalism undergirds efforts purportedly aimed to bring about equity, but it is this naturalness that should alert us to the toxicity and ensuing harm. The lesson seems to be that although School Improvement Grants may raise student test scores, they destroy schools, students, and teachers in the process. Change is clearly hard, but here it is also destructive. Business as usual is much easier, but as previous chapters highlight, the status quo is also destructive.

The liberalism undergirding SIG policy and practice cannot be divorced from the neoliberal transformation of schools taking place across the nation. Describing similar federally driven school-reform efforts in Chicago, Pauline Lipman (2011) articulates this transformation and its implications:

> Neoliberals naturalize market forms, processes, and ways of thinking as the only way to organize society (Leitner, Peck, and Sheppard 2007). Neoliberal policy discourses are thus "politically neutral," based on technical criteria of "efficiency" and "effectiveness," thereby excluding discussion of values, philosophies, and social interests. Pragmatism or doing "what works" is the order of the day, allowing those in power to dismiss criticism as politically motivated, ideologically driven, and change resistant. Discourses of change are mobilized to naturalize certain kinds of change and to paint the opposition as defenders of the status quo. President Obama evoked this trope when he contended criticism of his neoliberal Race-to-the-Top, federal-education program "reflects a general resistance to change. We get comfortable with the status quo" (Obama 2010, 11–12).

The "discourse of change" was similarly adopted by the Birch administrative team and central office leadership. I was told numerous times that the SIG reforms were "necessary" and "if teachers aren't on board, good riddance to them, they can go elsewhere." Echoing this sentiment were comments from individuals in leadership positions about "a lot of dead weight" and "resistance to do anything new" among the teaching staff at Birch. Teachers were well aware of these discourses among their leaders and highly offended by them. Most teachers I spoke with admitted that some teachers fit that category (which would be true at any school, they added), but that it was an inaccurate representation of the majority of Birch teachers.

The problem, as Lipman points out, is that the discourse of change adopted by SIG leaders becomes the default position so that *any* questioning or criticism of SIG work gets immediately labeled as "resistant to change," "stuck in their ways," or "obstructionist." This discourse of change is compelling. "If neoliberals have succeeded in appropriating the discourse of change, in part this is because the power to act as a consumer has resonance in the face of entrenched failures of the welfare-state model and administration of public education, particularly in cities (Pedroni 2007)" (Lipman 2011, 65). Clearly, change is needed in education, and most of all in the spaces meant to serve youth of color and low-income youth. But this discourse of change has become a powerful tool of whiteness because of the way it shapes common sense and thus policy and practice in schools. The discourse of change implies a decidedly nice kind of change—that is, change that fails to acknowledge systemic inequity and pervasive whiteness. As we see through the implementation of the School Improvement Grant at Birch, change is defined in particular ways and through difficult negotiations of power, control, and meaning making. Too often, students and systems of power are lost in the race to engage an idealized notion of change.

The liberal discourse surrounding the School Improvement Grant is seductive, which is partly why it is so hard to see that it is also problematic. The seductiveness of these liberal tropes and tenets was not lost on me as an evaluator, researcher, and writer. I found myself enthralled with the quest for "truth" in which the teachers and administrators were engaged. I went around and around trying to figure out who was accurately representing what was "really happening at Birch." I found myself usually on the side of the teachers but also tentatively sympathizing with administrators. This is exactly what whiteness wants. This is how whiteness maintains its absent presence among educators. Lost in the so-called quest for truth is an active commitment to justice and real, material equity. This is not unlike whiteness writ large. Whiteness is also seductive—at least for those of us who benefit from it. Whiteness is strategic in that it is not cast as a seductive, winner-take-all sort of phenomenon. Rather, it is nicely cast as neutral, as open to everyone, even as empathetic to the downtrodden and compassionate toward those who may need a little boost.

It is here that we can see how whiteness, liberalism, and neoliberalism intertwine. Rather than simply abstract ideas with no bearing on reality—on schools, on teachers, and on students—whiteness and liberalism shape the way we engage and are in turn engaged by policy and practice. With a grounding in classical liberalism and related notions of the individual and social change, "neoliberals redefined democracy as choice in the marketplace and freedom as personal freedom to consume . . . Competitive individualism is a virtue and personal accountability replaces government responsibility for collective social welfare" (Lipman 2011, 10). Indeed, the SIG program operationalizes these characteristics: Schools compete for funds, and students and teachers consume resources under the assumption that they will produce particular results. Individualism frames everything from the grant application to merit pay to student success, and individuals are held responsible for outcomes largely dependent on structural factors. What is important to understand here are the foundational principles of classical liberalism and the way liberalism shapes what becomes common sense.

The SIG policy is a structure created by someone else on which individual teachers and students are judged. The policy and overall reform model act as a seemingly neutral, and actually generous, effort to "improve" and "turn around" schools. It is, in part, this supposed neutrality and goodwill that educators at Birch have bought into. They have embraced the idea that individual teachers matter, irrespective of the larger process of schooling. It makes sense that educators would buy into the idea that they matter; it would, in fact, be surprising if they did not believe this. Most teachers become teachers because they want to matter in the lives of students. Our daily work has meaning because we believe that what we do matters fundamentally. What teachers do does matter fundamentally, but it is not *all* that matters. And perhaps unfortunately, what teachers do matters much less if structures and systems are in place that exert intense pressure to maintain whiteness. Educators have also bought into the structure of the School Improvement Grant because their pay is tied to the idea that they matter and what they do matters more than anything else. Even teachers who are not primarily motivated by increased pay can easily get swept up in the tide of school reform that pounds particular notions of the individual and social change into the shore.

Engagement and Struggle within the "Culture of Nice"

Racism is inside the schools and outside the schools, but we must struggle where we are.

—DAVID GILLBORN, *RACISM AND EDUCATION*

In writing this book, I set out to answer a number of questions. Primarily, I hoped to examine how schools contribute to inequity given educators' good intentions. This question includes some others: How are popular educational discourses employed in contradictory ways? How do potentially transformative agendas get taken up in ways that run counter to the initial intent? How do individuals with good intentions (re)produce structures that harm children? A simple answer to all these questions is whiteness. And yet, it is also an incredibly complex answer. Whiteness, as a system of ideological and institutional race dominance engaged by everyone to various degrees, composes an elaborate and extensive set of mechanisms that work to sustain and mask dominance. As such, whiteness stands in the way of equity. How does this happen? And specifically, how does this happen in schools? Of any social institution, schools should be the place where fairness and justice are most obvious, most valued, and most sought after. Educators are typically nice people with good intentions of serving youth and communities. But educators are just as invested in dominant American ideologies and institutions as any other individuals in our society. They may even be more invested in things like equality, meritocracy, colorblindness, and politeness because of the way schools are positioned as fundamental to helping anyone—and everyone—achieve the American dream. Schools also worked, and continue to work, for most educators, so educators are understandably invested in this institution that provided an avenue for their own success.

Through the voices, scenes, and texts in this book, I have attempted to illustrate what these investments look like, how they interact with one another, and what their implications are. In doing so, I hope to have made clear how being educated in whiteness works. Central to this understanding is that whiteness often works through nice people and well-intended policies and practices.[1]

As the stories from the Zion School District highlight, "educated in whiteness" has multiple meanings. In part, it means that we are all surrounded by whiteness daily, and it therefore permeates our learning and experiences even when we are not aware of it. In this sense, whiteness is like the water fish swim in or the air we breathe. Teachers are educated in whiteness, students are educated in whiteness, our schools as institutions are built on foundations of whiteness, and the list could go on. An alternative meaning of "educated in whiteness" refers to the process of coming to see, learning about, and thinking through the implications of whiteness. Indeed, through reading the stories and discussion in this book, I hope we become more aware of how, when, where, and why whiteness is operating in our schools and communities. In other words, we all need to be educated *about* whiteness so that we do not continue to educate *for* whiteness.

Being educated about whiteness requires that a particular set of glasses be worn, because it is only with these glasses that we can really see the mechanisms at work in our everyday, well-intended efforts to address diversity in schools. The glasses this book provides include the concepts of niceness, responsibility, colorblindness, powerblindness, politeness, equality, meritocracy, individualism, and liberalism. With an understanding of these theoretical notions, including what they look like in practice, we should be better equipped to see how whiteness permeates our educational system.

Niceness is a critical component to the operationalization of whiteness in schools, and previous chapters highlight multiple ways educators in the Zion School District engaged niceness. But niceness is not always fully subscribed to. In fact, we see a number of instances where Birch and Spruce teachers acted, talked, and engaged in ways that could easily be considered "not nice." Even when niceness breaks down (e.g., in relation to social class or sexual orientation) at the individual or interactional level, it continues to operate at an ideological and institutional level in service to whiteness.

So even when we witness individuals like the Spruce administrator who explicitly linked poverty with drug abuse, lack of interest in schooling, and a host of other social problems, whiteness is engaged through the ideological investment in deficit thinking and the institutional distancing of the school from holding any responsibility for ensuring equity. In fact, these discourses are commonly justified as being "real" or "the hard truth"—thus positioning the speaker as being helpful through their identification of the problem and willingness to be "honest." Niceness breaks down when it can be framed as telling "hard truths" about the deficiencies of *other people*. Niceness obfuscates power, and it absolves individuals from needing to address what are actually deficiencies in the system. While the norms of niceness are acceptably broken in these cases, the influence of niceness to protect one's in-group (in this case other educators and the middle-class communities surrounding Spruce) and one's institution (in this case the school) is unwavering. In other words, although an individual's actions or beliefs toward another individual or group of individuals may not be "nice," the actions and beliefs are always nice in relation to institutional and structural power because niceness masks structural dominance.

As we have seen in the Zion School District, educators are engaged in multiple diversity-related policies and practices in schools that they believe will be effective and useful and will appeal to shared norms around niceness. But the foundations of these efforts, while consistent with prototypical American values, are harmful in their ability to obscure systemic inequity, institutional oppression, and whiteness. Though difficult to locate, whiteness is a public hazard that thrives in our schools.

Toxicity

Superfund sites are the worst hazardous waste sites in the United States, and they offer a poignant metaphor for the patterns described in this book. They exist in communities across the nation. Some are ugly, smelly, and discouraging to visitors. Others are beautiful, perhaps heavily treed, sometimes including slides and elaborate climbing structures. The attractive ones rarely disclose what lies beneath, but their foundation is just as toxic as the obviously hazardous ones. Superfund sites are most often located in low-income, urban communities, and they always pose serious risks to the health and well-being of the people nearby. Although thousands of these spaces have been purportedly cleaned up over the past thirty years, there are still more than a thousand superfund sites waiting to be remediated. One approach to dealing with superfund sites is to cover over them; this solution leaves the toxicity in place but attempts to contain it. Containing the toxic site underground means it is still present, but it is now out of sight and, presumably, out of mind. Another approach to dealing with superfund sites is to remove them, but removing them obviously means that the hazardous waste must be relocated elsewhere. Often paired with either of these approaches is to beautify the site—that is, to develop it into a neighborhood park or some other visually pleasing and potentially useful space for the local community. The usefulness and attractiveness does not, however, negate the toxicity.

Before remediation of superfunds can occur, these sites must be identified and officially recognized on the National Priorities List—a process that is often the result of significant work, lobbying, research, and pressure from concerned community members. The federal government has broad authority to clean up releases or potential releases of hazardous substances that may endanger public health or the environment. The Environmental Protection Agency is charged with identifying those responsible for superfund sites and compelling them to clean up the site. However, when a responsible party cannot be found, the Environmental Protection Agency cleans up the site itself through a special trust fund. Federal law allows two types of responses to superfund sites: short-term responses that remove immediate hazards to a local community and long-term responses that reduce the risk of anticipated hazards by either neutralizing the toxic waste or preventing the migration of toxic waste. Currently, the superfund trust lacks sufficient funds to address most of the toxic sites across the nation. This trust was funded by taxes imposed on industries that produce pollution, but the superfund tax was discontinued in 1995, and the funds in the trust were gone by 2003. Since that time, the superfund has relied on annual congressional appropriations.

And so it is with whiteness and niceness in schools. There are, in fact, a number of parallels that can be drawn here. The toxicity associated with superfund sites impacts everyone, but the most significant damage is done in communities immediately surrounding the site—that is, in low-income neighborhoods and communities of color. Whiteness, too, is pervasive and seeps into every place it can, but its most deleterious effects are experienced by people of color. Recognition of a superfund site results in a search for the individual who created the hazard. If that individual is found, he or she is responsible for cleaning up the mess. Once an inequity and injustice associated with whiteness is identified and made obvious—usually only as a result of hard work on the part of individuals and groups—the most common responses are to locate individual culprits. Viewing racism as individually perpetuated and the result of isolated events leads to approaches that attempt to change individual opinions, move individual people from a bounded situation, or otherwise contain the injustice from spreading.

But as I have illustrated throughout this book, whiteness and inequity are structural, systemic, and patterned, and they are located in our ideologies and institutions. Similarly, superfund sites might alternatively be thought of as the result of beliefs and decisions about industry, progress, and capitalism. If, for example, the health of everyone in the nation was equally valued, and if our health was prioritized as a national collective interest, perhaps we would have different laws and regulations in place regarding hazardous waste. The same can be said of whiteness. If every member of our nation and every student in our schools was understood as being important, valuable, and destined for success, we would prioritize equity and justice over all else. Whiteness would no longer be central because we would understand that the investments we make in whiteness are contrary to the investments we need and want to make in equity. The success of certain individuals would not be achieved on the backs of other individuals.

A Nicely Bundled Package

Schools can ultimately either engage in practices that reproduce and reify whiteness or engage in practices that undo whiteness. Whether we look at educational attainment, earning power, net worth, crime statistics, hate crimes, infant mortality, or health patterns, we know that there are consistent trends indicating that White people fare much better in this country than people of color. We can choose either to maintain current inequities or to actively work for equity. While schools are certainly not the only institution with a responsibility for ensuring equity, schools do play a significant role. I assume that schools and educators can make a difference in chipping away at patterned inequity, and I believe that most educators share that assumption. I also assume that race and power matter fundamentally in every one of our lives, but I am not convinced that most educators share this assumption. I hope that the stories and discussion in this book have helped illuminate how, and to what extent, they do matter.

What also becomes apparent through the stories and discussion in this book is that whiteness is a significant and important enemy of equity. Over and over, we see that the ways teachers and administrators in the Zion School District understood and implemented diversity-related policy and practice were intimately shaped by whiteness and our investments in whiteness. At the same time, whiteness is reified through the diversity-related policy and practice in which educators engaged.

To be labeled as *racist* or *prejudiced* is a significant social disgrace, and perhaps even more so for those who are charged with educating and socializing our nation's youth. As a result, the language of "diversity," and at times "equity," has been embraced by most educators in diverse school settings. Ironically, however, the way diversity is taken up, understood, and even implemented merely serves to maintain the business-as-usual work of schools, which in turn supports and perpetuates the status quo of racialized hierarchies and systems of power and privilege. In other words, typical, well-intended approaches for addressing diversity in educational policy and practice act as allies to whiteness.

In the Zion School District, diversity-related policies and practices were always engaged in nice ways that would not upset the status quo. Powerblindness came to life in educators' attempts to ignore, silence, or explain away any power-related hierarchies, inequities, or injustices. Specifically, powerblindness was operationalized through appeals to learning styles and varied teaching techniques, human relations and character education, and by politely erasing heterosexism and homophobia. Colorblindness was evident in the ways teachers silenced race talk and racialized issues. When students tried talking about race, they were schooled in—and through—politeness. When confronted with racialized achievement gaps or race inequities at school that could not be silenced, educators turned them into issues related to language, social class, or refugee status. Deficit ideologies were another mechanism at work when explanations for student failure were located in student and family characteristics. In each of these instances, patterned and pervasive racial inequity was left unnamed, unexamined, and unchallenged. At the same time, educators operationalized equality, meritocracy, and individualism in their efforts to build particular school cultures, create conditions for certain students to succeed, and compete in the new school-reform race. All these mechanisms work in service to whiteness. They are also so common and prevalent that they allow whiteness to thrive without much effort.

Grounded in ethnographic data, this book illustrates how people, both individually and in groups, create and maintain the conditions within which whiteness thrives. But individuals do this through institutions and ideologies, so the mechanisms of whiteness are systemic. The fact that whiteness is systemic and systematic goes against the typical way Americans understand our reality. We are staunchly committed to the individual: We believe in individual rights and entitlements, and we value individual merit and reward individual effort. When something goes awry, we tend to look for a singular and individual culprit. This commitment to the individual certainly informs the typical understanding of racism as an individual act of race-related hostility, which then leads to approaches that focus on educating, remediating, or otherwise fixing individual racists. But whiteness must be understood as a patterned, ideological, and institutional phenomenon. As such, addressing and undoing whiteness must entail an examination of dominant ideologies and institutions and then working for change in the foundations of our schools and larger U.S. society.

This sort of change is difficult because of the way educators protect their investment in whiteness. In fact, we all do. *Of course we do.* It would be absurd to not keep, shelter, and cultivate that which one has and that which is such an important aspect of one's personhood. There is a general consensus that individuals should diversify their investments so that if some of the investments do poorly, one's entire portfolio does not suffer significantly. A wise investor has money in various stocks, bonds, real estate, and mutual funds; a wise investor trusts that this strategy will yield high profits and minimize loss. In a similar way, most educators invest in colorblindness, powerblindness, meritocracy, equality, individualism, and niceness. We count on these investments to collectively produce a meaningful, high-yield, and consistent return. The return is that our daily work in schools and with youth makes sense, feels good, and hopefully helps students succeed. But the return is also more of the same status quo—consistent patterns of inequity and persistent whiteness. This is why whiteness works so well; it is also why the arguments I have tried to make in this book are so difficult. I am asking us to look at the foundation of our schools, which is also the foundation of how we understand the world around us and our place in that world. Equality, meritocracy, colorblindness, powerblindness, niceness, individualism—these are so taken for granted that it is almost impossible to see how and why they might be problematic. But the usefulness and attractiveness of whiteness does not negate its toxicity.

Educating against Whiteness

We cannot allow niceness, and indeed whiteness, to stand in the way of equity and justice. Although in theory most diversity-related educational policies and practices promise to bring about greater equity, too often in practice they actually maintain, legitimate, and thus perpetuate whiteness. This book has illustrated multiple disconnects between the promises and practices of diversity-related initiatives but also some understanding of *why* the disconnect persists. As one of the teachers in the Zion School District eloquently noted, "I just think probably most teachers in schools pay lip service to multicultural education and diversity. . . . So multiculturalism is real, but I think it's hard to deal with because there's a giving up of some things that maybe you don't want to give up." Indeed, it is expected for teachers to "pay lip service" to diversity and equality—to not do so would be neither nice nor professionally acceptable. But "giving up" things one has and/or believes is not only asking a lot, it is also generally understood as unfair. Being nice does not entail inviting discomfort or unfairness on oneself, but this may be necessary for achieving equity.

The Zion School District is, of course, a singular place with its own history, context, nuances, actors, relationships, and culture. Birch and Spruce are similarly uniquely positioned secondary schools that cannot be equated to any other schools in the nation. But these places serve as windows through which to view larger patterns operating in other places. In this way, the data in this book should be read as an illustration—though not an exact replica—of how, why, and to what effect diversity-related policy and practice works in other communities throughout the United States.

Although the Zion School District has adopted the language of equity and has implemented a multicultural education policy and in-service opportunities that address diversity, like other districts across the country, there is clearly much work to be done if the goal is to disrupt whiteness by improving the schooling of all students and ultimately bringing about educational equity. District leaders, principals, and teachers need clearly articulated plans for learning about and practicing power-related and race-related discourse alongside equitable resource distribution. Curricular and pedagogical changes alone will not change schools, but that does not mean such changes should not be encouraged. Educators must come to see issues of power as structural and systemic rather than individual. This is not to say, of course, that individual people do not act in oppressive ways—certainly we all do at times. It is to say, however, that by shifting the emphasis to the ways in which systems of power work, we might be more successful in addressing the pervasive and continual inequities in schools. Understanding race as a structural phenomenon will help us make better sense of educational inequity, achievement gaps, and whiteness. We need education that combines critical investigations of whiteness, race, and equity with an affective component in order to address the discomfort, guilt, and embarrassment that is likely to ensue from these investigations. Teachers especially need to be supported in this work, which will include mistakes, parental discontent, and community discomfort. This ongoing process is not easy work, but it is both necessary and long overdue.

I have made, and continue to make, my own mistakes in this work. After completing the first year of ethnographic research for this book, I was invited back to the district to share the results. I embraced this opportunity since I hoped that the things I learned would be actually useful to teachers, educational leaders, and students in the Zion School District. I was invited to join central office leaders and principals over a two-day period to report on what I had learned and to facilitate conversation. I initially envisioned also engaging teachers in these conversations, but leadership in the Zion School District decided that it was best to let the principals think through how to share and address the research within their school communities. In framing my comments, I drew on the district's own use of the term *equity* and framed my comments around "providing an equitable and excellent education to all students" since I believed that this was language to which they could relate. My presentation and the ensuing conversation looked very similar to what has ultimately ended up in this book, but with one major difference.

When consulting with one central office leader who was not part of my study but knew the results well, I decided to not frame the research around the term *whiteness* when I shared the results in the district. As a young scholar and an outsider to the district, I thought this was the best approach at the time. I was nervous about how my ideas—and, by extension, *me* as a person—would be received if I talked about whiteness. I did not want to close people off to the conversation. I did not want to cause White people in the room to get defensive or guilt ridden. So I played into whiteness and, in turn, added to its power by not naming it. I substituted "the status quo" for "whiteness." This strategy was at least partially successful. Nobody walked out of the room, nobody attacked me, and nobody got visibly upset. I succeeded in maintaining a nice conversation. My effort and strategy was reinforced when a handful of leaders of color shared that they appreciated my research, they agreed with it, and they hoped "others would hear it" coming from me. I understood what they meant. I was not sharing anything groundbreaking for them, but my White identity sheltered me in ways that they could never access.

Although more than five years have passed since those two days I spent sharing my research with the district, I continue to think about the experience and have conflicting feelings about it. Indeed, in my current teaching with preservice and practicing teachers and administrators, I often encounter the same dilemma around how best to say what needs to be said about inequity, race, and whiteness in schools. We are all educated in whiteness. It is impossible not to be because the norms around niceness and whiteness are powerful. But White scholars, educators, policy makers, and leaders have a responsibility to engage those around us in ways that shine a light on those norms and the implications of subscribing to them.

Niceness is a key mechanism of whiteness among educators, but a simple reversal of niceness would not necessarily educate against whiteness any more effectively. Indeed, there were plenty of instances in the Zion School District where niceness at the individual and interactional levels broke down. In these instances, whiteness was actually strengthened. While there are instances where niceness breaks down in relation to social class, sexual orientation, language identity, and refugee status, it is extremely rare to witness a breakdown of niceness related to race. This is true even at the individual and interactional levels that at times permit digressions related to other power-related categories. Whiteness helps make sense of this pattern. Whiteness must allow some ideological flexibility to maintain its hegemony, but the consistency around race illustrates its centrally operative status. Niceness functions to at once neutralize dominance and maintain it. Dominance, inequity, and fundamentally whiteness are neutralized through niceness because educators' nice diversity-related efforts gloss over and thus obscure the very presence of whiteness.

What, then, are educators to do? Part of the answer lies in David Gillborn's call to "struggle where we are." This struggle will surely look different for different people and in different contexts, but at a minimum it must entail struggling with the reality of inequity, racism, dominance, and whiteness. Whiteness and the various mechanisms of whiteness illustrated throughout the previous chapters make it very difficult to keep this reality in view. Keeping whiteness in focus for ourselves, in collaboration with others, and for those who are otherwise resistant to seeing it requires both vigilance and an ability to name whiteness in ways that are able to be heard.

I try to remember Derrick Bell's (1992) call to be strategic and outmaneuver policies, practices, and systems that appear neutral but actually result in persistent inequity. In fact, the stories in this book suggest that this outmaneuvering may require difficult ideological and structural work. If our allegiance to equality, meritocracy, colorblindness, and powerblindness results in patterned inequity and the reification of whiteness, perhaps we need to let go of those ideologies. If our schools are built on assumptions that equal opportunity exists and meritocracy is fair, perhaps we need to restructure our schools for the obviously unequal society in which they operate. The only way to get to equity is through unequal means. It is impossible to get to equity through equality. And it is only through equity that we might actualize our ideals of "equality and justice for all" (Brayboy, Castagno, and Maughan 2007).

This is why equity ought to be what drives our work in schools. Currently, whiteness drives our work. Sometimes this is purposeful, and sometimes it is more of a default position. When we continue to make the same investments and operationalize the same ideologies, we allow whiteness to do the driving. It requires vigilance and strategic engagement to ensure that equity drives our work. With equity driving our educational policies and practices, we would be staunchly committed to every child in our schools. We would set up structures in which every child could succeed. We would not see the kinds of losses we see under whiteness. These losses are explained, justified, and even expected as long as whiteness frames our education. Only by educating against whiteness and investing in equity can we expect change.

ACKNOWLEDGMENTS

I am mindful of the many relationships that have made this book possible. For as much as this has been an independent project, it has also been a collaborative one.

I am indebted, of course, to the people in the Zion School District who allowed me into their classrooms, hallways, offices, and daily interactions. I have learned so much from this community, and I hope the time, experience, and knowledge they shared with me is beneficial to youth, educators, families, and leaders both within and outside of the Salt Lake area. I am especially grateful to the person who initially vetted my project, permitted my access, and then later read my entire dissertation and felt it was important enough to arrange an extensive dialogue with district leaders about the research. His belief in my work and his continued encouragement have meant a lot over the previous eight years.

This research was first conceived under the guidance of Stacey Lee, Michael Olneck, and Gloria Ladson-Billings. I was fortunate to be surrounded by such incredible scholars as a young graduate student. My good fortune has continued to grow as I find myself now surrounded by friends and colleagues who are far smarter than I. Bryan Brayboy's work around equity, tribal critical race theory, and colonization has been integral to developing my ideas around whiteness in education; he also models the kind of engaged, politically savvy, and compelling work I aim to do. Sabina Vaught's work around race and power inspires me, advances my own thinking, and provides yet another model for the methodologically and theoretically rigorous work I attempt. Both Bryan and Sabina read and commented on various iterations of this manuscript, and it is a more coherent and compelling book because of them.

Many of my ideas in this book evolved as I taught a doctoral-level course on race and whiteness during two different semesters at Northern Arizona University. I am grateful to all the students in those courses for engaging and learning with me, especially Robert Kelty, Nathan Velez, Wanda Tucker, Patrick Williams, and Derrick Span. Chapters 1 and 5 are based on collaborative work with Charles Hausman, and I am grateful for his ongoing support and thoughtful conversation. I am also grateful for the wisdom provided by the anonymous reviewers, both of whom pushed my thinking and analysis. Incredibly helpful editorial assistance was provided by Sylvia Somerville at NAU's IDEA Lab and Pieter Martin at the University of Minnesota Press. Jaclyn Pace, a graduate student at NAU, provided thoughtful and timely assistance with the index.

Various writing groups have been integral to my progress, thinking, and writing for the past ten years. From a graduate school group in Madison, Wisconsin, to a dissertation group in Salt Lake City, Utah, and finally a faculty group in Flagstaff, Arizona, I am grateful to my writing group friends and colleagues who have supported and pushed me in countless ways. Most recently, Frances Riemer, JeanAnn Foley, Susan Longerbeam, Melvin Hall, and Christine Lemley have helped to keep my writing focused, interesting, and moving forward.

Without some nudging and a belief in the potential of my work from both Peter Demerath and Pieter Martin, this book would not have happened. I'm grateful that they, and many others listed here, had faith that this was worth pursuing, even when I was ready to let it collect dust on my shelves.

There were many months during which I'm sure my family may have preferred that I let this manuscript collect dust. Tarek, who was three and a half at the time, asked at least weekly when I was going to be done writing this book—a question that was always followed by "and what are you going to do after you're done, mama?" I know my husband and Keelan, our younger son, probably had the same questions and implied eagerness to see this project completed. My mom provided time for me to actually do this work, as well as a lifetime of encouragement and unwavering support. Throughout the process, my husband, Tyler, provided much-needed comical relief, as well as reminders that this work needs to be accessible.

In the final months of writing this book, I attended a family celebration honoring the tenth anniversary of my Uncle Jim's passing. In 2002, at the age of forty-nine, he died after a long battle with cancer. Speaking about him in 2012, my aunt noted the gifts of *tenacity* and *truth* he left with her and their young daughter. Coincidentally, or maybe not, my father-in-law also died from cancer in 2010 at the age of fifty-nine, and tenacity and truth are similarly fitting of his character and the legacy he left with his kids. As I think about my two young sons, just three-and-a-half and two years old, I hope that they grow into boys, and later men, who embrace tenacity and truth. These characteristics are not always "nice" ones, but they are necessary in the struggle against whiteness and the related pursuit of equity and justice.

Introduction

1. All names of schools, districts, and people are pseudonyms.

1. "Equity Has to Be a Priority"

1. Referencing the sources of the quoted material in this paragraph would compromise the anonymity of the district and schools. For this reason, I have not included citations, but I have them on file.

2. There were also many refugee students from Sudan and the Congo in the Salt Lake area, but this was not articulated to me by anyone in the Zion School District and rarely recognized in the efforts with which I was familiar.

2. Engaging Multicultural Education

1. For a more complete articulation of these approaches, please see Castagno 2009.

2. Despite common understandings of the word *co-opt*, I am not convinced that it requires conscious intent on the part of the actor. In the tradition of Derrick Bell's (1992) work, I am more concerned with the effects of people's actions than with the reasoning or motivations driving the actions. This is similar to David Gillborn's (2008) analysis of racism in the United Kingdom's educational system and his use of the word *conspiracy* (which builds on a long history of African American scholarship on conspiracy).

3. For another discussion of the tension between a focus on individuals and structural racism within the dominant racial paradigm among teachers, see Vaught and Castagno 2008.

3. Practicing Politeness through Meaningful Silences

1. This is the criterion-referenced test the Zion School District used to comply with NCLB regulations.

2. In the Salt Lake area, *Pacific Islander* and *Polynesian* are used interchangeably to denote the significant number of people in this community from Samoa and Tonga. Among the teachers in my research, the diversity within these labels was rarely noted.

3. MESA stands for "mathematics, engineering, and science achievement." This was a program in the Zion School District that aimed to involve students of color and low-income students in these fields where they are traditionally underrepresented.

5. Obscuring Whiteness with Liberalism

1. I conducted this evaluation collaboratively with Charles Hausman.

Conclusion

1. Whiteness also obviously works through mean people and ill-intended policies and practices. Indeed, as I watched voter-suppression tactics being employed during the U.S. presidential elections in 2012, I was vividly reminded of this.

REFERENCES

Abu El-Haj, Thea Rhenda. 2006. *Elusive Justice: Wrestling with Difference and Educational Equity in Everyday Practice*. New York: Routledge.

Anderson, James A. 1995. "Toward a Framework for Matching Teaching and Learning Styles for Diverse Populations." In *The Importance of Learning Styles: Understanding the Implications for Learning, Course Design, and Education*, edited by Ronald R. Sims and Serbrenia J. Sims, 69–78. Westport, Conn.: Greenwood Press.

Apple, Michael W. 1993. *Official Knowledge: Democratic Education in a Conservative Age*. New York: Routledge.

Applebaum, Barbara. 2005. "In the Name of Morality: Moral Responsibility, Whiteness, and Social Justice Education." *Journal of Moral Education* 34:277–90.

Au, Kathryn Hu-Pei, and Jana M. Mason. 1981. "Social Organizational Factors in Learning to Read: The Balance of Rights Hypothesis." *Reading Research Quarterly* 17:115–52.

Baker, Gwendolyn C. 1994. *Planning and Organizing for Multicultural Instruction*. 2nd ed. Menlo Park, Calif.: Addison-Wesley.

Ball, Deborah, and Margery Osborne. 1998. "Teaching with Difference." *Journal of Research in Science Teaching* 35:395–98.

Banks, James A. 2001. "Multicultural Education: Characteristics and Goals." In *Multicultural Education: Issues and Perspectives*, edited by James A. Banks and Cherry A. McGee Banks, 3–30. 4th ed. Hoboken, N.J.: John Wiley and Sons.

Bartolome, Lilia I. 1994. "Beyond the Methods Fetish: Toward a Humanizing Pedagogy." *Harvard Educational Review* 64:173–94.

Bell, Derrick A., Jr. 1979. "*Bakke*, Minority Admissions, and the Usual Price of Racial Remedies." *California Law Review* 67:3–19.

———. 1980. "*Brown v. Board of Education* and the Interest-Convergence Dilemma." *Harvard Law Review* 93:518–33.

———. 1987. *And We Are Not Saved: The Elusive Quest for Racial Justice*. New York: Basic Books.

———. 1992. *Faces at the Bottom of the Well: The Permanence of Racism*. New York: Basic Books.

———. 2004. *Silent Covenants:* Brown v. Board of Education *and the Unfulfilled Hopes for Racial Reform*. Oxford, U.K.: Oxford University Press.

Bennett, William J. 1988. *Our Children and Our Country*. New York: Simon and Schuster.

Blanchett, Wanda J. 2006. "Disproportionate Representation of African American Students in Special Education: Acknowledging the Role of White Privilege and Racism." *Educational Researcher* 35:24–28.

Bloom, Allan. 1987. *The Closing of the American Mind*. New York: Simon and Schuster.

Boler, Megan, editor. 2004. *Democratic Dialogue in Education: Troubling Speech, Disturbing Silence*. New York: Peter Lang.

Bonilla-Silva, Eduardo. 2009. *Racism without Racists: Color-Blind Racism and Racial Inequality in Contemporary America*. Lanham, Md.: Rowman and Littlefield.

Brandt, Ron. 1990. "On Learning Styles: A Conversation with Pat Guild." *Educational Leadership* 48:10–13.

Brayboy, Bryan McKinley Jones. 2004. "Hiding in the Ivy: American Indian Students and Visibility in Elite Educational Settings." *Harvard Educational Review* 74:125–52.

———. 2005. "Transformational Resistance and Social Justice: American Indians in Ivy League Universities." *Anthropology and Education Quarterly* 36:193–211.

Brayboy, Bryan McKinley Jones, Angelina Elizabeth Castagno, and Emma Maughan. 2007. "Equality and Justice for All? Examining Race in Education Scholarship." *Review of Research in Education* 31:159–94.

Brayboy, Bryan McKinley Jones, and Emma Maughan. 2009. "Indigenous Knowledges and the Story of the Bean." *Harvard Educational Review* 79:1–21.

Buendia, E., Ares, N., Juarez, B., & Peercy, M. 2004. "The Geographies of Difference: The Production of the East Side, West Side, and Central City School." *American Educational Research Journal* 41:833–63.

Burch, Patricia Ellen. 2002. "Constraints and Opportunities in Changing Policy Environments: Intermediary Organizations' Response to Complex District Contexts." In *School Districts and Instructional Renewal*, edited by Amy M. Hightower, Michael S. Knapp, Julie A. Marsh, and Milbrey W. McLaughlin, 111–26. New York: Teachers College Press.

Bush, Melanie E. L. 2004. *Breaking the Code of Good Intentions: Everyday Forms of Whiteness*. Lanham, Md.: Rowman and Littlefield.

Canham, Matt. 2005. "Mormons in Utah: The Shrinking Majority." *The Salt Lake Tribune*, July 24.

Castagno, Angelina Elizabeth. 2008. "'I Don't Want to Hear That!': Legitimating Whiteness through Silence in Schools." *Anthropology and Education Quarterly* 39:314–33.

———. 2009. "Making Sense of Multicultural Education: A Synthesis of the Various Typologies Found in the Literature." *Multicultural Perspectives* 11:43–48.

Castagno, Angelina Elizabeth, and Stacey J. Lee. 2007. "Native Mascots, Ethnic Fraud, and Interest Convergence: A Critical Race Theory Perspective on Higher Education." *Equity & Excellence in Education* 40:3–13.

Chennault, Ronald E. 1998. "Giving Whiteness a Black Eye: An Interview with Michael Eric Dyson." In *White Reign: Deploying Whiteness in America*, edited by Joe L. Kincheloe, Shirley R. Steinberg, Nelson M. Rodriguez, and Ronald E. Chennault, 299–328. New York: St. Martin's Press.

Cochran, David Carroll. 1999. *The Color of Freedom: Race and Contemporary American Liberalism*. Albany: State University of New York Press.

Connell, R. W., Dean Ashenden, Sandra Kessler, and Gary Dowsett. 1982. *Making the Difference: Schools, Families, and Social Division*. Crow's Nest, New South Wales, Australia: Allen and Unwin.

Crenshaw, Kimberlé Williams. 1988. "Race, Reform, and Retrenchment: Transformation and Legitimation in Antidiscrimination Law." *Harvard Law Review* 101:1331–87.

Dawson, Michael C. 2003. *Black Visions: The Roots of Contemporary African-American Political Ideologies*. Chicago: University of Chicago Press.

Dee, Thomas. 2012. "School Turnarounds: Evidence from the 2009 Stimulus." Unpublished manuscript, JEL No. H52,I2. NBER Working Paper No. 17990.

Delgado, Richard, and Jean Stefancic. 2001. *Critical Race Theory: An Introduction*. New York: New York University Press.

Delpit, Lisa D. 1988. "The Silenced Dialogue: Power and Pedagogy in Educating Other People's Children." *Harvard Educational Review* 58:280–98.

———. 1995. *Other People's Children: Cultural Conflict in the Classroom*. New York: New Press.

Duncan, Arne. 2012. "Statement from U.S. Secretary of Education Arne Duncan on 'School Turnarounds: Evidence from the 2009 Stimulus,'" Paper by Thomas Dee, Professor of Public Policy and Economics at the University of Virginia. http://www.ed.gov/news/press-releases/statement-us-secretary-education -arne-duncan-school-turnarounds-evidence-2009-st.

Dunn, Rita, Jeffrey S. Beaudry, and Angela Klavas. 1989. "Survey of Research on Learning Styles." *Educational Leadership* 46:50–58.

Duster, Troy. 2001. "The 'Morphing' Properties of Whiteness." In *The Making and Unmaking of Whiteness*, edited by Birgit Brander Rasmussen, Eric Klinenberg, Irene J. Nexica, and Matt Wray, 113–37. Durham, N.C.: Duke University Press.

Dyson, Michael. 1996. *Race Rules: Navigating the Color Line*. Reading, Mass.: Addison-Wesley.

Erickson, Frederick. 1993. "Transformation and School Success: The Politics and Culture of Educational Achievement." In *Minority Education: Anthropological Perspectives*, edited by Evelyn Jacob and Cathie Jordan, 27–52. New York: Ablex.

Erickson, Frederick, and Gerald Mohatt. 1982. "Cultural Organization of Participation Structures in Two Classrooms of Indian Students." In *Doing the Ethnography of Schooling: Educational Anthropology in Action*, edited by George Spindler, 132–75. New York: Holt, Rinehart, and Winston.

Fine, Michelle. 1987. "Silencing in the Public Schools." *Language Arts* 64:157–74.

———. 1991. *Framing Dropouts: Notes on the Politics of an Urban Public High School*. Albany: State University of New York Press.

———. 1997. "Witnessing Whiteness." In *Off White: Readings on Race, Power, and Society*, edited by Michelle Fine, Linda C. Powell, Lois Weis, and L. Mun Wong, 57–65. New York: Routledge.

Fine, Michelle, Linda C. Powell, Lois Weis, and L. Mun Wong. 1997. "Preface." In *Off White: Readings on Race, Power, and Society*, edited by Michelle Fine, Linda C. Powell, Lois Weis, and L. Mun Wong, vii–xii. New York: Routledge.

Fletcher Stack, Peggy. 2005. "Keeping Members a Challenge for LDS Church." *The Salt Lake Tribune*, July 26.

Frankenberg, Ruth. 1993. *White Women, Race Matters: The Social Construction of Whiteness*. Minneapolis: University of Minnesota Press.

———. 1997. "Introduction: Local Whiteness, Localizing Whiteness." In *Displacing Whiteness: Essays in Social and Cultural Criticism*, edited by Ruth Frankenberg, 1–34. Durham, N.C.: Duke University Press.

———. 2001. "The Mirage of an Unmarked Whiteness." In *The Making and Unmaking of Whiteness*, edited by Birgit Brander Rasmussen, Eric Klinenberg, Irene J. Nexica, and Matt Wray, 72–96. Durham, N.C.: Duke University Press.

Fraynd, Donald. 2004. "The Politics of Controversy and Public Opinion in and around pK–12 Education." Unpublished dissertation, University of Wisconsin-Madison.

Frutcher, Norm. 2007. *Urban Schools, Public Will: Making Education Work for All Our Children*. New York: Teachers College Press.

Gay, Geneva. 2000. *Culturally Responsive Teaching: Theory, Research, and Practice*. New York: Teachers College Press.

Gibson, Margaret Alison. 1984. "Approaches to Multicultural Education in the United States: Some Concepts and Assumptions." *Anthropology and Education Quarterly* 15:94–120.

———. 1988. *Accommodation without Assimilation: Sikh Immigrants in an American High School*. Ithaca, N.Y.: Cornell University Press.

Gillborn, David. 2005. "Education Policy as an Act of White Supremacy: Whiteness, Critical Race Theory, and Education Reform." *Journal of Education Policy* 20:485–505.

———. 2008. *Racism and Education: Coincidence or Conspiracy?* New York: Routledge.

Gittell, Marilyn. 2005. "The Politics of Equity in Urban School Reform." In *Bringing Equity Back: Research for a New Era in American Educational Policy*, edited by Janice Petrovich and Amy Stuart Wells, 16–45. New York: Teachers College Press.

GLSEN (Gay, Lesbian & Straight Education Network). 2005. "Academic Performance and College Aspirations Suffer when Harassment Goes Unchecked." http://www.glsen.org/cgi-bin/iowa/all/library/record/1413.html.

Gonzalez, Norma, Luis C. Moll, and Cathy Amanti, editors. 2005. *Funds of Knowledge: Theorizing Practices in Households, Communities, and Classrooms.* Mahwah, N.J.: Lawrence Erlbaum Associates.

Gorski, Paul. 2006. "The Classist Underpinnings of Ruby Payne's Framework." *Teachers College Record.* http://tcrecord.org.

Gotanda, Neil. 1995. "A Critique of 'Our Constitution Is Color-Blind.'" In *Critical Race Theory: The Key Writings That Formed the Movement*, edited by Kimberlé Crenshaw, Neil Gotanda, Gary Peller, and Kendall Thomas, 257–75. New York: New Press.

Grant Hoefs-Bascom, Carl, and Christine Sleeter. 1996. *After the School Bell Rings.* London: Falmer Press.

Haney-Lopez, Ian. 2006. *White by Law: The Legal Construction of Race.* 10th anniversary ed., revised and updated. New York: New York University Press.

Harris, Cheryl I. 1993. "Whiteness as Property." *Harvard Law Review* 106:1707.

Harris Interactive and GLSEN. 2005. *From Teasing to Torment: School Climate in America; A Survey of Students and Teachers.* New York: GLSEN.

Heath, Shirley Brice. 1983. *Ways with Words: Language, Life, and Work in Communities and Classrooms.* Cambridge, U.K.: Cambridge University Press.

Helms, Janet E. 1995. "An Update of Helm's White and People of Color Racial Identity Models." In *Handbook of Multicultural Counseling*, edited by Joseph G. Ponterotto, J. Manuel Casas, Lisa A. Suzuki, and Charlene M. Alexander, 181–98. Thousand Oaks, Calif.: Sage.

Hogben, Matthew, and Caroline K. Waterman. 1997. "Are All of Your Students Represented in Their Textbooks? A Content Analysis of Coverage of Diversity Issues in Introductory Psychology Textbooks." *Teaching of Psychology* 24:95–100.

Hollingshead, Todd. 2005. "Study Ranks Mormon Teens No. 1 in Religiosity Nationwide." *The Salt Lake Tribune*, May 20.

Howard, Gary R. 1999. *We Can't Teach What We Don't Know: White Teachers, Multiracial Schools.* New York: Teachers College Press.

Human Rights Watch. 2001. *Hatred in the Hallways: Violence and Discrimination against Lesbian, Gay, Bisexual, and Transgender Students in U.S. Schools.* New York: Human Rights Watch.

Hunter, James Davison. 1991. *Culture Wars: The Struggle to Define America*. New York: Basic Books.

Hyland, Nora E. 2005. "Being a Good Teacher of Black Students? White Teachers and Unintentional Racism." *Curriculum Inquiry* 35:429–59.

Johnson, Allan G. 2001. *Privilege, Power, and Difference*. New York: McGraw Hill.

Johnson, Lauri. 2002. "'My Eyes Have Been Opened': White Teachers and Racial Awareness." *Journal of Teacher Education* 53:153–67.

Kailin, Julie. 1999. "How White Teachers Perceive the Problem of Racism in Their Schools: A Case Study in 'Liberal' Lakeview." *Teachers College Record* 100:724–50.

Kauffman, David, Susan Moore Johnson, Susan M. Kardos, Edward Liu, and Heather G. Peske. 2002. "'Lost at Sea': New Teachers' Experiences with Curriculum and Assessment." *Teachers College Record* 104:273–300.

Kincheloe, Joe L., and Shirley R. Steinberg. 1997. *Changing Multiculturalism: New Times, New Curriculum*. Philadelphia: Open University Press.

———. 1998. "Addressing the Crisis of Whiteness: Reconfiguring White Identity in a Pedagogy of Whiteness." In *White Reign: Deploying Whiteness in America*, edited by Joe L. Kincheloe, Shirley R. Steinberg, Nelson M. Rodriguez, and Ronald E. Chennault, 3–30. New York: St. Martin's Press.

Kosciw, Joseph G., Emily A. Greytak, Elizabeth M. Diaz, and Mark J. Bartkiewicz. 2010. *The 2009 National School Climate Survey: The Experiences of Lesbian, Gay, Bisexual, and Transgender Youth in Our Nation's Schools*. New York: GLSEN.

Kumashiro, Kevin J. 2004. "Uncertain Beginnings: Learning to Teach Paradoxically." *Theory into Practice* 43:111–15.

Ladson-Billings, Gloria. 1995a. "But That's Just Good Teaching! The Case for Culturally Relevant Pedagogy." *Theory into Practice* 34:159–65.

———. 1995b. "Toward a Theory of Culturally Relevant Pedagogy." *American Educational Research Journal* 32:465–91.

———. 1998. "Just What Is Critical Race Theory and What's It Doing in a *Nice* Field Like Education?" *International Journal of Qualitative Studies in Education* 11:7–24.

———. 2006. "From the Achievement Gap to the Education Debt: Understanding Achievement in U.S. Schools." *Educational Researcher* 35:3–12.

Ladson-Billings, Gloria, and William F. Tate IV. 1995. "Toward a Critical Race Theory of Education." *Teachers College Record* 97:47–68.

———. 2006. *Education Research in the Public Interest: Social Justice, Action, and Policy*. New York: Teachers College Press.

Lee, Carol D., Margaret Beale Spencer, and Vinay Harpalani. 2003. "'Every Shut Eye Ain't Sleep': Studying How People Live Culturally." *Educational Researcher* 32:6–13.

Lee, Stacey J. 2005. *Up against Whiteness: Race, School, and Immigrant Youth*. New York: Teachers College Press.

Leonardo, Zeus. 2009. *Race, Whiteness, and Education*. New York: Routledge.

Levin, Henry M. 1988. *Accelerated Schools for At-Risk Students*. CPRE Research Report Series RR-010. New Brunswick, N.J.: Rutgers University, Center for Policy Research in Education.

Lewis, Amanda E. 2003. *Race in the Schoolyard: Negotiating the Color Line in Classrooms and Communities*. New Brunswick, N.J.: Rutgers University Press.

Lipman, Pauline. 1998. *Race, Class, and Power in School Restructuring*. Albany: State University of New York Press.

———. 2004. *High Stakes Education: Inequality, Globalization, and Urban School Reform*. New York: Routledge Falmer.

———. 2011. *The New Political Economy of Urban Education: Neoliberalism, Race, and the Right to the City*. New York: Routledge.

Lipsitz, George. 1998. *The Possessive Investment in Whiteness: How White People Profit from Identity Politics*. Philadelphia: Temple University Press.

Lipsky, Michael. 1980. *Street-Level Bureaucracy Dilemmas of Individuals in Public Services*. New York: Russell Sage Foundation.

Locke, John. 1986. *The Second Treatise of Civil Government*. Amherst, N.Y.: Prometheus Books.

Loutzenheiser, Lisa W. 1996. "How Schools Play 'Smear the Queer.'" *Feminist Teacher* 10:59–64.

Maher, Frances, and Mary Kay Thompson Tetreault. 1998. "'They Got the Paradigm and Painted It White': Whiteness and Pedagogies of Positionality." In *White Reign: Deploying Whiteness in America*, edited by Joe L. Kincheloe, Shirley R. Steinberg, Nelson M. Rodriguez, and Ronald E. Chennault, 137–58. New York: St. Martin's Press.

Marx, Sherry. 2006. *Revealing the Invisible: Confronting Passive Racism in Teacher Education*. New York: Routledge.

McCormick, John S. 2000. *The Gathering Place: An Illustrated History of Salt Lake City*. Salt Lake City: Signature Books.

McIntosh, Peggy. 1988. "White Privilege and Male Privilege: A Personal Account of Coming to See Correspondences through Work in Women's Studies." In *Critical White Studies: Looking behind the Mirror*, edited by Richard Delgado and Jean Stefancic, 291–99. Philadelphia: Temple University Press.

McIntyre, Alice. 1997. *Making Meaning of Whiteness: Exploring Racial Identity with White Teachers*. Albany: State University of New York Press.

McLaren, Peter. 1994. "White Terror and Oppositional Agency: Towards a Critical Multiculturalism." In *Multiculturalism: A Critical Reader*, edited by David Theo Goldberg, 45–74. Malden, Mass.: Blackwell.

———. 1998. "Whiteness Is . . . The Struggle for Postcolonial Hybridity." In *White Reign: Deploying Whiteness in America*, edited by Joe L. Kincheloe,

Shirley R. Steinberg, Nelson M. Rodriguez, and Ronald E. Chennault, 63–76. New York: St. Martin's Press.

Meyer, Elizabeth J. 2009. *Gender, Bullying, and Harassment: Strategies to End Sexism and Homophobia in Schools*. New York: Teachers College Press.

Mill, John. 1982. *On Liberty*. New York: Penguin Classics.

Moll, Luis C., Cathy Amanti, Deborah Neff, and Norma Gonzalez. 1992. "Funds of Knowledge for Teaching: Using a Qualitative Approach to Connect Homes and Classrooms." *Theory into Practice* 31:132–41.

Morrison, Toni. 1992. *Playing in the Dark: Whiteness and the Literary Imagination*. New York: Vintage Books.

Nieto, Sonia. 2004. *Affirming Diversity: The Sociopolitical Context of Multicultural Education*. 4th ed. Upper Saddle River, N.J.: Pearson.

Oakes, Jeannie. 1985. *Keeping Track: How Schools Structure Inequality*. New Haven, Conn.: Yale University Press.

O'Connor, Carla, and Sonia DeLuca Fernandez. 2006. "Race, Class, and Disproportionality: Reevaluating the Relationship between Poverty and Special Education Placement." *Educational Researcher* 35:6–11.

Olneck, Michael. 2004. "Immigrants and Education in the United States." In *Handbook of Research on Multicultural Education*, edited by James A. Banks and Cherry A. McGee Banks, 381–403. 2nd ed. San Francisco: Jossey Bass.

Olsen, Laurie. 1997. *Made in America: Immigrant Students in Our Public Schools*. New York: New Press.

Olson, Joel. 2004. *The Abolition of White Democracy*. Minneapolis: University of Minnesota Press.

Omi, Michael, and Howard Winant. 1994. *Racial Formation in the United States: From the 1960s to the 1990s*. 2nd ed. New York: Routledge.

Payne, Ruby K. 1996. *A Framework for Understanding Poverty*. 3rd rev. ed. Highlands, Tex.: aha! Process.

Perry, Pamela. 2002. *Shades of White: White Kids and Racial Identities in High School*. Durham, N.C.: Duke University Press.

Philips, Susan Urmston. 1983. *The Invisible Culture: Communication in Classroom and Community on the Warm Springs Indian Reservation*. New York: Longman.

Pierce, Chester. 1974. "Psychiatric Problems of the Black Minority." In *American Handbook of Psychiatry, Vol. II*, edited by Silvano Arieti, 512–23. 2nd ed. New York: Basic Books.

Polite, Lillian, and Elizabeth Baird Saenger. 2003. "A Pernicious Silence: Confronting Race in the Elementary Classroom." *Phi Delta Kappan* 85:274–78.

Pollock, Mica. 2004. *Colormute: Race Talk Dilemmas in an American School*. Princeton, N.J.: Princeton University Press.

Powell, Linda C. 1997. "The Achievement (K)not: Whiteness and Black Underachievement." In *Off White: Readings on Race, Power, and Society*, edited by Michelle Fine, Linda C. Powell, Lois Weis, and L. Mun Wong, 3–12. New York: Routledge.

Powell, Rebecca. 2001. *Straight Talk: Growing as Multicultural Educators*. 2nd ed. New York: Peter Lang.

Rasmussen, Birgit Brander, Eric Klinenberg, Irene J. Nexica, and Matt Wray. 2001. "Introduction." In *The Making and Unmaking of Whiteness*, edited by Birgit Brander Rasmussen, Eric Klinenberg, Irene J. Nexica, and Matt Wray, 1–24. Durham, N.C.: Duke University Press.

Ravitch, Diane. 1990. "Multiculturalism Yes, Particularism No." *The Chronicle of Higher Education*, October 24, A44.

Reid, D. Kim, and Michelle G. Knight. 2006. "Disability Justifies Exclusion of Minority Students: A Critical History Grounded in Disability Studies." *Educational Researcher* 35:18–23.

Roediger, David R. 2000. *The Wages of Whiteness: Race and the Making of the American Working Class*. Rev. ed. London: Verso.

Romo, Harriett D., and Toni Falbo. 1995. *Latino High School Graduation: Defying the Odds*. Austin: University of Texas Press.

Ross, E. Wayne, and Rich Gibson. 2007. "Introduction." In *Neoliberalism and Education Reform*, edited by E. Wayne Ross and Rich Gibson, 1–14. New York: Hampton Press.

Sanchez, Jennifer W. 2005. "Beyond English." *The Salt Lake Tribune*, August 7.

Schlesinger, Arthur Meier, Jr. 1998. *The Disuniting of America: Reflections on a Multicultural Society*. Rev. and enlarged ed. New York: W. W. Norton.

Sears, James T. 1991. "Helping Students Understand and Accept Sexual Diversity." *Educational Leadership* 57:53–56.

Sims, Ronald R., and Serbrenia J. Sims, editors. 1995. *The Importance of Learning Styles: Understanding the Implications for Learning, Course Design, and Education*. Westport, Conn.: Greenwood Press.

Skrla, Linda, and James Scheurich. 2001. "Replacing Deficit Thinking in School District Leadership." *Education and Urban Society* 33:235–59.

Sleeter, Christine E. 1996. *Multicultural Education as Social Activism*. Albany: State University of New York Press.

———. 2005. *Un-Standardizing Curriculum: Multicultural Teaching in the Standards-Based Classroom*. New York: Teachers College Press.

Sleeter, Christine E., and Carl A. Grant. 2003. *Making Choices for Multicultural Education: Five Approaches to Race, Class, and Gender*. 4th ed. Hoboken, N.J.: John Wiley and Sons.

Smith, Anthony. 2005. "Conferring with Young Second-Language Writers: Keys To Success." *New Horizons for Learning Online Journal*. http://education.jhu.edu/PD/newhorizons/strategies/topics/literacy/articles/conferring-with-young-second/index.html.

Solomon, R. Patrick, John P. Portelli, Beverly Jean Daniel, and Arlene Campbell. 2005. "The Discourse of Denial: How White Teacher Candidates Construct Race, Racism, and 'White Privilege.'" *Race, Ethnicity and Education* 8:147–69.

Solórzano, Daniel. G., and Octavio Villalpando. 1998. "Critical Race Theory, Marginality, and the Experiences of Students of Color in Higher Education." In *Sociology of Education: Emerging Perspectives*, edited by Carlos Alberto Torres and Theodore R. Mitchell, 211–24. Albany: State University of New York Press.

Solórzano, Daniel. G., and Tara J. Yosso. 2001. "From Racial Stereotyping and Deficit Discourse toward a Critical Race Theory in Teacher Education." *Multicultural Education* 9:2–8.

Spillane, James P. 2002. "District Policy-Making and State Standards: A Cognitive Perspective on Implementation." In *School Districts and Instructional Renewal*, edited by Amy M. Hightower, Michael S. Knapp, Julie A. Marsh, and Milbrey W. McLaughlin, 143–59. New York: Teachers College Press.

Stanhope, Kate. 2012. "*The New Normal* Gets New Home in Utah." *TV Guide*, September 2. http://www.tvguide.com/News/New-Normal-Utah-1052572.aspx?rss=news&partnerid=spi&profileid=05.

Starr, Paul. 2008. *Freedom's Power: The History and Promise of Liberalism*. New York: Basic Books.

Tate, William F., IV. 1997. "Critical Race Theory and Education: History, Theory, and Implications." *Review of Research in Education* 22:195–247.

Tatum, Beverly Daniel. 1997. "*Why Are All the Black Kids Sitting Together in the Cafeteria?*" *and Other Conversations about Race*. New York: Basic Books.

Taylor, Edward. 1999. "Critical Race Theory and Interest Convergence in the Desegregation of Higher Education." In *Race Is . . . Race Isn't: Critical Race Theory and Qualitative Studies in Education*, edited by Laurence Parker, Donna Deyhle, and Sofia Villenas, 182–201. Boulder, Colo.: Westview Press.

Thompson, Audrey. 1999. "Colortalk: Whiteness and Off White." *Educational Studies* 30:141–60.

———. 2003. "Tiffany, Friend of People of Color: White Investments in Antiracism." *International Journal of Qualitative Studies in Education* 16:7–29.

———. 2005. "Schooling Race Talk." *Educational Researcher* 34:22–29.

Thompson, Becky. 1997. "Home/Work: Antiracism Activism and the Meaning of Whiteness." In *Off White: Readings on Race, Power, and Society*, edited by Michelle Fine, Linda C. Powell, Lois Weis, and L. Mun Wong, 354–66. New York: Routledge.

Valdes, Guadalupe. 2001. *Learning and Not Learning English: Latino Students in American Schools*. New York: Teachers College Press.

Valenzuela, Angela. 1999. *Subtractive Schooling: U.S.-Mexican Youth and the Politics of Caring*. Albany: State University of New York Press.

Vaught, Sabina E. 2011. *Racism, Public Schooling, and the Entrenchment of White Supremacy: A Critical Race Ethnography*. Albany: State University of New York Press.

Vaught, Sabina E., and Angelina E. Castagno. 2008. "'I Don't Think I'm a Racist': Critical Race Theory, Teacher Attitudes, and Structural Racism." *Race, Ethnicity, and Education* 11:95–113.

Villenas, Sofia, and Donna Deyhle. 1999. "Critical Race Theory and Ethnographies Challenging the Stereotypes: Latino Families, Schooling, Resilience, and Resistance." *Curriculum Inquiry* 29:413–45.

Vogt, Lynn A., Cathie Jordan, and Roland G. Tharp. 1993. "Explaining School Failure, Producing School Success: Two Cases." In *Minority Education: Anthropological Perspectives*, edited by Evelyn Jacob and Cathie Jordan, 53–66. Norwood, N.J.: Ablex.

West, Cornel. 2004. "Race Matters." In *Race, Class, and Gender: An Anthology*, edited by Margaret L. Anderson and Patricia Hill Collins, 122–25. 5th ed. Belmont, Calif.: Wadsworth/Thomas Learning.

Wheelock, Anne. 1992. *Crossing the Tracks: How Untracking Can Save America's Schools*. New York: New Press.

Williams, Patricia. 1995. *The Rooster's Egg: On the Persistence of Prejudice*. Cambridge, Mass.: Harvard University Press.

Winant, Howard. 2001. "White Racial Projects." In *The Making and Unmaking of Whiteness*, edited by Birgit Brander Rasmussen, Eric Klinenberg, Irene J. Nexica, and Matt Wray, 97–112. Durham, N.C.: Duke University Press.

Wing Sue, Derald. 2010. *Microaggressions in Everyday Life: Race, Gender, and Sexual Orientation*. Hoboken, N.J.: Wiley.

Yosso, Tara J. 2005. *Critical Race Counterstories along the Chicana/Chicano Educational Pipeline*. New York: Routledge.

Angelina E. Castagno is associate professor of educational leadership at Northern Arizona University.